A
WELCOME
ON THE MAT

A WELCOME ON THE MAT

Father Tom Dunlea
A Memoir

by

John McSweeney PE

OMP Publications

First published in Australia in April 2004 by

OMP Publications

Copyright © John McSweeney, 2004

All rights reserved. No part of this book may be reproduced or transmitted in any form or by any means, electronic or mechanical, including photocopying, recording or by any information and storage system without permission in writing from the publisher.

National Library of Australia
Cataloguing-in-publication data:

McSweeney, John, 1919–
A Welcome on the Mat — Tom Dunlea — A Memoir

Bibliography
Includes index
ISBN 0 646 43396 2

1. Dunlea, Thomas Vincent, 1894–1970. 2. Catholic Church — Australia — Clergy — Biography. 3. Boys Town (Engadine, NSW) — History. 4. Alcoholics Anonymous (Australia) — History. I. Title.

282.092

Cover and colour sections designed by Graphic by Design,
    Erina NSW 2250
Printed by Ligare Pty Ltd, Riverwood NSW 2210
Typeset by Turn-Key Systems Pty Ltd, St Leonards NSW 2065

Table of Contents

	Foreword	vii
1	That was a Boy	1
2	Life at Roran House	9
3	Capacity "to let go"	16
4	Sydney in the 1930s	23
5	A boy's cry for love	29
6	Evicted	38
7	The grand march	46
8	The tent village	53
9	The ugly man competition	61
10	The Clergy Conference	70
11	De La Salle Brothers	81
12	Alcoholics Anonymous	91
13	Christmas House	96
14	Riding into the silence of the bush	107
15	Father Ciantar takes over	118
16	Sobriety attained	127
17	Matt Talbot Hostel	139
18	The concursus	150
19	All God's creatures	161
20	Australiana — Arthur Maher	173
21	GROW is born	183
22	The Bell	192
23	Hands can speak	202

24	Striking a balance	210
25	He Loved his Bishop	220
26	Weakness accepted — power released	228
27	Fifty golden years	236
28	His final gift	244
29	He returns to Boys Town	253
	Epilogue	257
	Bibliography	263
	Selected References	264

Dedication

This memoir is inscribed to Bishop David Cremin, who with Father Ron Harden succeeded Dunlea in Hurstville. Like his predecessor, Bishop David has walked the extra mile with so many people and in addition has been an esteemed *Anam Cara* (soul friend) to the Sydney clergy.

By the same author

A Meddling Priest — John Joseph Therry
St Pauls 2000

The sale of this book
will benefit
Father Chris Riley's *Youth off the Street*
Boys Town Engadine
and
Matt Talbot Hostel, Sydney

Foreword

This book brings together the written (and spoken) viewpoints of many correspondents. Some of their names appear in the text. Others, although not acknowledged individually, made invaluable contributions. They are (in alphabetical order):

Mrs D Atkinson, Grace Barnes, Joan Blood, Alice Brady, S Browne, Mary Budden, Bill Butcher, Hilary Calwell, Joan Gortley, Ken Chriton, Paddy Coleman, Mick Croot, Dawn Crowe, John Cummins, Anna Dee, Mary Dolan, Laurie Doran, Yvonne Duffy, Beryl Green, Edna Green, Gwen Green, Laurie Grundy, Maria Hall, Chris Hernon, Noeleen Hewitt, Brother Howard, Jock, Doris Jones, Eileen Kavanagh, Ivy Kerry, Mrs Leary, Laura Lennox, Richard Love, Lil Lyle, Leo Massey, Eric McClement, Gerard McGuire, Maree McHugh, Bernie McMahon, M. McNeil, Alice Meas, Patricia Metcalf, Brother Moe, Frank Morgan, Eve Nathan, Valmarie Nethery, E Neville, Frank Noonan, Jim Noonan, June Noonan, Brian O'Brien, Kath Pearce, Father Gabriel Pedron, Terry Pollard, Bill Priest, Frank Priest, Les Ramsay, Iris Regan, Jimmie Robertson, Violet Simmons, Noreen Simons, Claire Slocum, Florence Stover, Doreen Verlin, Alice Warwick, Patricia Waterford, George Wilson, Hazel Wilson, Moana Woods and others whose names I have mislaid.

I am deeply indebted to them as I am to two priests who, although much younger than Dunlea, were very close to him and allowed me to use the published and unpublished material they so expertly recorded about him. They are Peter Morrisey and Pat Kenna. They also took the time to read over the text and make some very helpful suggestions and corrections. As did Tony Newman, Ted Kennedy, Chris Riley, Ted Cooper and Margaret Bouffler.

My honorary secretary Shirley typed the various drafts with patience and good humour. Peter Finneran has very generously shared his publishing expertise with me. The staff at Turn-Key Systems, Brother Brian Greiner CFC (Brisbane), Catherine Hammond Editorial Services, Mario Villareal and Father Terry Brady and staff at OLF Kingsgrove have been helpful, supportive and encouraging.

John McSweeney PE
March 2004

The subject of "A Welcome on the Mat" was, by any standard, an extraordinary human being. Few, if any Australians could realistically claim to have done more to have helped the most vulnerable of Australians. Indeed most of us would be proud to have managed a small fraction of the achievements which mark his life.

As the founder of Australia's first Boys Town, he achieved mighty things for the most disadvantaged boys of Australia's largest city and beyond. His special gift of establishing real contact with troubled homeless youngsters and encouraging them to turn around their lives was firmly based upon an extraordinary generosity of spirit and an oft stated conviction that there is no such thing as an innately bad boy.

As if Boys Town was not enough, he was one of the founders of Alcoholics Anonymous in Australia. As well, he filled the role of friend, helper and guide for Sydney's homeless men. While Parish Priest of Hurstville in Sydney he was involved in founding GROW, the self-help movement for the mentally ill.

In short, his life was an embodiment of the teaching of Chapter 25 of St Matthew's Gospel. This book, written with wit and insight by Father John McSweeney PE, tells the story of the man and his achievements. I warmly recommend it.

The Honourable Sir William Deane AC KBE
Governor-General of Australia 1996–2001
June 10, 2003

I am happy that the memory of the founder of the first Boys Town Australia is being kept alive. His passion to alleviate homelessness has been an inspiration to me and his way of approaching the problem of disadvantaged children, in many ways, parallels my own.

I feel this easy-to-read interesting book will move many people to help stamp out the growing problem of homelessness in our increasingly affluent society.

Fr Chris Riley SDB
June 6, 2003

Founder and Director of *Youth Off The Streets*. Comprising seven farms, three schools and over ten other programmes for street kids, including the Dunlea Detox centre.

In Engadine, I saw a scene,
Drawn from my dreams, a dream of leonine Tom:
An atom Tom, this atom, Tom;
The yet dynamic atom; lion-like Tom.

In Engadine, I saw a scene,
Drawn from my dreams, a dream of lamb-like Tom:
An atom Tom, small atom, Tom;
Dynamic, little atom; lamb-like Tom.

I dream the twentieth century all night long,
Ten thousand Engadines throughout the world:
And all are atom bombed out of their minds;
And yet, in time, the lion lies with the lamb.

Once, ever AA'd, Job-like, broken Tom,
Yet always Tom Dunlea, but now at one:
This simple man binds all in love as one;
Tom, lion and lamb; Christ dreams at Engadine.

Maurice Crittenden (Priest-poet)

August 22, 2002
Composed for the 32nd anniversary of
Father Tom Dunlea's death

1

That was a Boy

In the early 1930s, when Australia and the industrialised world were in the throes of a paralysing depression, a horseman was slowly wending his way along the banks of the Woronora River, not far from the township of Sutherland in Sydney's south. He was the local priest, visiting families who had been evicted from their homes because of inability to pay rent and were finding temporary shelter in the rock caves on the eastern bank of the river.

Out of nowhere a boy appeared and called to him. "My mother is sick, she wants to see you," he shouted. As he led him along the track towards the woman's sick bed, the boy was amazed to find he could talk to the priest. That was the first of many visits to this family.

Then one day news came that the lady was dying and wanted to see him urgently. She had a very special favour to ask, a dying wish, which was so important to her that she had kept it till this last precious moment. It concerned her son, whom the priest had come to know by this time. The father had cleared out, and his older brothers, unable to control him, had resorted to beating him up. As a result, he had run away and begun to sleep rough. The priest had actually helped him find a job, but it hadn't lasted and he was in trouble with the police once more.

The dying woman told the priest she had no-one else to turn to. Apart from herself, the one person he related to and respected was the priest. Could he take him in and look after him?

Although he had received many and varied requests from different people before, this was new and frightening — a big ask, one could say. It was serious stuff. As he felt her eyes fixed on him with the intensity of that other mysterious world she was slowly sinking into, he found himself answering "Yes" with a confidence and assurance he certainly didn't feel. That "Yes" solved her one remaining problem on this earth and released her peacefully into the realms of eternity.

Before I realised what I was doing I had said "Yes". Like many a man who says "yes" to a lady and lives to regret it, so did I. But the mother was laid to rest in a few days and my particular responsibility, in the midst of multitudinous other responsibilities, commenced. (Petrus p38)

On his way back to the small weatherboard presbytery, some of the consequences of his yes slowly began to dawn on him. He already had a couple of dogs, as well as his old white horse. To these he related without trouble; caring for them was a joy. Caring for a boy was a different matter altogether. It would entail paternal and even maternal skills — that worried him. Although he needed relational skills as a pastor, he didn't have to be father and mother to anyone.

Disturbing thoughts of finance, accommodation, food, clothing, schooling, supervision ... darted in and out of his mind as he trundled along the dusty track on that fateful day in 1934, with young Eric in tow. The April sun was glistening on the rippling flow of the Woronora River, the budgerigars were darting to and fro, proudly displaying their beautiful rainbow colours.

As priest and boy came to a newly thrown-together shanty of fibre and hessian, the horse automatically stopped, evidently aware of his master's social habits. The family had just moved in and, like so many other new families in the area, they had that depression look about them. And still they welcomed the priest and the boy and would have gladly shared their meagre rations with them. This spontaneous generosity and hospitality, coming from impoverished people, somehow banished his troubled thoughts. The hearts of ordinary people were like his own. The financial institutions had gone to the wall, but the goodness of people was still intact.

Although neither the priest nor the boy nor, indeed, anyone else, was aware of it at the time, Eric was to be the foundation member of Sydney's first-ever Boys Town, founded some years later by this priest, Thomas Vincent Dunlea.

The priest's home now had a small and very unusual extra resident who, it was said, adapted rather well to his changed circumstances. Parishioners went out of their way to get a look at him. They liked to chat with him and went to great lengths to satisfy their curiosity about his background and the reason for his being in the presbytery. They discovered he had three older brothers and a sister Gwen, all of whom were being helped by their pastor, who had given his mother such a fine funeral.

The adjustment was difficult for the priest. Eric had to be included in his day-to-day life, even in his pastoral planning and in his response to the many calls for help. Although his was an open house, with people coming and going continually, a permanent boarder like Eric required much attention and care.

* * * * * * * *

Some months after Eric's arrival, three members of the Society of St Vincent de Paul, Jim Noonan, Fred Moclaire and Bernie McMahon, came to talk to Father Dunlea about the growing number of destitute people drifting into the Sutherland Shire.

After the meeting, as they stood with Dunlea at the door chatting, they were distracted by some small creature darting across the path in the dark, disappearing into the scrub.

"That's a joey," one of them ventured. "The drought is drawing them in close." "More likely a dog," said Jim. "It was neither," said Dunlea as he began to follow into the bushes. "That was a boy."

He fished him out and, bringing him into the light, saw a blond-haired, cheeky-looking youngster, standing with arms folded and looking defiantly at him.

"Aren't you the bloke who's supposed to like kids?" the child blurted out.

This, the priest's second adopted child, Eddie by name, was on the run, one could say. He had run away from home in the first place and, after some months on the street, he was placed in a welfare home. Somehow he had managed to hide in the back of a van delivering bread to the institution and thus made it onto the street once more. He had come to Sutherland because he had heard about a bloke who might be worth trying out.

The boy was known to be subject to uncontrollable fits of temper. He had quite a reputation, in fact. He could be violent, even to the extent of wielding a knife to attack people. No wonder the Welfare people were happy to let Eddie join Eric in the little presbytery.

By talking to him, the priest got the full picture. Eddie's mother was an alcoholic, not due to weakness, the boy believed, but as a result of the bad influence of her so-called friends. These were the people who had destroyed his mother. Otherwise, he believed, she would have been a loving, caring human being. Brooding on this filled him with such outrage that he would take a knife and try to avenge himself on society.

Listening to his story and understanding where he was coming from had a deep effect on the priest and on his attitude to the problems of the scores of boys he was eventually to become responsible for.

The third boy to join the little community was Ray, called "Monkey" by his former companions, who made fun of him because he couldn't speak properly. Shunned and, at times, tormented by other kids, he lived rough on the banks of the Woronora River. Dunlea came across him when one of the priest's brown setters began to chase a bullock in a paddock by the river. The boy, who was in some way responsible for the cattle, ran for his life, causing the dogs to run after him.

Dunlea had to come to the rescue quickly, assuring the boy that the dogs were harmless and were happy playing with the boys in the presbytery. The boy's speech was little better than an unintelligible stammer. Dunlea quickly surmised that he was merely unable to control his facial muscles, probably because of a brain injury. As he tried to make conversation, he saw that the lad was not stupid, even though he had been to no less than forty-three schools without learning anything. He looked severely neglected, but wasn't afraid of the priest.

Giving no signs that he wanted to disappear into the scrub as was his wont, his eyes held Dunlea in a steady gaze, with a hint, a vague hint, of hope that this, at last, might be a friend. Answering questions with noises and wide gesticulations, he seemed at ease and relaxed.

"Will you come and stay with me?" Dunlea asked. Smiling gratefully, Monkey nodded his head.

On the way back to the presbytery, they met Patrick Moriarty, one of three men who had to co-sign parish cheques with the parish priest. They made up what was loosely called "the Parish Committee". Patrick, unemployed himself and living from hand to mouth, had great sympathy for what the priest was doing. He became somewhat apprehensive, however, when he learned that Dunlea had no real plan for the future of his (now) three boys. Nor had he any idea where the extra food and the other necessities of life would come from. Dunlea next to penniless himself, would remark, with a smile and somewhat ambiguously, his bank "was the bank of Providence in the hearts of the Australian people"!

At the little presbytery, space for Monkey was found through Dunlea leaving his bed and sleeping on the settee. He continued to teach his newly acquired family the arts and graces of civilised living. Patiently, he showed Monkey how to use his lips and tongue and teeth to form vowels and words. Words were a problem for all three. Their vocabulary, limited almost entirely to slang, profanity and obscenity, had to be expanded and developed.

The biggest problem was convincing them that people were good, that people were not their enemies, that people didn't hate them. Probing into their past, Dunlea got to know where each one was hurting, where the anti-social attitudes were rooted. This opened up the possibility of healing and acquiring a more positive outlook.

The key to Dunlea's success in changing these boys' way of looking at life, however, was in the boys themselves, who were convinced that the priest cared about them, believed in them, and believed they had the potential to become successful respected members of society.

To develop that potential, Dunlea knew he needed to have his parishioners on side. He started with the material elements of life. He knew that even the most poverty-stricken of his flock had pots and pans and household utensils they could do without. They were delighted and sometimes bemused at being visited by their horse-riding priest. His ability to make himself at home in their sparse and unkempt homes, his cheerful humorous attitude to life, raised their spirits and opened their hearts. They were happy to be able to contribute something, no matter how small.

Sometimes, as he returned to the presbytery, a small blanket or maybe a child's mattress would be draped over the horse's neck!

Even though the boys looked a bit wild and uncivilised to most people, Dunlea advised people in his own humorous way that they didn't bite! They weren't dangerous — in fact, they were good. In his preaching and teaching, he went out of his way to pluck, with a mischievous smile, little phrases out of the air: "Let the children come to Me and do not stop them ..." (Luke 18:16) or, "Taking a little boy, He put his arms around him saying Anyone who welcomes one of these ... welcomes me" (Mark 9:37).

Because they liked their parish priest, people linked into his concern for homeless boys and his desire to find a place for them. Even though they just couldn't imagine where such a place could be found and who would run it, they were beginning to feel that the priest's house wasn't that place. And even though the priest obviously loved children and had a great rapport with them, they felt he was too soft and disorganised to insist on the firm discipline boys needed.

A fourth ambassador from God's pathways appeared — a man with a long flowing beard, several overcoats and as many coverings as an onion; a swagman, one of those wanderers who tramp the outback roads and who have given us one of our most loved folk-songs, "Waltzing Matilda". I asked him to stay the night — he stayed for ten years! I later learned that this man had had the spiritual history of a Matt Talbot. (Petrus p27)

He was housed in a little tent Dunlea erected in the backyard (against Council Ordinances). He recalled later:

> One day I'd been out on my morning calls when I returned to the presbytery to find our swagman and Ray on their knees praying. I believe Boys Town is built upon the knees of those two, just as the Sydney Harbour Bridge is built upon its concrete pylons.

As the days became months and months melted into years, other boys, seeking temporary accommodation, would stay for a day or a week or sometimes a month or more.

From the mid to the late 1930s, more and more boys knocked on his door, some in such a desperate state that he had to add them to the original three, on a more or less permanent basis. By 1938 the little house in Merton Street was bursting at the seams with seven permanent boys, as well as what parishioners referred to whimsically as the passing trade. As Dunlea searched for a bigger place, the war clouds gathering over Europe were filling him with forebodings. The sufferings occasioned by the Great Depression would be small in comparison to those occasioned by a new world war.

On December 12, 1938, a letter in Latin from the Archbishop brought the good news that, as of that date, Sutherland had been raised to the status of Parish and Dunlea to the rank of Parish Priest. Up to this point it was a parochial district and Dunlea was priest in charge. The change didn't mean much in practice, except that it now enjoyed a higher status in canon law, which the Bishop had to respect when contemplating future changes.

2

Life at Roran House

West Tipperary is part of what is called the Golden Vale, a rich fertile valley extending into parts of Counties Limerick and Cork, where crops like wheat and barley flourish, changing in the autumn from deep green to bright gold. Lying between the two ranges of the Knockmealdown and Galtee Mountains, it is a kaleidoscope of forty shades of green, where cattle and sheep luxuriate in the soft lush paddocks.

Here at the family residence called *Roran House*, five kilometres east of Ballina on April 19, 1894 Thomas Vincent Dunlea was born, the tenth of eleven children, to parents Michael and Bridget. The house, a two-storey with a single-storey extension and entrance porch, provided fairly tight accommodation for the Dunleas. A great open hearth fire in the living room warmed the whole house including the small attic where Tom and one or two others slept.

Surrounded by a large family he grew into a bright happy intelligent youngster. From childhood he was interested in the farm animals, the weak and the ailing, as well as the healthy and strong. He had two hunting dogs, with whom he spent sometimes whole days tramping through the heather and the scrub of the foothills, chasing the odd badger or hare or wild deer.

Reminiscing on his childhood, he told the *Catholic Weekly*:

> My mother would say of me: "This Tom of ours talks to dogs by the hour, but seldom thinks of his books". I loved running races like the 100 yards and upwards.

Even the three-mile distance wasn't too much for me. In the scholastic field, however, I fear I was a backbencher.

Walking featured largely in his young life, as his senior primary schooling at Killaloe was over six kilometres away. Sometimes one of the family horses or donkeys provided transport; normally, however, the distance was covered on foot. If the weather was too bad, he could have the day off from school.

That daily trip to and from school, as well as the days spent in the foothills with his dogs, aroused in him an awareness of and a love for nature. Trees held a special fascination for him, the way they developed from seedlings, responded to the changing seasons by acquiring and shedding leaves, creating colours that delighted the eye. There was one old oak tree that he particularly loved to sit and look at. Its bark was crusted and dry and shrivelled. It looked lifeless and dead, and yet the juices of life pulsed invisibly within it, travelling silently and secretly from the roots right up to the most distant branches.

The mystery of life in that old seemingly lifeless tree provided, at an early age, a window into the natural world which he began to see as mysteriously animated and living, indeed as continuously developing and full of creativity.

A teacher in Killaloe used a quote from G K Chesterton which his young pupil never forgot: "The world will never starve for want of wonders but only for want of wonder". The capacity to wonder was a strong enriching influence in Tom's youth and continued to be so during all his adult life. He didn't feel alone in the woods or the fields or the foothills. He felt good, as if surrounded by friendly company, company to which he related, as he disclosed to a friend later in his life, not so much in an I/it as in a I/thou way!

Long before he encountered Aboriginal spirituality, he felt an affinity with the earth as a living organism. To him, as to his Celtic forebears, it was mother earth, a nurturing mother to be treated with respect and even affection. This mystical relationship with nature, with trees and flowers and stars, opened his mind to the mysterious, even to the mysterious source of everything, the one in whom we live and move and have our being (Acts 17:28).

This mystical element in his life didn't make it any easier to deal with the ghost stories told around the fireside in Roran House by his father and the other local farmers who gathered during the long winter nights. These tales of encountering someone who had recently died in some stretch of lonely road at the dead of night in the pitch dark just scared him witless. Nor did the mystic bent save him from the messiness that attended the oncoming of puberty and the consequent (on the part of some) interest in the male and female body. The struggle to control the sensual impulses at that time, he remembered later, was exacerbated by the telling and hearing of dirty jokes — so much so that Peter Morrissey maintained, "In this free and easy age, I never ever heard Father Dunlea tell a dirty joke of any kind, and if someone else did, he changed the subject instantly". This was somewhat counter-cultural at a time when some of the more sociable clergy didn't regard it as improper to laugh at or even tell the odd mildly lurid joke.

Although his encounter with the mysteries of life didn't begin when he came under the influence of the Cistercians, his long association with these contemplative monks did give it a fresh impetus. For his senior high schooling he entered Mount St Joseph's Monastery, operated by the Cistercian Order in the next-door town of Roscrea, County Tipperary. Although he loved the warm, free and easy atmosphere of his home, he adapted well to the constraints and the rough and tumble of a boys' boarding school.

As well as being a fun-loving, carefree, happy youth, he was rather good at sport. That in itself was the passport to the esteem and affection of his peers. He was recruited for the various sporting teams and was unbeatable at handball. At the numerous athletics carnivals that were a feature of summer life in the area, he managed frequently to bring home gold. This, as well as his good looks and charisma, caught the attention and admiration of the girls. When Tom was home on holidays, his brother Jack recalled, the rest of us didn't get a look in with the local lassies.

During his last year in Roscrea, one of the monks read to the senior boys a letter he had received from a Father Galvin, an Irish priest who had worked in Brooklyn N.Y. From there the priest had felt the call to minister in the great land of China. (He later became the founder of the Maynooth Mission to China, a society of priests known as the Columban Fathers, and also Bishop of Hanyang.) The letter was optimistic and passionate about the possibilities for evangelisation in the mysterious Far East, as it was then called.

Young Dunlea was greatly impressed. Like others, he already had dreams of some day treading the golden road to Samarkand, or discovering the mysterious and far away Valparaiso. Going to China, in one way, was to him a dream come true.

The idea of devoting his life to God in the priesthood had been percolating within him for some time. Being a priest in Ireland seemed to him to be a bit tame and unadventurous, and thus China was very appealing. However, the World War I influenza epidemic struck him, leaving him with a weak chest that would make ministry in the demanding mission fields of the Far East out of the question. Nonetheless, the desire to follow a missionary vocation remained firm.

His thoughts turned to Australia, which was the favoured overseas country in the Dunlea household. His brothers Tim and Jack, in Australia since 1912, embraced the occupations the Irish immigrants favoured at that time. Tim became a policeman in Brisbane and Jack a publican in Melbourne, eventually the proprietor of the Silver Gate Hotel in North Melbourne. In letters home they reported on the conscription debate and Tom felt a country free enough to consider both sides of the great question and eventually vote no would be a good place to put down roots.

He opted for Sydney, where Archbishop Michael Kelly was seeking to attract priests from Ireland to cater for his rapidly growing diocese. His sister Delia followed him to Australia, settling in Brisbane, and brother Edmond settled in the United States, where he died at a comparatively young age.

Tom's decision in 1914 to enter the clergy training College of Mount Melleray was a defining moment in his life. It was his first positive public indication that he had priesthood in mind. It was quite a surprise to most people.

Mount Melleray, like Mount St Joseph's Roscrea, is run by the Cistercians, whose primary call is to contemplation. Like their counterparts in Tarrawarra in Victoria, they invite people to come and stay with them, to savour the contemplative atmosphere and join in their chanting of the Hours. They also conduct a junior Seminary, where students for the priesthood study philosophy for two years. Although it was against the Seminary rules, Tom sometimes sneaked down into the back of the monks' chapel at 2 a.m. just to watch the monks in their dark robes and white cowls quietly shuffling into their stalls. There in the dim candlelight, they'd open the huge illuminated Books of the Hours.

The resultant beautiful Gregorian chant filled the darkened chapel with the fascinating sound of what Tom felt was divine music. Like the strong Latin words of the chanted psalms, he felt carried on angels' wings right up to the throne of Yahweh. This experience reinforced in him a sense of the mysterious, of the transcendent, which he never lost.

To study theology the students seek admission to one of the major seminaries, like All Hallows in Dublin, St John's Waterford, St Patrick's Carlow, St Peter's Wexford or St Kieran's Kilkenny. Because his best friends were attracted to St Peter's, that became Tom's choice too, and he entered in September 1916.

During Tom's seminary years, the momentous events of World War I were taking place in the European mainland. One of the greatest tragedies of all time was being enacted within a few hundred miles off Wexford, but such was the isolation of seminaries in those pre-radio days that the one source of news, the daily paper, was deemed to be a distraction, and so no newspaper was allowed into the students' part of the building. The only information regarding the progress of the War, apart from the odd crystal set or letter from home, was the professor of hermeneutics, who saw how ridiculous it was to cut the students off from what was happening in the real world in which they were going to minister. At the beginning of each lecture he gave his class a rundown on the politics and progress of the conflict. He amazed them by reflecting that the God revealed by Jesus was the same God who was suffering in the trenches of France and the landing beaches of Gallipoli. Jesus, whose Word they were coming to discover, was present in the blood and guts and gore of the Western Front, in which many of their own kith and kin were involved. This immanence of God in the nitty-gritty of human life and this capacity of God to suffer with people (cum passio) were two piers on which Tom's future ministry was to be built.

Although he was a popular and well-liked student in Wexford, Tom's tendency to pursue outside activities and interests didn't go down well with some of his professors. They felt his capacity to make prudent judgments as confessor and counsellor would be impaired by his laissez faire attitude toward moral theology and canon law. They felt, too, that his Franciscan orientation would be a handicap when dealing with the more practical aspects of life as a pastor. However, he was devout and mystical and related so well to everyone that they had little hesitation in calling him to Orders.

When he was ordained a priest on June 20, 1920 at St Peter's College Chapel there were three other young men ordained for the Australian Mission: Dan Galvin (late Parish Priest Ashbury), Maurice Kennedy (late Parish Priest Eastwood) and Michael Moylan (late Parish Priest Wingham). They travelled together to the antipodes on the *SS Olympic* arriving in Sydney in December 1920.

3

Capacity "to let go"

When home on holidays from Roscrea and Wexford, Tom spent some time during the long summer break coaching the local youngsters in gaelic football, equipping them to compete with teams from other parishes in the district competition. Although not that skilled in the code himself, Dunlea was an enthusiastic coach.

Training began at about 9.30 pm, after the day's work in the farms was completed and the cattle were assembled, milked (by hand) and driven back into the paddocks for the night. The lads were eager, so the training went well. From their usual place at the bottom they began the slow climb back, winning the competition for the first time in years.

Dunlea felt that the players, who had trained so arduously, should be given some token of appreciation, — only to find out, to his great disappointment, that no prizes were available. What to do? He then realised that Roran House had some old clocks, a very scarce commodity in the Irish countryside at that time. Somehow the Dunleas had managed to acquire timekeepers from various sources, some even coming from America. Tom prevailed on his brothers Jack and Tim to collect some of them. These he dusted off and polished and handed out as prizes to the perplexed but delighted footballers.

There were however, two substitute players who came on the field only when one of the regulars was injured. Because these two were weak players, he couldn't bear to leave them out. But the clocks were all gone. No more prizes. Then he remembered. There were two more, the most recent arrivals, just unwrapped. Next day the Dunleas discovered the sad fact that their most valuable time-keepers had disappeared, nowhere to be found.

This Robin Hood aspect of Tom's character was to surface many times during his life, even during his seminary days.

At the Armistice celebrations in Wexford on November 11, 1918, one of his professors noticed a returned one-legged soldier sitting on a park bench wrapped up snugly in Dunlea's one and only warm topcoat! The fact that a poor man was being protected from the bitter northerlies gave Dunlea so much satisfaction that, as he recalled later with a twinkle in his eye, his weak chest rebuffed every incipient attack on it during that very harsh winter — even without the extra protection a topcoat could give.

Many years later, one of his assignments in Sydney was to the rather affluent Mary Magdalene parish, Rose Bay, where the parish priest, Monsignor O'Regan, was reputed to be hard on curates. One day when the Monsignor was away on holidays, a parishioner reported that an unemployed man, with his wife and family, was being evicted from their weatherboard house for inability to meet his mortgage payments to the bank. With three children and a fourth due any day, they were sitting on their few possessions outside their locked-up home when Dunlea visited. It transpired they literally had nowhere to go, so he invited them to the presbytery to tide them over while awaiting a more permanent arrangement.

Now it happened that as the parish priest's companion, Monsignor Collender, the Vicar General of the Archdiocese, was suddenly called back from holidays, the parish priest came back with him, arriving at the Rose Bay Presbytery ten days before he was due. Opening the door, he went to his room, to be greeted by a bevy of children and a mother sitting on his bed nursing a newborn baby! He was speechless. In fact, he was so taken aback that the words he wanted to say just wouldn't come out.

At this juncture the curate arrived back from parish visitation and, in his utter surprise at the incongruity of the situation, with the Monsignor surrounded by the children and the mother on the bed, he spontaneously burst out laughing. It broke the tension. To his credit the Monsignor laughed heartily too, and was soon joined by the children and their parents. They all had a really good therapeutic laugh and felt better for it.

Monsignor O'Regan spent the next couple of nights in his neighbour's presbytery. Being a man of influence he contacted Labor leader Jack Lang who managed to persuade the bank to let the family back into their home forthwith. Versions of this story became part of Sydney clerical folklore for many years.

In the *Australian Women's Weekly* of August 1992, journalist Betty O'Brien recalls a story from her childhood in Sutherland:

> It seemed funny to me that though everyone loved Father Dunlea to pieces, someone always seemed to be upset by something he'd done. I mean like the time Mrs Coberg knitted him a nice woolly scarf. He said it was perfect and would keep him warm when he was off here, there and everywhere, saying Masses. But after two or three wears, we never saw it again. A neighbour told my Auntie Kath that when she went to Sydney to see the doctor, she saw, walking along the street, as happy as Larry and wearing the Father's scarf ... a most awful boy. Dreadful. A real larrikin! "Pray to God," said the neighbour, "that Dora Coberg never finds out what happened to that scarf. That's all she needs to put her back on the bottle!"

Shortly after he became parish priest of Sutherland, a friend from his Rose Bay days opened a shoe business a few doors from the church. Being Depression times, he was fearful about how viable the business would be, and he invited the pastor to come and pray God's blessing on it. To add a little *oomph* to the blessing, he asked the priest to sit on one of the stools while he fitted him with a pair of shoes from among the most expensive range he had in stock. They fitted like a glove, looked great and, unlike their equivalent today, they remained dry inside in all sorts of weather.

Dunlea was delighted with them. Keeping his feet dry and warm helped his weak chest.

A few weeks later, on a wet cold night, his good friend and adviser, Dr Eric Miles, was returning from a late night call when he caught up to him on the road and gave him a lift. As Father settled into the front seat of the old Chevrolet, Eric noticed that even though he was otherwise fully clothed, he had no shoes on. The good doctor found this rather worrying, but also amusing. Here was a man of the cloth complete with black trousers, collar, coat and even umbrella — and in his bare feet!

Knowing that he was dealing with a somewhat unconventional cleric, Miles tried to suppress the laughter that was changing the contours of his face and his lips. With a whimsical tremor in his voice, he enquired how this odd situation had come about. Dunlea evaded the issue by treating it flippantly and of no consequence, so it was only after Miles persisted that he admitted what really had happened.

He had taken some groceries to a family who were having a bad time. The father, the breadwinner, was in bed with tuberculosis. The mother, who couldn't go out because she had no decent clothes to wear, told him someone was offering the son a cleaning job, but he had no shoes to wear for the interview. She was praying to St Anthony that somehow he might find him a pair of shoes. Dunlea asked her if she had told St Anthony the size required. He knew he had to help St Anthony, but not directly, as they were proud people.

As he left the house, he noticed it was one of those that had a closed-in verandah with a screen door that wasn't locked. When he saw the lights go out behind him, he removed his shoes, dried them as best he could and placed them quietly inside the screen door. He would love to have written "a present from St Anthony" and put it near them, but he didn't have the paper! He felt, however, that the lady of the house would be in no doubt about St Anthony's role in the affair.

Even in those Depression years, people went to great lengths to make things. Ladies like Dora Coberg, mentioned above, loved to make him items of clothing or knit him things like jumpers or socks. These he accepted with much elation and profuse thanks and, indeed, wore them for a while. Then they would disappear mysteriously.

His good friends the Giddings of Cronulla, startled him once when they told him they had heard that half the street people in Sutherland were attired in assorted articles of black clerical apparel!

The ladies who looked after his personal needs from time to time, especially Joan Paranthoine, Mrs Sullivan, Mrs Shoveller and Molly Cooney were driven to distraction "as he would often return at evening time after his rounds, minus socks, shoes and occasionally even his shirt. At times the blankets from his bed were gone." (Sutherland Saga p14)

According to Ken Scully, Molly Cooney used to lock up his shirts and singlets, but he would break the drawers open and give them away. Scully also reports:

> Father often came to our home for a chat. We kids used to smile as he related how grand things were going — for we could see the newspaper stuffed under the soles through the holes in his shoes.

Caught in a very heavy downpour after visiting Hilary Coldwell's parents' home in Sutherland one cold July day, he could find nothing to wear except an old pair of shorts procured by one of the boys; his spare trousers were keeping someone else warm.

Joan Blood's mother received the Last Sacraments in her sick bed with a degree of distraction. She just couldn't help but notice, somewhat in awe, that her parish priest was in his bare feet. She didn't ask questions. She knew. And that knowledge somehow gave her an experience of deep peace as she drifted towards the portals of eternity.

Thea Trembath, a catechist, knew one of Dunlea's curates whose main complaint was coming home at night and finding that his bed had been given away!

Emeritus History Professor Ed Campion summed up this aspect of his character rather well: "Someone said of him: if he had given away anything else, he would have been charged with indecent exposure".

Steve Allen, who spent many of his adult years in gaols in N.S.W. and Queensland, writes:

> It was Christmas time in 1938. My mother sent me up to give a note to Father Dunlea. The note said we had no food at home. He gave me a piece of paper (like a voucher) to take to Derrin Bros. grocers, Main Street, Sutherland. That afternoon a delivery of groceries came to our house — young chap with a three-wheel bicycle with a box in front. My memory says it probably cost as much or more than three pounds. I first remember Father when he was curate at Surry Hills and came down to Central cells and stood bail for me. I have been and have known others to have been bashed, starved and brutalised by officialdom for being a Depression boy. I will always remember Father Dunlea as being one of the real great caring blokes in my life.

Individuals or families with a specific urgent need were etched in Father Tom's memory, to such an extent that when he saw the required item in someone else's house, he felt compelled to appropriate it. Frances Massey writes:

> My father was sick, so, of course, Father Dunlea visited. Noting all our umbrellas on the stand, he would remark: "What a lot of umbrellas", and (tucking one under his arm), "I'm sure you won't miss this one". We didn't. We knew it would find an owner who needed it more than we did.

The contemplative monks in Roscrea and Mount Melleray would have influenced this amazing capacity to let go. By word and example they would have alerted him to the fact that less is more, that addiction to material things is best dealt with by living simply in this world, as Jesus did. As Franciscan Richard Rohr puts it:

> All spirituality is about letting go. How to let go of our security, how to let go of our good reputation, how to let go of our identity and our self-image. Because we no longer understand any of this, we have become an addictive society and an addictive Church. (p107)

"This capacity to let go, to give away possessions to those in need, remained with him to his death. He didn't change." (Hazel Wilson)

No wonder Cardinal Gilroy said that no priest has done more to make the Church loved.

4

Sydney in the 1930s

During his Rose Bay days, Dunlea and his pastor, Dick O'Regan, were both associated with State Premier Jack Lang. O'Regan knew him personally, but disagreed with his policy of defaulting during the Great Depression on interest owed on loans obtained from English banks for public works in New South Wales. Apart from questions of justice and morality, he felt it wasn't in Australia's long-term interests to alienate the mother country, whose financial apron-strings kept Australia afloat.

Dunlea, on the other hand, was among the thousands in New South Wales who felt that Lang was right in resorting to this desperate ploy. He was putting people first at a time when bankruptcies and suicides, heartbreaks and dole queues were biting deep into the Australian psyche. During his curate days in Surry Hills, he enthusiastically supported the 1925 Lang Government social reforms, especially those that recognised the plight of widows and young families, leading to the granting of widows' pensions and child endowment. He applauded Lang's insistence that compulsory insurance should be paid by employers and his fight for better conditions for rural workers. He saw at first hand the human misery caused by unemployment which, by 1932, involved 30% of the work force.

Dunlea saw too that for many, unemployment meant losing their prized possession, the home they had been struggling to pay off. He kept in touch with the dispossessed homeless under the trees in the Sydney Domain, where families were huddled together in cardboard and tin shanties after Lang had insisted that the park land be opened up to them.

The construction of the Sydney Harbour Bridge during the late 1920s and the early 1930s was a focus of interest for many Sydneysiders like Dunlea. A priest friend, Jim Meaney, founder of Radio Station 2SM, managed to get two tickets to the VIP enclosure at the official opening on March 19, 1932, but decided not to go because he was disappointed that some overseas dignitary wasn't invited to cut the ribbon instead of Premier Lang. By now Lang was in the bad books of many Australians. Meaney passed the tickets to Dunlea who was delighted that Lang was doing the honours himself. He invited a colleague, Dr Pat Tuomey, to accompany him as part of the Premier's entourage. Tuomey, who had previously clashed with the Empire-loving anti-Lang group calling themselves the New Guard, was apprehensive that they might attempt something. But the protocol was being observed without a hitch until Lang was handed the scissors to cut the ribbon and declare the bridge open.

At that moment, seemingly out of nowhere, appears on horseback New Guardsman De Groot dramatically brandishing a sword with a bright shiny blade and defiantly cutting the ribbon before the Premier's scissors could touch it. De Groot stood to his full height on the stirrups and triumphantly declared the Harbour Bridge open!

Afterwards en route to the Dolphin Hotel Surry Hills, as Dunlea and Tuomey were recovering from shock, they came to see the amusing side of this extraordinary turn of events which had Sydney and all Australia talking and laughing for months.

A short time later on May 13, 1932 to the great disappointment of Dunlea, Jack Lang was sacked as Premier by the State Governor, Sir Philip Game. He recalled how offended he felt when people would solemnly proclaim that it had to happen or the country would be ruined. To show his defiance and support, he urged parishioners to attend the rally in the Domain a few days after the Big Fella, as he was called, was defeated in the election held a month after the sacking. The pro-Lang rally attracted 300,000 people, the biggest crowd ever assembled in one place up to then.

1932 was a bad year for Dunlea and Australia in another way. From his earliest days he had a feeling for all animals, especially for dogs and horses. Although not a betting man, he would have loved to go to the races to see the horses in action, but that was forbidden to clerics in New South Wales. Once, in November 1930, with a clerical colleague and neighbour, Tom Wallace, he had stretched the law somewhat by heading south across the state border to see his favourite horse line up for the Melbourne Cup. Although Phar Lap was New Zealand-bred, he was trained in Australia and part-owned by a friend in the Rose Bay Parish. He had hit some headlines in the racing world by coming third in the 1929 Melbourne Cup.

Dunlea being a hands-on person insisted on going to the saddling paddock to get the feel of the horses and experience the smells that were part of life in his home farm in Ireland. He met Jim Pike, Phar Lap's jockey, who allowed him to stroke the great champion. Jim asked him to give the horse a quick blessing and himself, too. After Phar Lap's stunning Melbourne Cup win on that beautiful November day, Jim sent him, through his friend in Rose Bay, a very gracious note of thanks for the blessing.

Although never putting on a bet, over the next two years Dunlea followed Phar Lap's spectacular career, as he won an amazing 35 out of 39 starts. He recalled how Phar Lap had added a little sunshine, a ray of hope, to countless Australians during those depressed years. With pride they acknowledged that Australia was home to the world's best cricketer, Donald Bradman, and the world's best horse. To prove the latter, Phar Lap was shipped overseas to make his debut in Los Angeles. From there came the news that made headlines in Australia and indeed around the world: the great horse had died suddenly in California. Dunlea admitted that he went to his room and cried.

Dunlea often remarked that Australians, like the Irish, had a great capacity to see the lighter side of life, especially when clouds were gathering overhead. The best expression of this, he felt, was the cartoon character Ginger Meggs. It first appeared in the Sydney *Sunday Sun* newspaper in 1922 when Dunlea was a curate in St Francis Church Albion Street, Surry Hills. Like millions of Australians of all ages, he became a regular devotee. He felt that Ginger, with his mop of red hair and black waistcoat, was the typical Aussie battler-larrikin, at once both philosopher and comedian.

Sometimes Ginger added familiar down-to-earth spice to Dunlea's Sunday sermons. This was received with a chuckle, people being so much at home with Ginger, his girlfriend Minnie, his enemy Tiger Kelly, his rival for Minnie's affection, Eddie, his mates Bennie and Ocker, and Mrs Meggs, the typically sensible unflappable Aussie mother. In the depths of the Depression years, people laughed with them, hoped and dreamt with them and even worried with them.

A few months after Dunlea went to Surry Hills, the poet-author Henry Lawson died. He never forgot the date, September 2, 1922 and admitted Lawson had quite an impact on his life. Dr Pat Tuomey, an outspoken priest, passionate about social justice and given to what were then looked on as inflammatory pro-Irish statements, gave him a collection of Lawson poems and *Bulletin* articles. These he studied and treasured and quoted. Although perturbed by Lawson's rather bleak attitude to life in the bush as contrasted to that in the city, he was intrigued at how the hopelessness of life was so beautifully combined with an attitude of stoic endurance. This attitude was for him epitomised by Mrs Spicer, one of Lawson's famous bush women, whose last dying words to her children were "feed the pigs and the calves and be sure and water them geraniums".

To Dunlea, Lawson was typical of the misunderstood visionary whose sad but far-seeing eyes witnessed the degradation of the land and the flora and the fauna that he loved.

That Australian flora and fauna became very dear to Dunlea. On his days off and during his annual holiday, he didn't head for the golf course like most of his contemporaries. Even after his fellow curate, Jim Meaney, had created St Michael's out of the scrub of Little Bay in East Sydney (a Catholic golf course!), he still didn't frequent the Monday clergy competition. His interests lay elsewhere: in the country bordering on the coast and, when time permitted, in the more distant bushland. Valleys like the Hawkesbury, the Hunter and the Kangaroo, as well as the Blue Mountains and the Snowy he found awesome and inspiring.

When he landed in Sydney in the early summer of 1920, the bewitching music of the cicada was the first unusual wild-life sound to come to his ears. He quickly learned that the cicada was an inoffensive creature, unlike the locust, of the grasshopper family, which could do such devastating harm to food production in the country. The cicada, after years of a sort of still life underground, suddenly finds itself in a new world of dazzling sunlight, blue skies and lovely landscapes and that, he was told, was good reason to make a joyful sound. This insect passes through an amazing transformation after emerging from the earth. It kind of walks out of itself with a new body something like wax. At this stage it is incapable of flying or much movement until it has been hardened and changed in colour by exposure to the sun and the air.

Dunlea liked to use the cicada's remarkable transformation as a metaphor for the transformation effected in human lives by baptism or union with Jesus Christ. Always he would add a witty caution to the effect that he hoped the joyful music of the newborn Christian wouldn't be as loud or piercing as that of the cicada.

His interest in poets like Lawson, who highlight Australian flora and fauna, got a new boost years later when Arthur Maher, a country priest, joined him in Sydney. He was particularly moved by the fact that a man of such literary talents as Lawson should spend the last years of his life clouded by advanced alcoholism and dire poverty and living in a rented shack. This sad fact troubled Dunlea greatly and had a bearing on his own attitudes, especially towards alcoholism.

Although not an Irish nationalist of the same ardour as his colleague Dr Tuomey, Dunlea readily tuned into the stories coming through the grapevine from Melbourne when he first landed in Sydney. He had known about Archbishop Mannix's pivotal role in defeating the two conscription referenda proposed, during World War I by Prime Minister Billy Hughes. He hadn't known, however, about the anti-catholic backlash that followed after the war. The St Patrick's Day parade, an annual event of enormous significance to Mannix and Victorian Catholics, was black-listed at the urging of Herbert Brooks a leading monarchist in Melbourne. This unprecedented ban threw the southern capital into turmoil. A solution had to be found and it was found eventually by John Wren, a millionaire friend of Dr Mannix. Wren arranged for ten Victoria Cross winners to lead the parade on white horses. The opposition grudgingly had to allow it to go ahead but only on one condition: it must be led off by the Union Jack. That was a sore point in Victoria. Mannix, Dunlea was assured, infuriated many people by his well-publicised preference for things Australian, especially the Australian flag and Australian nationality, over that of Britain.

The parade was indeed led off by the Union Jack, an almost invisible mini-Union Jack, carried slovenly by one of Melbourne's best known drunks. Behind him were the Australian and Irish flags full sized and carried aloft on white horses by two of the VC winners.

Dunlea found this solution to the flag problem, which generated such heat in Melbourne, both imaginative and funny and loved to retell it years later.

5

A boy's cry for love

On the evening of Australia Day, January 26, 1927 Dunlea was called to a dying man in Abercrombie Street, Surry Hills. He was horrified to find that the man had had his throat cut and was bleeding to death. The instrument used was a razor blade, a weapon that was to cause havoc in the area for the next couple of years.

Desperate to stem growing street violence, the New South Wales Government had passed a law against guns. Anyone caught with an unlicensed firearm faced an automatic prison sentence. Overnight, gangsters, thieves and standover merchants began to terrorise people with a new weapon. Easy to conceal, the old cut-throat razor proved to be even more effective than the revolver as an instrument of attack. Men who might be ready to face the muzzle of a gun would panic before the shining blade held menacingly to their face. In the month of April alone in that year, 1927, the priest visited over ten parishioners in St Vincent's Hospital who were razor victims.

Much of the blame for this new wave of violence was attributed to two notorious women who operated in the Surry Hills area and were well known to Dunlea and to the parishioners of Surry Hills. Many times when visiting his flock, he spotted Kate Leigh, the queen of the East Sydney sly-grog trade. She invariably had a large black handbag, which was said to contain a heavy revolver, and some thousands of pounds in cash for emergencies. Many times he reminisced with amusement on the fur stole she wore in all weather and, on top of her greasy dyed hair, the dark wide-brimmed hat that sprouted feathers!

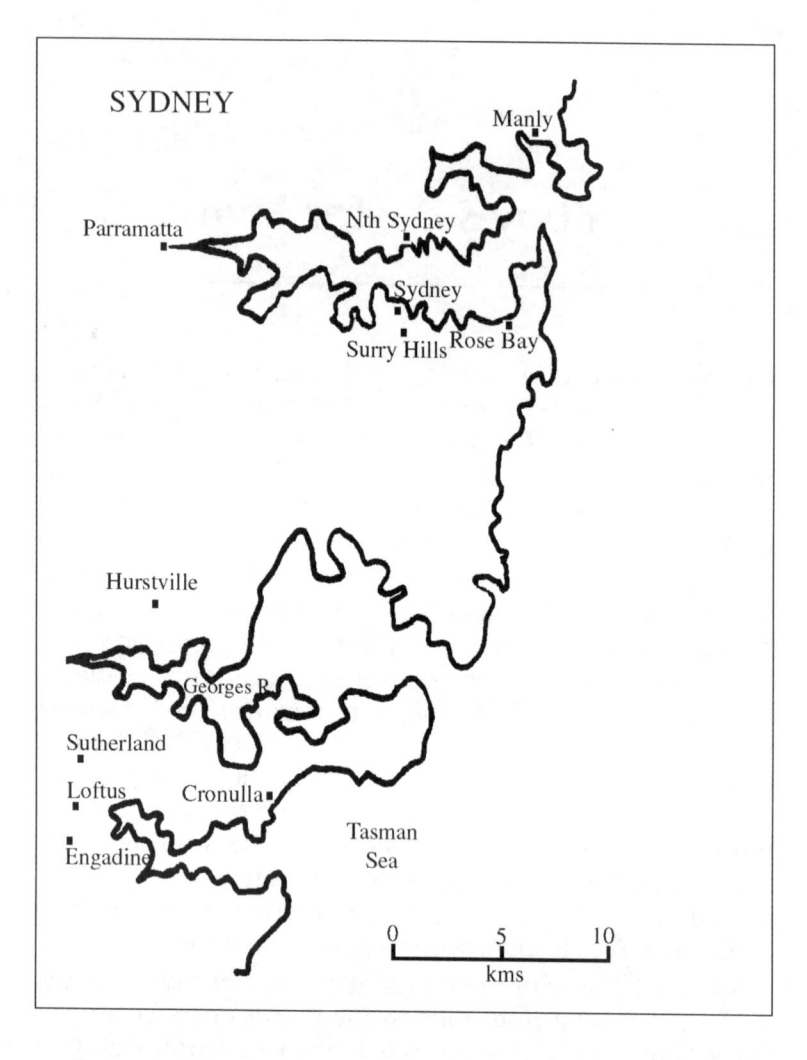

Government regulations had forced pubs to close at 6 p.m., thus providing people like Leigh with a very lucrative business.

The other vice queen and rival of Kate Leigh was Londoner Matilda (Tilly) Divine, the gaudily dressed, chain-smoking madam who sported twice as many diamond rings as she had fingers. She operated many brothels in the East Sydney area, but the ones that most impinged on the clergy and the local police were in the seedy rat-infested terraces in nearby Palmer Street. Tradesmen and factory workers flocked to the place where the star attraction was the blonde pert-nosed prostitute, Dulcie Markham. So popular was this well-endowed Ginger Rogers look-alike that at least eight of her clients were done to death by rivals for her attention.

After answering one bogus sick call to the place, Dunlea would only respond subsequently if the policeman on duty at Surry Hills accompanied him. Even then he was likely to be passionately embraced by one of the scantily dressed ladies. Although this was regarded as quite a joke by those present, what worried him most was the erotic thoughts and feelings that tantalised him for days afterwards.

His Surry Hills years influenced Dunlea in one very important way. In his own words:

> Our presbytery was next door to a Children's Centre for underprivileged boys ranging in age from five to eighteen years. They came from broken homes, some had been abandoned while others had been committed on various delinquency charges. As my bedroom window looked straight down into their courtyard, I could see all too clearly how much these boys needed someone to help them.
>
> One dead hour of night, I heard a whole family of boys being brought in by a kindly police officer, their guardians having abandoned them. I could hear their loud protests as they were compulsorily showered and bathed. Later on, just as dawn was breaking, one of these little urchins, who had broken out of the dormitory, came and sat underneath my window. I could hear him softly singing to himself a popular song of that era:
> I wish I had someone to love me
> Someone to call me their own ...
> I listened and there and then I resolved that if ever a chance should come my way I would try to do something for boys such as he, I would respond to

that primordial hunger to belong that echoes deep down in every human being even in the most macho cool street kid. (Petrus p37)

The words resonated in his own heart, too. They expressed a deeply felt need in Dunlea himself. He was a warm touchy-feely kind of person, but being intimate with someone in any real sense was not on the cards for him. He was in his late twenties, an age at which most of his contemporaries, including his own brothers, were settled into permanent relationships. The need to belong to someone, to create a family of his own, knocked at his heartstrings, causing a sort of empty feeling to surface every now and then. He had many colleagues with whom he was close and lots of people who, as Betty O'Brien said, loved him to bits. But still that inner hunger was largely unfulfilled.

His commitment to celibacy involved keeping women at arms' length, even though he loved their company. He had that roving eye that at gatherings spotted the best looker, and without in any way passing over or neglecting anyone else, had him floating almost automatically towards her orbit as, similarly moved, she moved towards his. The attraction was mutual, as was the animated banter. This gave him a great buzz.

At the time, it did satisfy the need within, but most certainly didn't take it away. Being a hands-on person, he found the current celibate's norm of keeping one's distance (especially regarding females) very limiting, yet he knew that breaking it could lead him over a line he did not want to cross. The fact that the good women who were attracted to him didn't want to cross that line either probably saved him more than once.

He loved his priestly duties, especially his involvement with the victims of the great Depression, and that just about absorbed all his energies. To cope with the suffering and hardship he was touching daily, he found comfort in the Prophet Micah's vision of what God wanted of him, namely:

> To live justly
> To love tenderly
> And to walk humbly with your God. (Micah 6:8)
>   After seven or eight years in the crowded and very interesting parish of Surry Hills my venerable graduate of Wexford College, Archbishop Kelly, was anxious that my lines should be cast in pleasanter surroundings, so I was appointed to the aristocratic suburb of Rose Bay. Here I spent close on two years, pining a little for more democratic and troublesome appointments in spite of the great kindness and open heartedness of all concerned. (Petrus p37)

During his last month in Rose Bay parish, a generous and wealthy widow offered Dunlea her late husband's car at a much reduced price. It was an old Chevrolet in poor condition, which he paid for from some funds he had inherited from his parents' estate. For the curate in Rose Bay, however, a car was seen by the Archbishop as an unnecessary luxury. As a result, Dunlea was quickly removed from Rose Bay and posted to Hurstville parish which was soon to be hit badly by the sudden and nationwide depression.

Plans to establish a new mass-centre in the nearby suburb of Kingsgrove being fairly well advanced, people were anxious that a date be set. Even though the pastor was away, Dunlea characteristically proposed Easter Sunday, the biggest feast day of the year, as the appropriate one for the first Mass. And so on April 5, 1931 some one hundred and twenty people gathered at a garage owned by William Sivertsen in Staples Street. There over a table used for cutting furniture covers, Dunlea made history by being the first priest to celebrate the sacred mysteries in a suburb that became the Parish of Kingsgrove-Bexley North. Its founding pastor would be his own cousin, Edward Clune.

1932 was a special year for Dunlea in that it marked his twelfth year in Australia. When he first arrived in 1920, Archbishop Kelly unwittingly scared him by saying, "You can go back for a holiday in twelve years' time". It had seemed like an eternity to him then. Although he dearly loved Australia and its people, he missed his home and family deeply. Many years later, when pastor of Hurstville, he confided in his curate Peter Morrissey that for some time after he arrived in Australia, he found it almost impossible to get out of bed of a morning to face the day, so unsure of himself was he, and homesick and apprehensive of he knew not what.

At the beginning of Passion Week in 1932, the letter from the Cathedral arrived with the exciting news that he could have eight months' leave of absence to visit his family in Tipperary and participate in the International Eucharistic Congress in Dublin. Leaving in April 1932, *en route* to Ireland he took in Egypt, Palestine and Rome and on the way back he managed to fit in the U.S.A.

Although he missed his father, who had died in the late 1920s, his first visit home was memorable and moving for himself and his family. After many wonderful gatherings in Tipperary and Clare, he joined his mother and other relatives and a large contingent of Ballina parishioners on board the train at Limerick Junction, heading for the Dublin Congress.

After he returned to Sydney in November 1932, there were several other temporary postings, including Newtown, Enfield and Golden Grove, as well as a further stint at St Michael's Hurstville where, predictably, he made a big impression, especially on the youngsters:

> All the children loved him. On the days we went to Confession, we would all huddle on Father Dunlea's side of the church. He regularly took us to Macinante's shop opposite the church in Croydon Road to buy us lollies. He got the boys the cricket pitch and was one of the first to recognise the skill of Ray Lindwall. (Alice Kinnane)

One of the Macinante children, Anne (who married Rowe Cuddy) remembers him as the pied piper of his day, leading troubled children into their shop to consume generous helpings of the Macinante icecream.

August 2, 1934 brought him very good news — news of a promotion he had been hoping for and looking forward to. He was being appointed pastor of Sutherland, not an already established parish, but one carved out of the parishes of Cronulla and Helensburgh in Sydney's South. Besides Sutherland the parochial district included Como, Woronora River, Menai, Loftus, Oyster Bay, Engadine, Grays Point, Kirrawee, Gymea, Miranda and Sylvania.

He recalls:

> Sutherland was an outlying district where a National Park of some 60,000 acres was situated and it also had many other unoccupied sites, which were a Godsend to the thousands of homeless families who had suffered the loss of jobs and homes. Those who were lucky enough to own tents pitched them on these unoccupied sites, but in most cases they simply erected "humpies" wherever they could. There was no need to consult learned treatises on economy to know that in the ministry of the Gospel, the first duty of Christian action, before the soul could be attended, was that the hungry had to be fed. As one of our great judges once remarked to me — "The devil dances on an empty stomach".
>
> The newly established parish had to be mobilised to visit the camps, with the St Vincent de Paul men leading the way. Sympathetic Protestants, would-be violent Socialists and even those with Communist learnings, saw that not only was charity preached but that it was also practiced. From then on they were all only too anxious to lend a helping hand.
> (Petrus p38)

As pastor, Dunlea's job would include working with the people to acquire the land on which the necessary buildings for a parish centre could be erected. Fundraising activities like fetes, bazaars, dances, raffles and so on would provide the where-with-all. Although labour-intensive, these did create a sense of interdependence and cooperation, the essential ingredients of a community of love and caring which Dunlea hoped to promote in Sutherland.

Little did he know, at that time, that his move south would be a catalyst leading to a response to the voice of the lonely street kid that had pierced the dawn air that fateful morning in Surry Hills:

> I wish I had someone to love me
> Someone to call me their own.

He arrived in Sutherland in his Rose Bay-acquired Chevvy but, on counting his first Sunday's collection, he decided there was no way he could afford to run a car. Happily he was able to trade it in for Bill Sykes, a white ex-racehorse he felt very much at home with. He also found a house in Merton Street that was small and old and basic, but just right for him. Gradually Bill Sykes and his owner became a familiar sight in that whole area south of the Georges River. Riding out of Sutherland, he visited everyone, irrespective of religion.

When visiting the children at Sutherland State School, he was delighted to see Alice Kinnane, whom he had come to know in Hurstville. Alice's family lived at Grays Point, then known as North West Arm. Her four-mile trek to school began in a boat, which she rowed across the river to Gymea Bay to catch the bus to Sutherland. Alice writes:

> My family were forced by the Depression from Hurstville to Grays Point, where there was no electricity or water or transport at that time. When my father was building a house by cutting down trees and making shingles and slabs, Father Dunlea tried to give him some money. My father, who was a lapsed Catholic, told him off and he went, but left behind a pound note, which my father found later. He grew to admire Father Dunlea and they became good friends. He it was who took the race game to functions to raise money for Boys Town. Father Dunlea used to bring my mother Communion, as she had no way of getting to the church.

There was an old man named Tom who lived in a shack behind McNeil's. Father met him while he was riding his horse and saw that his boots were worn through. He took off his own and gave them to Tom and rode home without boots.

Alice knew an eleven-year-old called Ray Shepherd, who lived with his father at Swallow Rock. His mother had died and his father drank and sometimes came home very late. Dunlea visited there and eventually adopted Ray. Years later Alice met Ray and noted how well and happy he was, with a good steady job. She adds:

> Father Dunlea, never asked anyone their religion or suggested they go to Church, but arranged transport for anyone who wanted to go. Even the most anti-Catholic at Grays Point liked him. Lots of things he did for people were not made public, and I have never heard anyone say a bad word about him. He really loved his fellow man. Later on, when he was Parish Priest of Hurstville, he was told that someone had stolen the candlesticks from the altar. His response was, "Oh, the poor man", which just about sums up Father Dunlea's philosophy.

After much fundraising activities by parishioners, St Patrick's School was opened at Sutherland. What particularly pleased Dunlea was securing the Presentation Sisters to look after it. He greatly admired Nano Nagle, their foundress, whose love of the poor was so like his own.

> "Whenever there was a school picnic at St Patrick's," writes Alice, "Father would gather up all the Catholics at the State school and take us to the picnic, and if anyone didn't have money for something, he would supply it."

Alice closes her report with an interesting assertion that certainly comes from deep conviction: "Father Tom Dunlea was as close as the human race will ever get to a saint, in my opinion".

6

Evicted

On Sunday September 3rd 1939, Dunlea was conducting an evening service for the Sacred Heart Sodality in the Sutherland parish church. In the middle of the sermon, the sacristan tugged at his soutane and handed him a note. He stopped in mid-sentence. It was one of those dramatic moments in which Dunlea excelled. A seriousness came over his normally bright, cheerful eyes and face. After a pregnant pause, he began solemnly: "I regret to inform you there is further bad news". (He had already spoken at the morning Mass about Germany's invasion of Poland and was actually commenting on the virtues of the Polish people, especially their strong Catholic faith, at the evening session when he was handed the note.) "News", he went on, "that is bad, bad for Australia and indeed for the world; however, news that is not unexpected. Britain and France have just declared war on Germany, and our own Prime Minister, Robert Menzies, has followed suit". Having paused for a couple of minutes for silent prayer, he went on to give the usual benediction. However, since the state of war was uppermost in their minds, he decided to invite the ladies to supper in the house he now called Boys Town, thinking that the distraction might ease the war nerves.

Earlier in the year he had moved out of the Merton Street presbytery, which had become so overcrowded that he just had to relocate. He had gone to the Sutherland estate agent and, in his own words:

> With a ten shilling deposit, we took a big old house nearby, belonging to Dorothy Boyle, on the corner of

Glencoe and Flora Streets. The walls were cracked, water seeped in here and there and it was condemned by the Sutherland Council, but it was a start.

Good friends like Eric Drew, Jim Walsh, Hilary Caldwell, Jim Noonan, the Colbrans and Moriartys and many others spent days cleaning and repairing, while Dunlea and the boys did the moving and settling in.

The boys made the ladies very welcome, and in general, this open-house venture was quite successful. Some of the ladies, however, were a bit nervous and ill at ease in the presence of these boys, many of whom they regarded as delinquents and petty criminals. The women loved their pastor, but couldn't at all share his strong affection for the boys, especially for the older tougher-looking ones. They recognised the ones who were fellow pupils with their own kids at St Patrick's school. There was a general perception that the younger boys, some as young as eight, might be in moral danger, living in such close proximity to fugitive street-wise teenagers.

This perception wasn't helped when the housekeeper informed them that many a time when Father Dunlea was engaged in parochial duties, he returned to find the place in a turmoil. She also informed them that more boys were knocking on the door of this cosmopolitan parent (as some called him), with the result that the number of boys in residence had now risen to seventeen.

As well as the war, another topic of conversation was being discussed animatedly by the boys and their visitors. Dunlea was very excited about it. In fact it was a turning-point for him, a catalyst that opened up a new future for himself and his boys. It had to do with an American film that had come to Sutherland some weeks before. A few parishioners had gone to the opening night and were so impressed that they couldn't recommend it highly enough.

Its name *Boys Town* attracted Dunlea, as did its main actors, Spencer Tracy and Mickey Rooney. It was the true story of a unique experiment in rehabilitating boys like his own, boys who were on the street and in trouble with the police. Father Flanagan, who was the founder and director of the so-called Town in Omaha, Nebraska, was played by all-time favourite Spencer Tracy.

Viewing the film with three of his boys, Dunlea became enraptured with the theme, kind of obsessed, as he told the ladies. The similarity between Flanagan's boys and his own was quite uncanny. Even the kids with him were fascinated. A boy called Steve, whose parents were non-Catholic and who lived in the neighbourhood, was already nominated the Mickey Rooney of Boys Town Australia. He writes:

> One of his horses, an ex-racehorse called Beau Ideal, he allowed me to ride around the area in the Mickey Rooney fashion. It was a very classy horse, which had been disqualified from racing in Sydney because of its continued resistance to accepting the standstill that was necessary at the starting barrier.

The fact that he had no long-term plan for his boys was a worry to Dunlea, as it was to others who were supporting him. He was succeeding in keeping them off the streets by giving them a home and sense of family. His way of relating to them was developing in the boys a feeling of belonging, of being cared about. His aim was to give them the confidence to grow into respected, responsible citizens. The way to do this in practice was not well defined or clear in his thinking, and this was causing him quite some concern.

Now as the Boys Town film unfolded before his eyes, a deep sense of relief began to come over him. Flanagan was ahead of him in that he had taken his boys that further step that hadn't yet entered Dunlea's thinking.

Dunlea knew that his boys should aim to be self-supporting, but creating a town for the running of which the boys themselves were to be responsible, was a brilliant idea, imaginative and exciting. The three boys with him at the film were equally excited. They kept prodding him with their elbows, urging him to follow Father Flanagan's lead.

When the film finished and the lights came on, Dunlea noticed some of his best helpers were present as well. As he moved out into the foyer, these came rushing excitedly towards him. At that moment, he knew in his heart that the key to his own future and that of his boys had been handed to him. Developing an Australian Boys Town there and then entered his agenda and henceforth preoccupied him almost full-time.

Even before this, he had embarked on a self-supporting programme. The vegetable plot at the back of Boyle's cottage was being cultivated by the boys with some success. A couple of them returning from a swim in the Woronora River, allegedly found some stray fowls, which were duly housed in the backyard for breeding purposes. These Dunlea accepted with some misgivings, knowing the boys were inclined to interpret the word stray in a wide sense! His good friend, Dr Eric Miles, kept a few goats to provide milk for those who were allergic to cows' milk. Two of these he donated to the cause. The boys also set up a little shop from which they sold small household goods. A committee consisting of Phil Brady, Rex McKenzie, Rupert Wiidhouse, Bert Townsend, Jim Walsh, Percy Ryan and Pat Hall whom Dunlea had got together to help with the finances, solicited goods from shops and farms to stock the shop and provide items for the boys to sell door-to-door on Saturdays.

The house had become quite a hive of activity. Dunlea, so single-minded and untiring in his work for the poor, set a pace that was too time-consuming for the adult committee, who had homes and families to look after. As a result their wives came to complain and although, quite taken aback by the seeming disorder and general mayhem in the house, they were very moved by the way Dunlea introduced his boys. His manner radiated good-humoured and affectionate respect, even pride. He seemed to know and trust the boys without hesitation, even though most of them looked quite disreputable and even somewhat obnoxious.

As usual, his charm and wit won the day with the young women — with all but one, that is. Mary Rose, a straight-shooter, was quite unimpressed with the whole enterprise and especially with her husband's role in it, and she wasn't leaving until she had said so in no uncertain terms. Her sudden outburst bowled Dunlea over somewhat. It did, however, alert him to the fact that he had to pay more attention to the often hidden turmoil boiling up within people, within men as well as women.

Did Mary Rose have a point? There are hints in some correspondence that perhaps she did. His powers of persuasion seemed almost irresistible according to Anne Cuddy and Thea Trembath.

> T.V.D. (Dunlea), writes Anne, was ruthless in pressuring his friends for his current cause. One Sutherland parishioner, an old lady he visited, was found playing the piano and he decided to work on her. Drops of water wear a rock and she finally agreed to let him have it for a home he had set up for alcoholics where so many poor fellows could enjoy it.
>
> Thea explains his modus operandi: with his silver tongue and musical laugh he handed out the compliments increasingly, knowing of course, that this was his bait for the numerous fish he was to catch. We in our turn fell for it, thinking it was our beauty that attracted him.

Perhaps he saw it as robbing the rich to help the poor as in the song *The Wild Colonial Boy* which he would have tuned into at Irish parties.

Her husband having retired from the committee, Mary Rose actually forgot about Dunlea and her confrontation with him. The next time she saw him was on a Saturday morning outside the local newsagency, where he was helping the Salvation Army make an appeal for funds. As Dunlea was lauding the work for the poor being done by the Army, he held up his little three-legged dog, Fred, saying, "Do you know how much it costs to keep Fred in a dog's hospital? One full pound! Do you know how much the dole is for one single man? Six shillings, and eight pence".

Mary Rose was singularly impressed. She liked the Salvos. After the appeal she came around and gave him a big kiss. He was delighted; it healed the still painful wound within him and endeared her to him. From then on she became one of his most loyal supporters.

Although on the one hand the Boys Town plan had Dunlea all buoyed up and full of energy and enthusiasm, the 1940s, on the other hand, saw crises of varying intensity gathering momentum and threatening to frustrate the plan. For one thing the leaking roof and generally poor condition of the building was worrying. Neighbours were complaining about the shabby, neglected look of the place, and parishioners were uneasy about the behaviour of the boys and the overcrowding. The number of boys was well past the twenty mark by mid-1940, not counting the couple of swagmen who had wandered in from the scrub and built themselves a tent in a corner of the backyard.

All this had been a turn-off for many in the area, but what got under their skin most was the fact that the Dunlea enterprise was diminishing the value of their properties! That was a very sore point indeed. And of course, the whole project was a thorn in the sides of the local Shire councillors, who were caught between a rock and a hard place! It was a permanent item in their meeting agenda for weeks. Some of them couldn't bring themselves to vote for closure, so beguiled were they by Dunlea and his total trust in God's providence and in the basic goodness of the boys.

The Health Inspector, Walter Cooper, had the final say, but he was also a good friend of Dunlea's. The prevalence of infectious diseases like polio and diphtheria was pointing to the urgent need to demolish premises like Dunlea's. The matter was raised in the middle of the

Woronora River, with Eric Miles present. The trio — the parish priest, the health inspector and the local G.P. — were making a trip to the south of the river. There was a settlement there euphemistically called Happy Valley. Workmen who were unemployed camped there in all sorts of humpies made of hessian, cardboard, cloth or whatever. Dunlea visited them frequently, bringing whatever goodies he could lay his hands on.

The doctor and the health inspector accompanied him this time, because they were concerned about the outbreak of poverty-induced epidemics. Dunlea administered the Last Sacraments and did the funerals of several Happy Valley non-Catholics, either because he was the only clergyman they trusted or the one the relatives wanted.

On the way back to Sutherland all three, the doctor, the health Inspector and the priest, agreed that something had to be done about the boys in the Boyle house. All Dunlea looked for was time enough to find alternative accommodation.

By mid-1940, however, the situation in the Boyle house had become so bad and the neighbours so irate that most of the pro-Dunlea councillors could hold out no longer. The motion to close passed by a narrow margin, and the document to that effect was signed by Walter Cooper.

Although saddened at the haste with which they were being thrown on the street, as it were, Dunlea managed to see in it the hand of God at work. His mother had taught him always to look for the silver lining, and although, in his native Tipperary cuteness, he didn't say so at the time, he felt certain the lining he saw was more gold than silver. He recalled the fact that many of the poorest in Sutherland had been driven out of rented properties in Sydney. Indeed, in the not-too-distant past, many of his forebears in Ireland had suffered a similar fate. He himself, and so many others he knew, felt a great sympathy for such people.

The word that described their predicament was a strong emotive one that would ring bells in the hearts of people of good-will — EVICTION. In that word, "eviction", he saw the possibility of turning dark tragedy into a bright future. The famous twinkle in his eye became more pronounced as he savoured it.

7

The grand march

July 17, 1940 was a red-letter day in the eventful life of Thomas Vincent Dunlea. It was a day that revealed his capacity for drama, for flair, for the creative gesture that would attract the attention of the media and, through the media, the public.

The media of the time, print and radio, was taken up with ominous war news. Northern Europe and Paris had fallen into German hands. Mussolini was entering the war as Hitler's partner, British forces were being evacuated from Dunkirk, and Australian servicemen and women were heading for Singapore, Northern Africa and Europe. Dunlea was a very small fish in a vast turbulent sea. If he were to secure the headlines he needed, he would have to earn them in some imaginative and appealing way. He needed a plan of action to create waves that couldn't but be noticed.

He began preparations early in July by calling together the boys and all his active helpers. As with all meetings when important decisions had to be made, he started with a couple of minutes of silent prayer. Most of his boys and many of his supporters didn't belong to his Church. Not wanting to impose his way of praying on them, he suggested they talk to God in whatever way they felt comfortable with. From their association with him they could be in no doubt as to his own conviction about God's presence and goodness and, indeed, the goodness of Australian people. He explained in some detail the discussions that had taken place in the Council and the growing concern of some people living nearby.

As he read the letter signed by Walter Cooper, his eyes seemed to fill up and his voice began to falter. During the ensuing silence, just about every boy in the room and many of the adults were sobbing or very close to tears. At this stage the three original boys, Eric, Eddie and Monkey, were at his side, assuring him that no-one would evict them and, if they tried, it would be over their dead bodies!

Dunlea, always quick to see the funny side, began to laugh, as did everyone present.

It was almost a year since Dunlea had obtained the Archbishop's approval to start an Australian Boys Town after the Father Flanagan model. His curate, Roger Wynne, had sent a press release to Brian Marien of the *Daily Telegraph* with the news that the foundation day would be August 1st, 1939. For weeks before, a campaign to elect the town's first Mayor was waged with vigour and excitement. The boys got their first experience of the democratic process and they just loved it. Dunlea was pleased that, after all the speechmaking and policy announcements, the mantle fell on Eric Green, his first boy. Eric was about to oversee the election of a number of aldermen when the news of closure broke.

Dunlea, of course, was aware for some time that a town would need more space than the quarter-acre suburban block they were occupying. They needed land, several acres, amenable to cultivation. They needed buildings of various shapes and sizes, arranged to resemble what they saw in the film. A tall order indeed, and not a shadow of an idea how it could possibly happen! The only trickle of light was Dunlea's unshakable trust in God's providence, together with his wit and imagination. He told the boys to rest assured that a place would be found. He didn't tell them how or where for the good reason that he just didn't know. He knew, however, the Council order meant that before they moved to a permanent home, they would have to bed down under the stars for a while. This he forewarned them about.

His friend, Eric Drew, knew a second-hand dealer in Sydney who had a supply of ex-army tents that he would sell at minimum cost. The committee and their wives, rounded up by Mary Rose, dealt with the logistics. They prepared for the relocating of the kitchen facilities, the food, the bedding, etc. D-day was to be July 10th but, owing to heavy rain and some floodings, it was put off for a week. His very good friends Yvonne and Brian Marien alerted the *Leader*, the Sutherland Shire newspaper, that the move was imminent. Newsreel was an important visual news medium and, in some undisclosed and indirect way, Dunlea's *bête noire* of Surry Hills days, the redoubtable Kate Leigh, alerted a Cinesound cameraman. Brian Marien made the front page of the *Telegraph* with the eviction factor.

The boys, now numbering twenty-seven, were advised again that the future was uncertain, and the move in midwinter would entail some quite rough living. They were also free to opt out. Dunlea would find them suitable alternative accommodation. Proof of how tightly he had bound the little community around him was the fact that every one of the boys then in residence elected to go with him. The move was announced in Sutherland and at the other mass-centres he visited regularly. Although Menai was bush then, he announced it there on Saturday when he rode out for the monthly mass, visiting homes as far as the Lugarno Ferry.

Radio 2FC forecast a dry cool day for July 17, with a maximum of 71 degrees Fahrenheit. Even though the morning temperature was only 30 degrees Fahrenheit, the boys lined up early for a big breakfast which, they were warned, would have to be their lunch as well. When the packing up was completed, Monkey led the larger goat, the one with the huge horns, out into the assembly area in the street in front of the Boyle cottage.

Attached to the goat's horns was a large placard on which was written in bold letters the name of the health inspector, Mr Cooper. The boys and some of the committee had insisted on this. A scapegoat made good copy for the media.

Behind the goat were six of the younger boys lined up in twos, followed by the two brown setters on the leash; then came six more boys followed by a hand-cart in which some four chooks clucked loudly. Boys carrying an assortment of banners were joined by Mary Rose, Yvonne and Brian Marien, Anne Macinante (Cuddy), some soldiers (from the nearby camp) and a handful of other adults. These were followed by more boys and other youngsters making up a sort of ragtime band. Bringing up the rear were two horses driven by two senior boys.

The banners, with messages neatly printed, communicated Dunlea's message very fluently. "We are Australian refugees", "We ask only for independence", "Give us a fair go" and "Australian homes for Australian lads" were a few of the messages.

At the stroke of noon, Dunlea, dressed in full clericals, mounted his old white charger and, taking his place in front of the large goat, led this most unusual procession slowly down into the town centre. Word had somehow got out; the bush telegraph was functioning. Quite a crowd gathered, some to support, some to be amused by this motley assortment of boys, animals, fowls and adults. The band, including some boys using pots and pans as drums, wasn't very harmonious, but it was loud and attracting. Some people clapped, some smiled and some looked on somewhat dumbstruck.

The procession veered a little off course towards the Council offices and halted in front of the building where, among the people gathered, were, amazingly, the Coopers. When they saw what was happening, they turned towards Dunlea, who was now walking with the boys. "Good on you, Father Tom!" shouted Mrs Cooper, "Please keep in touch". Dunlea responded with a smile, "Thank you, we will".

With banners aloft, the procession, continued to attract attention as it wound its way through the town. Dunlea's spirit got a great boost when he noticed some people, strangers to him, writing in their notebooks and taking photographs. At this stage the boys were holding their places well. The music of the band was keeping the goats from becoming too obstreperous, and the dogs from escaping from the leash and the horses from prancing around too much. The only one who insisted on doing its own thing was the rooster. Much to the amusement of the boys and the spectators, it crowed impressively every couple of minutes.

Jim Noonan had asked a friend in the police force to arrange some traffic control for their route along the Princes Highway. The occupants of cars and vans and even horsedrawn vehicles strained their necks to examine the unusual collection of marchers, by now becoming fairly ragged. The banners alone gave them an idea of what it was all about. When the procession reached the culvert marking the city limits, to celebrate the fact that they were now outside the jurisdiction of the Sutherland Council, they relieved the goat of the Mr Cooper placard. Much to the amusement of everyone, they nailed the sign on a clean barkless gum tree.

Further along the highway, seeing the road sign, Royal National Park — 1/2 mile, the boys' pace quickened, the chatter grew louder, the sense of excitement became more palpable. The goats alone were falling behind, finding it difficult to cope with the hard scraggy surface of the roadside.

There were no houses now, only old-growth forest on both sides of the road. The eucalyptus-scented air was clear and crisp, with just the semblance of a nor'-easterly helping them along. As the road veered to the right at the Loftus rifle range, a great cry of delight arose from the marchers. There, right in front of them, was a placard stretching from one gum tree to the next reading:

BOYS TOWN'S NEW HOME.

Eric Drew and a few boys who had been erecting the tents and Mary Rose and her helpers, who had been preparing the food, rushed to the road to give the marchers a big welcome. Dunlea, mounted on his horse again, halted near the big banner to congratulate and thank the boys and the helpers on completing a march that would bring their vision and their needs to the notice of the Australian people, who would not let them down.

As the boys were settling into their new environment, Dunlea had an interview with Brian Marien from the *Daily Telegraph*, followed by another with journalists from the *Mirror* and Cinesound. He was in his element. His wit, good humour and charismatic approach delighted the reporters, with the result that Boys Town was headline news in most of the print media the next day. It even featured that evening in the Radio News and in cinema newsreels all over Sydney.

Some weeks before the boys left Sutherland, Hurstville businessman, Jim Walsh, had met his namesake, Father Joe Walsh, one of Dunlea's curates, at a funeral service in nearby Woronora Cemetery. He had learned from Father Walsh that without massive support, Dunlea could not bring his plan for the boys to fruition. Having some entrepreneurial skills, Jim Walsh began to contact his many friends, especially politicians, hoteliers and other business people. Convinced that a public meeting was the way to publicise Dunlea's plans and needs, he booked the Hurstville Community Centre for Monday, July 25. However, the publicity resulting from the July 17 march was so effective that he had to look for a much bigger venue. With only a few days to go, he was at his wits' end looking for a suitable place when Dan Minogue, Member of Parliament for East Sydney, and Sydney City Councillor, Tony Doherty, procured the Sydney Town Hall free of charge.

Even though the notice was short and the night was wet and cold, a capacity crowd of one thousand five hundred people, from all classes of society, enthusiastically endorsed Dunlea's plan to make Boys Town a haven for the friendless and forsaken boy. Clive Evatt, brother of the redoubtable Bert, representing Leader of the Opposition, William McKell, declared "the

Opposition stood as a man behind Father Dunlea in his wonderful work".

Member of Parliament J Munro, and many Government officials were either present or represented. They declared Boys Town a sound and thoroughly praiseworthy cause. Together with a cheque, a letter was handed to Father Dunlea by Joe Munroe on behalf of the Premier, announcing that investigations had been made regarding Government aid to Boys Town. Father assured him that he greatly appreciated the Government's cooperation, but he preferred to work without state aid and outside Government control. (*The Voice of Boys Town*)

This freedom from Government control came at a price, but it was very important to Dunlea, who had his own unique plan for his boys, a plan radically different from any envisaged by Government agencies.

Jim Walsh's friend, T J Purcell, the well-known solicitor who chaired the meeting, felt that the size and mood of the gathering was a strong indication that Dunlea's confidence in the goodwill of the Australian people was well founded. The amount promised, one thousand pounds, was beyond all expectations and a pointer to the largesse to come.

Publicity, the limelight, front-page news — it all appealed greatly to Dunlea. He made no secret of the fact that he sought it and, indeed, revelled in it. He knew this was due to a streak of vanity in his make-up. He knew, too, that his vision for Boys Town could not become a reality without it.

8

The tent village

On July 24, 1940 one week after the Tent Village was set up, George Nathan, a bookmaker, a Jew and well-known philanthropist, was busily receiving bets at Moorefields Racecourse, Kogarah, when two women approached him. Both were great supporters of Dunlea. Dorothy Coleman was having a flutter on the next race, but her companion, Margaret Gray, being a devoted Methodist, was not a betting person, although interested in the horses. As they were placing Dorothy's bet, Nathan's assistant, who knew Margaret, asked them about the boys in the tents and their friend, the priest. Nathan overheard and, realising that they were talking about what he had seen in the paper, was curious to find out more. He decided to see for himself en route to Wollongong for the late evening race meeting there. Having got the necessary information, he did call into the Tent Village, to find Dunlea in the middle of one of his formal/informal chats with the boys.

Nathan noticed the rapport between the boys and the priest. Their faces, tough and unkempt as most of them were, were not only attentive, but were reflecting back to the priest the good humour and wit and affection he was directing towards them. Dunlea, on hearing George's family name, Nathan, savoured it with obvious relish. "Your namesake and kinsman", he said, "was the prophet of Yahweh who befriended King David and secured the succession for his son Solomon, a great man of God. I am sure you are worthy of such a great name". Over the weekend Nathan had read bits and pieces about Dunlea and the grand march, but seeing him in person, experiencing the warmth of his welcome and, most of all, observing his free and easy, yet respectful way with the boys, quite overwhelmed him. The Dunlea charisma was working.

Dunlea never forgot that day. In and through George Nathan, he saw for the first time, the possibility of his dream for Boys Town becoming a reality. He felt Nathan could be the person in whom Dunlea's utter trust in God's providence and in the fair-mindedness of the Australian people would be fulfilled. Although as a bookmaker Nathan could be suspect in the eyes of some, he was a high-profile public figure in Sydney who could bring Boys Town that note of recognition Dunlea had hoped for.

The best-known and arguably the best-looking female in Sydney at that time was June Russell. A hairdresser by profession and somewhat well-endowed — a characteristic well regarded in the early 1940s — she had reinvented herself a few years earlier by converting her hairdressing operation into a beauty salon. This had enabled her to share her solutions and formulas with her clientele. So successful was this venture that, within a couple of years, several Sydney suburbs had similar salons bearing her name. Nathan's wife, one of her regular customers, invited her to join them at Loftus one Sunday afternoon. Like so many other good-looking women, she was a big hit with Dunlea, and he with her. June Russell became a major supporter and a regular visitor, as did Benny Bear, a wealthy furniture man and good friend of Nathan's.

C V Eastburn, a well-known horse trainer, was similarly introduced to the priest by Nathan. Having a nephew who had been quite uncontrollable until some weeks previously when he had joined the AIF, Eastburn immediately saw the potential in Dunlea's plan. It was, however, a down-time for him just then. Of all the horses in his stables, only one, Dublin Lad, looked like having any great prospects. As it happened, the horse was to make his debut in Moorefields the following Saturday. If he did well in his first city race, the Juvenile Handicap,

Eastburn promised to give Boys Town a share in the takings.

As an outsider at 25 to 1, Dublin Lad surprised everyone by going on to win the race by almost half a length. Eastburn was so pleased that he made Boys Town a beneficiary from every race Dublin Lad won.

Some weeks after the establishment of the Tent Village at Loftus, there was a news item in the *Mirror* newspaper regarding a move to start Sunday car-racing at the Sydney Showgrounds. The City Council, it said, would give permission on condition that some charity would benefit. The next day Dunlea had a visit from a passing motorist who, it is said, had had a phone call that morning from George Nathan. The result: Sunday car-racing went ahead at the Sydney Showgrounds, with proceeds going to Boys Town. Eventually comprising lots of other attractive competitive events, it became known as the Sunday Carnival.

With its high-profile public figures on board, Boys Town was getting lots of media attention, and donations were coming from many quarters. Dunlea himself was in such demand that his chest gave out, and Dr Miles ordered him to Lewisham Hospital for a few days. Yvonne Marien, who had been on the march with him, found his hospital bed covered with letters and cheques, which she proceeded to acknowledge at his request. He was overwhelmed at the generosity of people, she noted.

His original Finance Committee, also overwhelmed at the response, felt their role was now completed. Boys Town had entered the big league, and it needed more financial experience than they were able to give. Accepting their resignation, he couldn't thank them enough for hanging in there and supporting him in the lean and difficult times they'd been through together.

Yvonne brought him a letter from his friend Dame Mary Gilmore, which Eric Drew had delivered to his hospital bed. It gave him quite a boost that Australia's greatly loved poet should be thinking of him. She enclosed a poem called *The Tree*, specially composed for him.

> Under the tree Man raised his tent — under the shining leaves
> The weary all came there and the spent — under the shining leaves
> Under the tree man set his tent — when at last the night had come
> Under the tree he laid him down — knowing that he was home.
> Birds came and rested in that tree — the ant climbed upwards from the sod.
> So, even as Man, all things came home
> Knowing the tree was God.

The boys' life in the tents, under the stars, was rough but, in a way, excitingly different. The challenge to survive appealed to them. Frequently gusts of wind knocked the tents around, and showers created puddles of muddy water under their feet. The boys of school age continued to go to their school in Sutherland. Urgent requests to accept new uncontrollable boys continued to come.

Heart-rending letters were received from invalid mothers and heartbroken relatives, asking that their lads be admitted to Boys Town. Also letters of pleading came from inefficiently trained mothers, relatives, friends and acquaintances, asking for the adoption of boys before disgrace and ignominy was brought upon the family.

The mothers had no inhibitions about recording the boys' delinquencies. What never ceased to surprise Dunlea was the fact that no matter how long the list or how bad the crimes recorded, mother still hung in there: "But he's not a bad boy, Father".

This refusal to give up, to write them off, delighted Dunlea. He saw in it the mysterious identity of mother with her child. Time and again in crisis situations, he experienced the motherly instincts silently and unconsciously bringing her back to that identity: he's my child, he's me, I see myself in him, in his eyes, in his laughter, even in his horrible actions. I cannot reject him because he's me.

Some years later, with his friend John McRae, a Boys Town teacher who became a priest, he explained how he had come to an illuminating application of the mother/child identity. He saw it as a reflection of the Creator/creature relationships. In his human creation the Creator sees his own image, his own likeness; he sees divinity, he sees his Godself. His love for people has no conditions, no cut-off point; even the worst of human badness doesn't stop it because God cannot stop loving himself. Father Tom felt this was the illumination that filled St John's mind when he penned the mysterious words: God is love (1 John 4:16).

* * * * * * * *

Feeling that a prolonged stay in the tents would lead to a slovenly, free-and-easy attitude that might later be difficult to shake off, Mary Rose and the other helpers kept up the pressure to search for a permanent home. Someone would see or hear of a place for sale that could be suitable, but it was either too far away, like a property in Robertson in the Southern Highlands, or too dear, like a big house and garden in Sans Souci on Botany Bay. When Dunlea returned after the few days in Lewisham Hospital, Dr Miles was adamant that he leave Loftus and the primitive outdoor living as soon as possible.

Even with all the support from so many people, finding suitable accommodation proved elusive and time-consuming. What kept the morale high was the priest's unshakable confidence in God's providence and the people's goodness.

"The right place will find us even before we find it" he would say cheerfully. And lo and behold! — on October 8, 1940 that did happen. It was almost next door, just four kilometres to the south along the Princes Highway, in Engadine.

Alice and Phil Brady, two of the tent helpers, had gone to Engadine to buy some eggs and fruit for the boys from the Lombe family who had a property there. Max Lombe, then a school boy, informed them that the lady next door, a Mrs Higgen in Waratah Street East, had told his parents she was thinking of selling and moving nearer to the city. Phil and Alice went to investigate and found there was a large old house and seven acres of good land.

The owner was a Presbyterian whose only son had been severely wounded in France some months earlier. She listened to the Boys Town story with interest, and having already heard of Dunlea, indicated she would be honoured to talk with him. A couple of days later, she succumbed as expected to the Dunlea charm, and Boys Town acquired its first permanent home for well below market price.

Dunlea couldn't get over his luck. Not only had he a large house, but a well-tended vegetable garden, a piggery and, most importantly, a dam. Pointing to the goldfish of various sizes playfully and excitedly darting about in the dam water, Dunlea and his companion, Bruce Aley, saw it as a happy omen, imagining the hectic activity and excitement that would soon transform this place. And, indeed, the transformation began within weeks. After Roger Wynne, the curate in Sutherland, contacted his friend Brian Marien, of the *Daily Telegraph*, the good news spread quickly. While George Nathan, June Russell and Arthur Cooper of Sutherland were shown over the new acquisition by Anne Cuddy and Val Marie Nethery, Dunlea and Bruce McMahon were giving the boys the first glimpse of their new town. In their excitement and delight, they wanted to move in immediately. Dunlea, however, explaining in some detail the work that needed to be done to the old house to make it habitable, indicated a wait of many weeks, maybe even until Christmas or longer.

In the meantime, a great variety of fundraising functions had begun or were about to begin. These contributed much to making wartime Sydney a rather pleasant place to be. Sunday, especially, changed from being a rather dour day of stringent Sabbatical observance to being, for some at any rate, a gala day with interesting options. The beach culture hadn't taken on as yet, and the Blue Mountains and other country destinations weren't very accessible because of petrol rationing. Hotels were forbidden to trade and to discourage Sunday dances or films or concerts, no charge could be made at the door.

In this milieu the Sunday Carnival at the Sydney Sports Ground attracted a capacity crowd who came to support the cause and enjoy the trotting, cycling and midget-car racing. For the first time, the doors of the old Tivoli Ballroom in Sydney opened on a Sunday, with proceeds from the sale of the programmes going to Boys Town. Sydneysiders, young and old, as well as lots of Australian and American servicemen and women participated in the dancing promoted by florist Bill Suit, and in the concerts organised by Phil Brady.

Gradually the friends and supporters of Dunlea brightened the Sydney social calendar with harbour cruises, gymkhanas, football matches promoted by well-known sports personalities, pet shows, and operas courtesy of well-known entrepreneur Reuben F Scarf, who proved to be a very generous benefactor to Boys Town and Dunlea.

In October 1940, learning that his brother Tim, a policeman in Queensland was seriously ill, Dunlea sought permission to travel to Ravenshoe in northern Queensland to see him. It was a difficult time-consuming wartime journey, entailing long sleepless nights.

Just two years later, in July 1942, Tim died in Sydney. Dunlea wrote to thank Archbishop Gilroy for visiting and praying for him and enclosed a cheque, which the Archbishop graciously declined to cash.

In the meantime, the new town was beginning to take shape in Engadine. Dunlea had succeeded in attracting a former religious brother, a Mr Duffy, to Engadine as his first trained teacher with Anne Cuddy (nee Macinante) as secretary. Anne, who knew Dunlea when he was curate in

Hurstville, remembers getting the 7 a.m. train from Hurstville to Sutherland. From there on the two-car rail motor to the tiny Engadine Station and then across the paddocks (where Woolworths is now located) to Boys Town.

> There, Ann recalls, Mr Duffy would be seated on an open verandah with the boys grouped around him, a big man with white hair, his bloodshot eyes told the tale of his alcoholism but his profession of faith before these boys was worthy of an apostle.

While Dunlea was away drumming up support for the town, the boys proved somewhat of a handful for Anne. So it was decided that a male live-in secretary was needed. A Mr Singh was found to fill the bill.

During most of 1940 and all of 1941, Dunlea had received leave of absence from Sutherland parish, so that he could devote himself totally to the boys and live with them. The town's mayor and his aldermen felt that his physical presence was very important, especially at that critical time. Fortunately, the Archbishop agreed, although most of his college of consultors did not.

9

The ugly man competition

A strong southerly-buster early in May 1941 brought much needed relief from the heat and humidity of the last days of April. Sunday May 4 saw the clouds give way to bright warm sunshine. Alex Mair, the Premier of New South Wales, looked forward to the afternoon function as he sped south on the Princes Highway towards Engadine in his comfortable government-supplied Buick. He had followed the Boys Town saga with keen and, to some extent, selfish interest. His Youth and Community Services Department found it very useful for placing their more intractable and difficult boys. When he arrived at the entrance in Waratah Street, East Engadine, he got a big welcome from the boys, who formed the guard-of-honour. As everyone knew Dunlea wasn't big on rehearsing and precise training, so there was a general chuckle when members of the guard-of-honour broke ranks to shake hands with the Premier and actually escort him towards the podium.

As was usual on occasions like this, Dunlea was in his element. It was one of the great days in his life. His cherished dream was at last becoming a reality! The foundation stone of the new Boys Town Engadine was being cemented into place by the Premier. After welcoming the guests and outlining the ambitious plans for the site, Dunlea addressed the generous benefactors and supporters, who were making it all happen:

> The years to come will show you more than buildings. They will show you worthy Australian citizens in the trades, in offices, in factories, who will

bear witness that they had been Boys Town boys, proud of the trust you had in their ability to go forward and conquer, despite unfortunate beginnings, mistakes, misfortune.

In reference to the dismal war news that weighed heavily on people's minds at the time, he expressed deep sympathy with the relatives of the six thousand Australian troops of the Sixth Division who had lately fallen under enemy fire in Greece and Crete. Everyone was conscious of the members of the Ninth Division holding out in Tobruk against a blockade and bombardment now in its sixth month. Dunlea was eloquent and dramatic as he lauded these young men (later known as the Rats of Tobruk) who, in their courage and self-sacrifice, were carrying on the heroic spirit of the Anzacs of World War I. He hoped his Boys Town boys would always remember them as heroes and role models.

He was grateful for the presence of the Italian Apostolic Delegate, Giovanni Panico. This was the Prelate who had assumed the role of Australianising the Hierarchy — filling vacant Sees with Australian-born Bishops, which made him less than popular with sections of the clergy and laity. Facetiously, Dunlea referred to two contemporary news items highly embarrassing to Panico. First, the almost effortless capture of some 40,000 of his fellow countrymen in Egypt by the Australian Army and then the sinking of the cruiser *Bartolomeo Colleone* by the Australian Navy ship, *HMAS Sydney*. The Dunlea humour and innuendo was not lost on most of those present, especially Archbishop Gilroy, who at the time was having his own disagreement with Bishop Panico.

Alex Mair, having referred to the splendid service being done by a small group of people under the guidance of Father Dunlea, went on to say:

> I earnestly believe that this magnificent creation will stand as a glowing example of self-service and, as such, give a stimulus to the whole community to

extend a helping hand to those less fortunate than themselves.

My earnest wish is that Boys Town will go from strength to strength and that the boys who pass through its care will, in the fullest sense, become the men of tomorrow.

Eric Green, the Town Mayor, responded by thanking the Premier (a non-Catholic) for his generous words and delighted everyone by quoting from the Casino Presbyterian *Church Standard* the words of its acting Rector, Rev G Stuart Watts:

Father Dunlea's Boys Town is one of the finest humanitarian crusades ever launched in Australia. In the spirit of his Master, the great-hearted priest and citizen is seeking to provide a home for the homeless, irrespective of creed or class, and to afford them a fair chance in life.

Boys Town is a work of national importance and deserves the wholehearted support of all sections of the community. God bless Father Dunlea, and may his efforts on behalf of the Australian citizens of tomorrow be crowned with success.

Dunlea then introduced Jimmy Jones, a homeless boy whose entry to Boys Town was occasioned by stealing bread and jumping the rattlers when searching for employment. He had written down some of his experiences at Boys Town, which Dunlea asked him to share with the gathering:

When I am hungry — in fact, when I am getting hungry — I find food is set out on a table for me. Father is not always reminding me of the loaf of bread and jumping the rattlers, and somehow he seems so different to the other people I have met. In fact, he often reminds me of my own father.

I like the police force in this town too, and when they get on to me, it is only when I deserve it. They are only the boys who sit with me at table, perhaps that is why I'm not afraid of them, but yet I can look a real policeman in the eye now. This whole place is changing me.

The Mayor of Boys Town is a good sport, so perhaps other mayors are not quite so inhuman as I thought.

I don't know why I ever ran away from school, but I think it was because a teacher could not understand a bloke like Boys Town teachers.

I never thought I would have the opportunity of choosing the job I would like best. It is interesting, too, what the other boys in Boys Town are going to do. I hear them talk of primary Industries — the rearing of pedigree sheep, cattle and poultry under all modern methods, with minimum cost and maximum returns.

Regarding secondary industries, there are the usual bookbinding, printing, leather workings and making of feltex mats. Also wireless construction and even a factory which, if possible, would embrace many trades, so as those boys who prefer city life would have their wishes fulfilled. Some of the boys are also interested in radio and aero-navigation.

Two years ago I ran a mile if I saw a policeman, but after Boys Town police force, I learnt that even the Police Force bore me no malice, if I abided by the laws.

Funny thing, only two years ago I did not realise stealing a loaf of bread was a crime. (Voice of Boys Town 1941)

****

Mayor Green, and his six newly elected aldermen, showed people over the only building on the site, the old house.

Extended and refurbished with the help of furniture man Benny Bear, it was being transformed by honorary architect, Francis Ryan, and builder, William Cruickshank, into dormitories, one honouring June Russell and the other George Nathan, Dunlea's two major benefactors.

Mrs Grayson, the Matron, with Mr and Mrs Fisk from Sutherland days, showed off the new kitchen-dining area. The plans for the new buildings were explained by two Boys Town teachers Miss M Knight, and Mr G Duffy, who had taught in many public schools in New Zealand and New South Wales. Neville Johnson, a full-blooded Aborigine from Menindee, proudly showed people over the temporary chapel, where he was chief altar server.

Dunlea's dream plan for the future included colourful garden plots, ornamental lakes, walkways and a variety of native trees and shrubs.

The Bread Manufacturers Association had earmarked the corner plot on which to build the bakery where the boys would be trained in the trade, also supplying valuable food for the Town and guaranteeing quality employment for the graduates when they eventually sought work. A carpentry workshop and boot-repairing facilities were within weeks of being up and running. A poultry run was being set up by the Hurstville Youngerset, led by Joan Gortley, and the vegetable garden tradition from the old Sutherland Boys Town was being continued and extended.

Through a long process of dialogue and consultation, Dunlea made sure the boys were in agreement with the plan and all its details. It had to be their plan, they had to own it. Thus, led by the Mayor and his alderman, they felt involved in its implementation. People were surprised at their detailed knowledge of the plan and their readiness to answer questions and consider suggestions. One important suggestion had to do with making space for a meat industry project.

* * * * * * * *

Peter Mutton and Tony Paul, two Australian pilots killed on war service, had been involved in the meat industry before joining the RAAF and had given every promise of returning to it when hostilities were over. However, this was not to be. Indeed, their sad loss sent through the meat industry a wave of sympathy for their fathers, who were executive members of the Meat and Allied Trade Federation of Australia. A memorial to these two young men, proposed by Fred Forest, a fellow executive member, was decided on, and an appeal for funds launched.

At first, the memorial in mind was the endowment of a bed or cot at the Children's Hospital. A worthy cause and politically and religiously neutral. However, Joseph Merritt, a colleague of Fred Forest on the Meat Federation Executive, had heard about Dunlea from his wife who was a June Russell customer. He suggested that the executive visit Dunlea at Boys Town before making up their minds. This, the first of many visits, led to a partnership that was to bring many fine buildings to Boys Town over the years and create a spirit of community and co-operation in the industry. The executive decided that:

> There was no finer method of perpetuating the memories of meat industry workers who died on war service than an endowment at Boys Town, which is doing magnificent work in preserving the lives of neglected boys and giving them a chance to develop into first-class men. No more appropriate memorial could be chosen than one which will give to our community self-reliant young men of character, whose original circumstances gave them a very poor chance of becoming good citizens. Those young men will, to some extent, replace men who made the supreme sacrifice, and the ex-citizens of Boys Town will in every way endeavour to prove themselves worthy of an endowment that is perpetuating the memory of our own members killed in war service.

The Meat Trade Training School was located next to the Bakery Training School, the buildings being similar in design and size. Like the bakers before them, volunteers from the meat trade generously gave their time and skill in helping the more senior of the boys to start in a skilled trade. The Boys Town programme and the boys' response so impressed the meat trade executive that they began to look at erecting another building. Many of the boys, they noticed, were suffering from malnutrition and various organic diseases, especially the more recent arrivals. A clinic, they deemed, was an urgent necessity. As they became more involved, however, they concluded that a hospital would be the ideal answer. Dunlea, who continued to respond to requests from the courts and from distraught mothers, wasn't totally convinced, but nonetheless gave the project his full support and blessing.

To build a hospital as a fitting memorial to their war dead, the meatmen would need to involve all their members in fundraising activities. This would mean presenting Dunlea's plan for wayward boys in a way that would touch the hearts and the pockets of thousands in New South Wales.

After a direct appeal for funds began to wind down, a memorial button was designed and sold throughout the industry. Someone then suggested a Beauty Queen Competition, which was becoming a popular money-raising activity at the time. Although this appealed to Dunlea, he humorously suggested a man's competition might be more appropriate in such a male-dominated industry. This suggestion, provoking much laughter and levity, led eventually to a decision to hold an Ugly Man Competition!

Fred Forest and meatman Jim McCormack, using their considerable organisational skills and powers of persuasion, prevailed on five enthusiastic members to be contestants. Each would represent a section of the industry, as follows:

> ALLIED TRADES: Tom Cranitch
> MEAT INDUSTRY EMPLOYEES: Sam Shelton
> COUNTRY MEATWORKS: Alf Anderson
> RETAILERS: Jally Beatton
> WHOLESALERS: Alf Smairl

The industry reported:

> This competition was a unique example of
> enthusiastic co-operation amongst all sections of the

meat industry and allied trades. Strange as it may sound, this co-operation had its main driving force in the rivalry between each section in supporting its Ugly Man candidate. It brought together many men of the meat industry who had not met before or perhaps who had met only in the hurly-burly of business life without that friendly touch of informality that adds sweetness to life.

The report went on to note that wholesalers, retailers, country meatworks, allied trades and employees shared the joy of striving for a common ideal — the building of a hospital that would be testimony to the industry's regards for the underprivileged boys, under the care of their friend, Father Tom Dunlea.

Many functions were organised by the supporters of the individual candidates, and the money raised counted as votes. Snowball auctions were held for such items as lambs, steers, body of beef, hides, drums of tallow, etc. One candidate went to the extent of purchasing and raffling a champion yearling, which was won by a lady from as far away as Tamworth in northern New South Wales.

After six months of fundraising, the Competition concluded in the Sydney Town Hall with a musical extravaganza called, The Glorification of Ugliness, produced by Radio 2UE's well-known presenter, Arthur Carr. When 2UE's popular announcer, Alan Toohey, called Dunlea and the five contestants to the stage, there was a great standing ovation by the three thousand or more people present. Before Alan Toohey announced the winner, Dunlea called Frank Lonie, the then Mayor of Boys Town, and his six aldermen to the stage. In a moment of high drama and to thundering applause, Mayor Frank Lonie placed the Ugly Man crown on the head of burly Alf Anderson, the representative of Country Meatworks.

Having expressed his thanks and congratulations, with his usual humour and panache, to Alf Anderson and the other contestants, Dunlea read a message from John Curtin, Prime Minister of Australia, saying how much he appreciated the splended contributions to the war by supporters of Boys Town and a message from State Premier McKell:

> Young Australians are being given a real chance in life. Boys Town has assumed an aspect of national importance because it is building up the youth of the country. (The Voice of Boys Town 1942)

He then held up for all to see two international cablegrams congratulating the winner, the meat industry and Boys Town Australia. He mischievously challenged the audience to guess who the authors were. Churchill and Roosevelt were among the names flippantly thrown up from the body of the Hall. Then, as silence crept over the vast assembly, Dunlea revealed that the cables were from the two most popular pin-up heroes of that time: Spencer Tracy and Mickey Rooney!

After boisterous and prolonged applause, Dunlea repeated the two names with obvious satisfaction. He referred to Spencer Tracy's Oscar for his performance in *Captains Courageous* in 1937 and the Academy Award for his playing of Father Flanagan in *Boys Town*:

> We will never forget that brilliant portrayal of Father Flanagan and our whole vision for Boys Town is summed up in that famous caption under the picture of Mickey Rooney's smiling, sweaty face as he carries a large wounded boy on his shoulders:
>
>> He's not heavy,
>> he's my brother.

10

The Clergy Conference

As Boys Town was establishing itself in Engadine, James Madden, President of St Patrick's College, Manly, surprised Dunlea by suggesting that he give a short talk at the autumn gathering of all the Sydney clergy. This rather unprecedented request was due to the prompting of Archbishop Gilroy who was aware that many of the clergy and some laity were worried about Dunlea and his brainchild, Boys Town. He was getting lots of publicity, and hundreds of people were involved in the growing number of social activities that were financially supporting him. Some clergy thought he was crazy.

"He's just a fool," opined Pat O'Rourke, a young Kerry man, expressing rather stridently what many were thinking.

Among other things O'Rourke was amused at Dunlea's unconvincing attempts at reading palms, especially those of the opposite sex. A young woman who knew Dunlea before entering a Poor Clare contemplative monastery, is the only other to comment on this:

> My sister and I, she writes, were regular visitors to Boy Town in the 1940's, the central attraction being Father Dunlea and his efforts to tell the future. I still remember his taking my hand in his and looking deeply and intently into my eyes (which I found a bit daunting). Then after a long, pensive (and for me, painful) pause, he said with a smile: "Judith, you were born to be great".
>
> Although it wasn't very original and didn't grab me at the time, I now realise it is true of everyone.

Indeed, growth in the Christian and contemplative life, has to do with being aware of and reaching for that greatness and helping others do likewise.

The foundation on which Dunlea was building his town didn't make sense to many of his younger colleagues who, themselves, were heavily involved in youth work. Their clientele was mostly from good homes, where there was lots of love and sensible discipline; and still, even among them, the odd bad apple surfaced, one that needed removing before it could contaminate others. The credo that there are no bad boys just didn't stack up, at least not in their experience.

In fact, there was the strong conviction that contamination has already taken root in every family tree, even going back to the embryo. In what was called original sin, badness was thought to be endemic in every human gene. It was said you were inoculated against it but it was not removed through water and the Spirit in Baptism.

In introducing Dunlea, the Archbishop referred facetiously to some parish priests who were restrictive regarding the areas of pastoral care alloted to their curates, thereby depriving them of the challenge to initiate and innovate. He noted that Father Tom, on the other hand, with amazing magnanimity and trust, had put the pastoral care of Sutherland into the hands of his assistants, Roger Wynne and Jerry Wallington. In his native Tipperary, there were many absentee landlords who nonetheless saw to it that the tenants paid their rent. Father Tom, a mostly absentee parish priest at present, hadn't followed their example, with the result that a major financial crisis was looming in Sutherland. The parish was in danger of going into receivership! (Actually a sort of receiver, a Father Tom Wallace, was sent to Sutherland to try to bring the parish out of the red. He became known as the estate agent priest, because he disposed of much vacant land bequeathed to the Church over the years, the rates and interest on which was a drain on the scanty parish reserves.) (Sutherland Saga p16)

A couple of days previously, Dunlea had received a poem by Ted Burns of Mudgee, which more or less summed up what he was on about. This he used to address the clergy, assuring them with humour and flair that he always believed they themselves were poets and mystics at heart and deserved to be addressed accordingly. He began slowly, with drama and satisfaction, knowing that the poem was relevant also to his financial deficiencies, mentioned by the Archbishop:

The Voice of a Child

You have spoken, my child, my heart throbs are
    quick at the flush of dawn.
Tis the pleading call of a lonely child in the eerie
    hours of morn.
The skies are grey while the stars look down like a
    million weeping eyes.
Is the heart of a man so hardened, child, that he does
    not heed your cries?
I must rise to your call, I must hasten, for my heart
    with unspeakable joy
has been touched by the hand of the Master,
At the call of a lonely boy
"I wish I had someone to love me" sang the child in
    his heart felt pain.
Oh God that your children love and pray for the lust
    of gold to wane.
Bold men have slaved in the early finds in the
    roaring days of old.
They have fought and died in the luring booms for
    the burning lust of gold.
Let us gild our hearts with a golden love, let them
    shine in the Shepherd's fold,
The soul of a child is more precious far than galleons
    filled with gold.

As he sat down to some mild applause, the Archbishop, sensing unfinished business, allotted some time for questions.

The school inspector, Tom Pearce, the first on his feet, gave voice to a question on most minds. It had to do with problem youngsters, a number of whom seemed to be quite incorrigible — even hopelessly bad. Dunlea introduced his response with the usual pursed lips and lofty tones, deeming the question a deep and important one, worthy of a clansman of the great Irish poet and patriot, Padraig Pearse. When the general chuckle subsided, he went on to extract from his case some copies of *The Voice of Boys Town*, a bi-monthly of which he was the editor. This, he told them, expressed aspects of his philosophy regarding delinquent boys. He passed them around.

In regard to what was wrong or bad, he said, he was interested in looking at the situation-generating problems, rather than singling out people who personified the problem for opprobrium, rejection or punishment. He always based his dealings with boys, he told them, on the truism that badness was not inherent in his charges. There were boys, of course, who did bad things, things that would be unpardonable if boys were responsible for their badness.

He referred to a previous clergy conference at which Joe Cusack, a high-profile cleric, held that dancing was evil and should be condemned. Noting that the clergy had wisely rejected that proposition, Dunlea called attention to other conditions that were indeed evil and should be condemned. He cited slum dwellings, grinding poverty, broken homes, addiction to alcohol, abandoned children, unsupported mothers, untended sickness.

These were the situations that disturbed the youngsters' equilibrium of outlook, often rudely and viciously, at a very immature age. The Depression, followed by the War, had created a veritable stream of boys who were misguided, neglected and failed by their parents, their home and their community. They were undernourished, underprivileged citizens, often wrongly classed as uncontrollable.

At this stage, Tommy Hayden, a fairly radical former seminary professor, raised many clerical eyebrows when he confessed he didn't see the doctrine of original sin as a satisfactory explanation of the existence of evil or badness in our world. He didn't believe that badness in any real sense was present at conception or birth. Badness was not inherited, it was caught or copied from significant adults or peers. Although some of the clergy were concerned at this seeming departure from orthodoxy, Dunlea picked it up with ardent relish:

> Myself and the staff at Engadine know from experience that even though a boy has done horrible things, he is not a bad boy. He is a victim of awful circumstances. The last decade has produced a generation of boys whose fathers have been worsted in the game of life, and some have poured their grievances into the minds of their children. The sons receiving these wrathful impressions have more or less grown up with a hatred of society. They come to us with their hearts starving for love and kindness. The mothers may do their best but, only too often, they themselves are worn out trying to love. In many cases, mothers have no idea of anything better in life than their own upbringing.

Frank McCosker, a priest psychologist, said something with which Dunlea totally agreed:

> Psychologists claim that up to two or three years of age, baby and mother/father are one, especially from the baby's perspective. The baby sees himself mirrored in his parents' eyes, especially the mother's. What her eyes tell him about himself, he believes and generally becomes. This original experience of life is not heard or seen or thought; it is primarily felt in his body. He knows himself in the security of the one who lovingly holds him and gazes upon him. Although he begins to grow out of that kind of knowing at around two or three years of age, it still continues to sustain him. In later life he may think himself smart and grown up, but when things fall apart, that original knowing is what he falls back on.

It enables the boy to know himself at a depth that cannot be shaken. Luke talks about causing a little one to stumble as the worst of sins (17:2). When that primal knowing is fractured or missing, a great blow is dealt to his self-image and self-esteem.

Although they had the gut feeling that this was true, the assembled brethren felt it was a bit highbrow and preachy. But a delighted Dunlea admiringly ruminated that only someone who had transversed the halls of academia with dignity and confidence could speak so succinctly and clearly. He himself had experienced the truth of what McCosker had said in his own personal life. On a daily basis he dealt with lives that were shattered through being denied that primordial love-relationship with a parent. That primal love had a parallel in the spiritual life, sometimes called the Garden of Eden experience. Even though the human family had to leave the garden, the communal memory of that primordial love relationship with the Creating Father, restored by the Son, was still the cornerstone of all Christian spirituality.

Dunlea went on:

> By providing for him a fair-dinkum town, a hometown of charity, unity and kindness, we give the disturbed boy a smooth landing-ground. Then we look for the key to his heart. Once that is found, turning it is easy. He is mentally and spiritually sick and only through kindly analysis of his problem can the seat of his trouble be found. It takes time and great patience. It takes a lot of listening, listening as an equal, listening as a child would listen to a fairytale: your brain will go stagnant, your imagination will be stimulated — until, in utter sympathy and understanding, you see yourself starving and stealing. Then and only then have you reached the stage of discretion. The process of rising up from the shadows now begins. The wound has been exposed, treatment can now be prescribed, but only with kindness and sympathy undiluted,

commanded by the heart, as the skilled surgeon is commanded by his brain.

Joe McGovern, an up-and-coming priest-historian, spoke about officiating at the funeral of a mother whose young son nobody wanted. The only option for him was an institution or orphanage. Dunlea felt that boys put into institutions are hampered unless these institutions are really homes, homes in which each boy can expect sympathy, can share in love, can expand naturally in the gracious atmosphere and can prove that he is worth being wanted. The basis on which a home is built is the unpredictable or ever-developing personality of a growing child. Cold lifeless rules and regulations can never cater for the thousand and one shades of development through which every adolescent must pass.

Boys Town, he said, is conducted in the spirit of love. Support is rendered in the spirit of love. That and nothing else was on my agenda from the beginning. The boys are inheriting that love. It is our most cherished hope that they will become givers to the limit of their capacity. It is already being manifested by the courtesies and goodwill-offerings to visitors and friends.

The Archbishop wondered about punishment and responsibility in the Boys Town setting. Dunlea explained that the battle on behalf of the homeless boy is a very difficult one chiefly owing to masquerading humbugs and false notions applied to the lives of children by people whose children they are not. Well-disposed parents will surround their own children with every comfort and luxury but, when they turn from their own to other children, they speak a penal language that advocates locking them away in a place of punishment, with plenty of rod and very little reasoning.

The policy of Boys Town is to put itself in the place of a really fond parent, said Dunlea, interpreting the kindly sentiments of parental love and applying them to the boys and defending their cause.

Boys Town dealt with with children sent from the courts, Crown Prosecutors, the police, child welfare officials, hospital almoners and the like. By the time boys from these sources arrive in Boys Town, Father Tom declared, they generally are severely traumatised. Gradually they are initiated into the philosophy of Boys Town by the Aldermen and the Mayor. The electoral system, the twice-yearly electoral campaign, the voting, the ballot box and competing for office are all explained. The democratic way in which all this is done greatly appeals and gives the new boy, maybe for the first time, an idea of how democracy actually works. Slowly, an appreciation of liberty and a sense of responsibility for his own life and the welfare of others begins to enter his consciousness.

After he has been through the initiation process, he is given a specific area for which he has sole responsibility. As well as the normal academic studies to which he is introduced, he picks the trade in which he is most interested. In this he is aided by the Mayor, the Aldermen and the Boys Town staff.

The clergy were amazed at the variety of choices available, choices outlined in technicolour by the effusive Dunlea. As well as the meat industry and bakery schools and a junior textile college, there were facilities for bootmaking and leatherwork, carpentry and woodwork, toy designing and making, cookery and kitchen management, laundry work, gardening, dairy farming, poultry rearing and, with the completion of the hospital, fitness and body-building.

Although punishment was not part of the Boys Town language, certain privileges could be withdrawn, such as going to the movies or using the swimming pool. What the boys regarded as grave offences were met by more severe measures, such as mowing the lawns or weeding the gardens. Dunlea found boys could go overboard at times.

One measure was having a repeater stand through a movie with his back to the screen. When Dunlea protested about this as being rather barbaric, the Mayor at the time replied laconically, "It works, nobody holds his chin out for that dose twice".

The last question from the clergy audience had to do with confronting anger. John Stack, a young curate, aroused some amusement by testily challenging the Dunlea method of reining in a really angry boy, whose fits of temper and destructive behaviour left parents and teachers powerless. After a pregnant pause, Dunlea began by referring to Stack as a worthy nephew of Charles Nolan, "one of our great seminary professors". He cited the case of a youngster called Aaron who had landed in Boys Town from the Childrens Court after he had been expelled from two juvenile detention centres. The first time they had met, Aaron's antagonism towards Dunlea was palpable. With hatred in his eyes, he had called him by every name he could think of, and "his vocabulary in that area was very rich indeed", Dunlea remarked with a chuckle.

In the playground he screamed and yelled and displayed the deep cuts in his arms and legs as signs of his readiness to destroy himself or anyone who got in his way. He would shout at the top of his voice, "I'm going to kill you!" Someone had to rush to protect his victim by placing their bodies in front of doors to prevent him from carrying out his threat. With hate eating into his heart, he yelled he was going to kill his father because he was the cause of all Aaron's problems. His father hated him and claimed that when Aaron walked into the house, everything went wrong. He brought out the worst in everyone, and as a result he has been banned from even setting foot inside the door again. And so he screamed that he had to kill the old man, as he lashed out with his tongue, his fists, or whatever he could get his hands on.

When Dunlea intervened, he noticed his own presence tended to inflame Aaron even further. He was finding it very hard to unlock the door to the boy's heart, until almost by accident, he asked him what caused his mother's death. In response Aaron glared at him with intense hatred, as he demanded several times, wildly and angrily, "Why do you ask? Why do you ask?"

"Then something happened inside him," Dunlea exclaimed.

> The storm abated, a change came over him and tears welled up in his eyes. He began to sob violently and cried like a baby. His mother, the only one who had been able to stand up to his father, had committed suicide, and Aaron felt he himself was in some way to blame. As we sat quietly, I helped him to articulate the fact that he felt driven to carry on his mother's hatred and anger towards his father and any father-figure he encountered, including myself. With deep sighs and pent-up emotion, he blurted out his tragic story, after which he gradually became rational and reasonable and peaceful — a peacefulness he hadn't lost for many months now.

In fact, Dunlea announced, with that certain dramatic effect in which he was quite an expert, Aaron has taken to composing beautiful poems, some of which were included in the *Voice of Boys Town* being passed around. Aaron was deeply impressed by the fact that even though he had called Dunlea by every name under the sun, there wasn't the slightest hint of unforgiveness or resentment in the priest's relationship with him. This, seemingly, empowered Aaron to forgive himself and to seek forgiveness from the many people he had hurt in his anger.

Dunlea concluded by assuring his audience that not only were poets and mystics, prophets and dreamers generously interspersed among the clergy, they were also part of the Boys Town scene. His job was to search for the hidden treasure in those rugged youngsters and provide the atmosphere in which it could bloom and grow.

Although the applause of the clergy was robust and sustained, some were still unconvinced. Clergy don't take well to enthusiasm and idealism. Living in the real world, they realise how difficult it is to change anyone, especially an anti-social boy. They gave Dunlea marks for putting his case well and they would consider recommending Boys Town, but many of the doubters brought their misgivings back home with them.

11

De La Salle Brothers

Benignus White sat somewhat apprehensively in the presbytery at St Mary's Cathedral. Being early June 1942, Sydney was having a bad attack of nerves. Three midget Japanese submarines had somehow slipped through what was supposed to be an impenetrable net blocking entry to Sydney Harbour to all but certified vessels. As the submarines began to direct their deadly cargo towards the unsuspecting shipping in the Harbour, Sydneysiders experienced the war on their very doorstep for the first time. The tragic impact of the fall of Singapore and the consequent capture of Australia's elite 8th Division of fifteen thousand troops was beginning to cause alarm among the populace. This was accentuated by the bombing of Darwin and the offshore shelling of Sydney and Newcastle by Japanese submarines.

White was the leader of a large group of teaching brothers of the De La Salle congregation. He had been called to the Cathedral by Archbishop Gilroy and that generally meant being invited to extend his already stretched workforce — an invitation from on high, as it were, that he could scarcely refuse. When he was ushered into the great man's presence, however, he found him in jubilant mood.

Gilroy had been a wireless officer with the Australian Navy in the first world war and had done duty at Gallipoli. Turning from the radio, he announced triumphantly that the Navy had just saved the day. The Japanese advance had been halted by Australian and American naval forces in the Coral Sea and Midway

Island. That, he felt, might be the turning point people had hoped and prayed for in the Pacific War. And, in fact, it was.

Over a cup of tea, the Archbishop spoke about a new challenging assignment he was hoping White's congregation might consider taking on. It was work for a type of youth they had not yet been involved with in Australia. He was assured, however, that it had been in the mind and heart of John Baptist De La Salle when he founded the congregation in France. Benignus White's apprehension was growing until, at last, Gilroy mentioned Boys Town.

White had followed the progress of Boys Town with great interest and, although he was full of admiration for its founder-director, he knew Dunlea's approach to the reformation and education of boys was unconventional and not shared by main-stream educators like the Brothers in White's congregation. Moreover, Dunlea had been adamant from the beginning that Boys Town should be non-sectarian. This, as his friend Eric Drew wrote, was part of his philosophy of life:

> The love of Father Tom for people didn't mean *some* people; it meant all people, irrespective of race, colour or creed, station in life, intellectual capacity, wealth or poverty (particularly the latter). It meant the underprivileged and the downtrodden. He recognised in all their faces the face of Christ.

One of the aspects of Dunlea's character that especially appealed to benefactors like George Nathan, June Russell and others, was the fact that the door of his heart and the doors of Boys Town were open to all comers. Boys of European stock mingled with boys of Aboriginal, Asian and Islander roots. Some were baptised Christians, Protestant and Catholic; a sprinkling were Buddhists or Muslims, and others again had no Church affiliation. Although the biggest single group were Catholics, they were a minority overall.

In theory De La Salle and other Catholic schools were open to other Christians, but Catholic applicants got first preference. This meant, in reality, that there were few places available for others. White wondered how he could motivate his Brothers to take responsibility for such a multicultural, multiracial and multireligious venture as Australia's Boys Town.

Gilroy explained that Dunlea's other role, that of a parish priest, was a very important one that demanded his living in the parish house and giving more time and attention than he was able to devote to it at present. Boys Town was now firmly established in its new location at Engadine. It was fast becoming a real town, with a life of its own. It was also becoming more complex and in need of the expertise and the academic orientation that a community of Religious Brothers was equipped to give.

White wondered if Dunlea was being pushed out. Gilroy however, assured him that Dunlea was the one who made the suggestion in the first place. He had discovered that De La Salle Brothers were working with Father Flanagan in Boys Town, Nebraska. Also, it seems, Dunlea's good friend, Brother Bill O'Riordan, had informed him that John Baptist De La Salle had himself opened a home for abandoned boys and those who appeared before the courts, in Rouen in France, at the beginning of the eighteenth century.

Gilroy felt that even though the Brothers would be responsible for the overall management and general supervision of the town, Dunlea's continuing presence would be essential because of his excellent rapport with the boys and his amazing capacity to attract sponsors and benefactors.

The Brothers knew that working with a charismatic leader like Dunlea would not be easy. He was the father-founder, the one who, almost alone, had called the tunes and decided play up to now. He had invaluable experience in dealing with marginalised boys and the rare gift of being able to see the goodness within, even under the most unpromising exterior.

A Sydney priest, Pat O'Rourke, had alerted the Brothers to the fact that a confrere of his, one of Dunlea's former curates, had found Dunlea difficult to work with because of mood swings. He was happily on the crest of a wave most of the time but, on the odd occasion when he hit the trough, he allegedly could be quite dejected.

One of the Brothers on an unofficial visit to Boys Town met the forthright Mary Rose, who told him that, even though Dunlea had countless friends and, to all intents and purposes, was the life of the party, he was nevertheless a rather lonely man. Maybe that's why he had what Ed Campion called "a brimming overconcern for any part of creation that was in need, especially stray dogs". Dunlea once said, "When Tom Dunlea doesn't take an interest in stray dogs any longer, you'll know that he's at the end of his tether".

Whereas this love for strays was highly commendable and praiseworthy, the Brothers realised it could lead to a certain amount of messiness, and even confusion, in the life of the town's citizens. Another similar matter that somewhat dismayed the Brothers was the trickle of homeless men who gravitated towards Dunlea. It was only a trickle, but it was a steady trickle. The Brothers came to realise that he just couldn't refuse hospitality to any of life's broken or wounded.

Many of these concerns were put into their proper perspective when the Brothers eventually met Dunlea. It didn't take long for them to see where he was coming from. The warmth and affection in his eyes and in his smile as he greeted and embraced them was sincere and fair-dinkum and had them on his side from that first meeting. They could work with a man like this, no matter how unconventional or even eccentric he might be.

Dunlea confided in Benignus over a drink that handing over the reins wasn't easy for him. During the last several years, the welfare of homeless boys had just about taken over his whole life. He thought and breathed and dreamt Boys Town. He knew in his head that, once established, the town would need to be directed by a trained professional staff. This conclusion hadn't yet fully registered in his heart, however. Although he did have a facility for letting go, Boys Town had become so dear to him that even a partial letting go was difficult for him. In the new arrangement, his role would be spiritual director to the boys and member of the committee responsible for fundraising. Brother Alban was to be the new Principal, with overall responsibility for the whole project.

He gave the Brothers a recent copy of *The Voice of Boys Town*, which carried messages from two prominent people. One, from Judge H R Curlewis, read in part:

> Few persons realise what an unpleasant task a judge has in dealing with young men, little more than boys, who come before him. Punish them and you send them to mix with criminals. Let them off and you are telling other lads that they may commit crimes with impunity.
>
> Father Dunlea is taking the boy who has every chance of becoming a criminal, and is endeavouring to let that lad see that his welfare is important to someone, and an ideal of good citizenship is being set before the growing youth.
>
> If the scheme meets with the success it deserves, there will be fewer problems for the judges to deal with. Better to spend money in making the boys decent citizens than to spend it in building gaols.

The other was from Mary Tennison-Woods, the much-loved relative of Father Tennison-Woods who was co-founder, with Mary McKillop, of the Sisters of St Joseph. It was mainly concerned with getting support for Boys Town, but she went on to say:

> I hope the *Voice of Boys Town* will be heard all over Australia, reaching the hearts of great-hearted people who will help you to build your town into something worthy of them and of you. I have only one fault to find — Boys Town is not big enough, There are so many under-privileged boys in this lovely country of ours to whom Boys Town would

mean the chance of becoming good and great citizens if only there were the room to take them in. It's not what a boy has been, but what he's capable of becoming, that counts . . .

She went on to point out that some confused people thought youngsters could not be trusted unless kept under the strictest supervision and discipline:

> You wisely plan the training to fit your young people to be useful and honourable citizens. This is done by giving them a large measure of responsibility and freedom before they have to go out into the world. You follow Father Flanagan, who has found that these privileges are rarely abused.

She then appealed directly to the boys:

> The experiment you are carrying out will be watched with keen interest by a great number of people — people who believe in you and your town — and by people who expect the venture to fail. So it's up to each one of you, by the way you train yourselves and what you become, to prove that your friends are right, and the doubters wrong.

* * * * * * * *

The same *Voice* also carried a little piece called *A Cow's a Cow*:

> Our latest admission — a modern cow. I had to meet her at Engadine Station at 2 a.m. and when she first looked at me, she as much as said, "Is it a modern farm I'm going to?"
>
> I knew she had no noble ideas of giving milk to Boys Town. Down came the first two young dairy farmers, swinging their bucket and singing merrily, just bursting to see how many cups of tea the modern cow is worth.
>
> They soon saw, though, that the representative of Cow Town was not at all friendly towards Boys Town. Shortly, the greatest free fight that had ever been fought on their soil was in full swing.

The regular wearers of football boots and boxing gloves were all in, and the youngest member pulled down the swing for a rope. Referee, Father Dunlea, saw no sense in this position, so he joined in the round-up.

Eventually, the cow was leg-roped and stood fast, held in position by four boys. Just as the bucket filled and the thought of black tea banished from the minds of the onlookers, she gave her last and most decisive kick and the boys got all the milk!

August 20, 1942 was voting day, when Boys Town's new mayor and new aldermen were elected. At supper that evening, after two senior boys who acted as scrutineers announced the winners, Dunlea made his dramatic announcement. He started in a rather roundabout way, as was his wont, by quoting a verse from St Mark's Gospel: "The grain of wheat must die in order to produce fruit". Holding up a green stalk of unripened wheat, he explained how it would never be there only for the grain of wheat dying and thereby bursting into new life. He talked about how the dying of Jesus led to resurrection and new life for all men and women.

Next, Dunlea showed them the little island of Midway in the battered world map they had used to cover the cracks in the dining hall wall. He told them about the thousands of Australian and American troops who were ready to die in order to save Australia from invasion. He himself had just made a decision which would involve a certain kind of dying — a dying to an aspect of his relationship with his boys that he deeply treasured, so that Boys Town could have the chance it needed to grow and bloom.

As he went on to explain in some detail what was about to happen, he became somewhat emotional, and so did some boys who were maybe more aware of what it was all about. His voice was husky and somewhat hesitant as he charged the newly elected mayor and aldermen with the preparations for the official handing over.

September 8, 1942 was one of those significant days etched in the memory of Thomas Vincent Dunlea. Spring was in the air, the sun was clear and bright and two important birthdays were being celebrated, the birth of the Virgin Mary and the birth of a new regime at Australia's Boys Town. The proceedings took place in the paddock near the original house. The new mayor welcomed the dignitaries, especially Monsignor Collender, who represented the Archbishop, and his driving companion, Dick O'Regan of Rose Bay, George Nathan and June Russell, as well as a number of meat industry and bakery representatives.

The boys were unusually quiet and just a little tense and apprehensive. Someone remarked afterwards that it felt like the calm before a storm, and, indeed so it was. The storm took off when someone opened the back door of O'Regan's car, sending two large brown setters, Rover and Rex, hurtling onto the paddock.

Dunlea's three-legged southpaw, Fred, and several other strays began to bark furiously; the goats and chooks and a couple of calves and pigs, together with Dunlea's pet wallabies, joined enthusiastically in the commotion. The boys, throwing restraint to the wind, exploded into a cauldron of noise and frenzy as they mixed in with the rampaging animals. It was the type of scene that didn't in any way faze Dunlea; in fact, he revelled in it, clapping and carrying on with the best of them.

Then as the confusion was gaining momentum, the mayor and the alderman led the new Boys Town Principal, Brother Alban Felix, onto the paddock! The more serious people present were aghast that this should be Brother's first introduction to the town in which he was about to take a leading role. What a disastrous and embarrassing way to be, as it were, thrown into his demanding new job! Alban, however, having weathered other difficult situations in his short life as a De La Salle Brother, was adept at turning problems into opportunities. When he realised what was happening, he almost spontaneously broke ranks with his minders and wading into the mclee, began to wave his arms and twist and turn and kick up his heels with glorious abandon. He patted the goat's mane, jigged with the wallabies and seemed to enjoy thoroughly this opportunity to let himself go and play the fool.

When eventually law and order was restored, Dunlea was convinced that Alban was the right man for the job. Like himself, he had the humour and sense of fun that enabled him to free up the child within and mix it with the boys with a certain wild freedom. In Alban, Dunlea knew he had a partner who seemed to share his own attitude, one with whom he could work harmoniously and happily. In welcoming the Brothers with joy, Dunlea assured them that he would canvass all the sympathy and practical kindness at his command to assist them in a work of such national necessity. He prayed that God would:

> Inspire himself and the friends of Boys Town to anticipate their every needful wish in their undertaking to lift little people from the scrap heap, placing them eventually among the leaders of the people.

Under the dual leadership of the brothers and the priest, Boys Town went from strength to strength. The boys and the committee and the many supporters were happy. The fact that complaints about the new regime were at a minimum was a great relief to Dunlea. He didn't have to play the role of go-between or buffer between the boys and/or committee and the brothers. He not only supported fully the changes the brothers were making, but he helped to explain and sell those changes to the boys and others. Although letting go wasn't easy, he was delighted at the way the brothers communicated with him, explained every move to him and, most importantly, included him in everything they did. He was now able to give more attention to his role as pastor of the parish of Sutherland, to work more committedly with the fund-raising committee, to attend the functions and, in his own inimitable way, to lobby the sponsors.

12

Alcoholics Anonymous

Lobbying prospective sponsors was a gift with which Dunlea was well endowed. A multitude of quotations, interesting anecdotes and references to real or imagined comical situations dotted his conversation. He was good to be with — he energised people. In western society alcoholic drink often accompanies human get-togethers. It too energises people. It stimulates conversation and, in moderation, frees people to relate to one another. Dunlea loved and needed company and conversation and enjoyed the alcohol that went with it. If, however, as Peter Morrissey testifies tea or water or lemonade were the beverage on offer, he would willingly stay up all night drinking it.

During the War years alcohol, especially Scotch whisky, was unavailable unless one had friends among the higher ranking American officers. A relative of Dunlea's, a Father Ned Clune, although himself a teetotaller, seemed to have had many such friends. He was happy to supply Dunlea with the where-with-all to entertain his friends and supporters. During the six weeks of Lent each year, he managed to give it up; during the rest of the year, however, alcohol normally accompanied his social and fundraising life.

When visiting a patient at the Rydalmere Hospital early in 1944, he ran into an old friend, Dr S J Minogue, a psychiatrist, who was said to have had some success in dealing with alcoholics. Minogue had tried many approaches with patients at Kenmore Hospital, but without success. Since he had become Medical

Superintendent of Rydalmere Hospital, someone had put him in touch with a Bobby Berger in New York, who informed Minogue about a new approach being investigated there that was showing great promise. Called Alcoholics Anonymous (AA), it was based on twelve simple truths, or steps as they were called. In taking these steps the addict admitted to himself and to others that he was an alcoholic, that he was powerless to overcome this condition by himself and that his only hope of attaining sobriety was through the help of a higher power.

As Minogue went on to talk about the AA Programme, it sounded like manna from heaven to Dunlea. For the first time he was hearing something that could be a solution to a problem that was proving so very intractable. Like Minogue, he too had tried many approaches, but they just didn't work. Even prayer and Sacraments, which he believed in so strongly, didn't counteract many people's tragic dependence on alcohol.

The philosophy of AA intrigued him in that it reflected so clearly his own attitude to life. The twelve steps called for a high degree of humility and honesty. Although given to flamboyant speech and lots of blarney when addressing others, Dunlea acknowledged his own faults and weaknesses with genuine humility. His letting-go attitude saved him from undue attachment to material possessions, security, reputation, self-image, and the like. In that, he was seen to be more liberated than his clergy colleagues. He was now discovering a new way of dealing with something that was enslaving so many of those unfortunate people he wanted to help most.

Having made this exciting discovery, he characteristically couldn't wait, he had to share it. He contacted Eric Drew, who erected a couple of large tents in the outskirts of Sutherland, not far from the Boys Town tents of a few years earlier. Dunlea collected the alcoholics from whose ranks he hoped to form a first AA group. In the tents they were clothed, fed and bedded down and even given a small ration of good liquor to replace the cheap grog to which they were accustomed. Things went so well that Dunlea felt the time had arrived to approach a certain wealthy businessman who had indicated that he was willing to make a substantial contribution towards anything practical in the way of rehabilitation of alcoholics.

So one day Father Dunlea left for Sydney to bring his benefactor back to look over the group at Sutherland.

> When the two men arrived at the camp, the group members were all there numerically, but all unconscious from the methylated spirits they had consumed in the priest's absence. The businessman did not make a contribution. After one look he fled to his car and drove away. So ended the first attempt to start AA in Australia. (McKinnon pp17–18)

Even though this was a great disappointment to him, Dunlea still believed in the power and effectiveness of AA.

In April 1945 he rang Archie McKinnon, a psychiatric nurse at the Reception House in Darlinghurst. Of the people who were undergoing psychiatric care at the Reception House, a large proportion were suffering from alcoholism. McKinnon, like Dunlea and Dr Minogue, was desperately searching for some way of treating this disease, when an American chaplain, visiting the reception centre, told him of the great breakthrough that had happened in Akron Ohio in June 1935. A stockbroker, Bill W, and a Dr Bob, both alcoholics had brought about their own recovery by developing a way of life that crystallised into the Twelve Steps of AA.

Ten years later, in April 1945, Dunlea invited McKinnon and Minogue to the Boys Town city office in the Australian Catholic Insurance Building, located at the corner of King and York Streets. The space had been made over to Dunlea by Mr Mooney, ACI Manager. Working separately up to then, McKinnon, Minogue and Dunlea decided to join forces in order to more effectively publicise and build up AA. This meeting of three men who, for different reasons, were driven to finding a solution to a major problem in society, laid the foundation on which

AA was established in Australia. They decided to meet weekly. They welcomed new members and became familiar with the twelve steps.

As word got round, many were attracted to the meetings; some benefited greatly and attained lasting sobriety. Others, who were greatly attracted to early AA, especially hard-core alcoholics, saw it as something new to be exploited. Others, like psychotic types, were unsuitable for the AA programme. Progress was being hindered also by the presence of non-alcoholic philanthropists, social workers and journalists.

The early meetings were held in Dr Minogue's quarters at Rydalmere Hospital. This was a long way to travel for most people, so other locations had to be found. When it was found out that the participants were alcoholics, however, even though no drink was involved at meetings, they were forced to move on. Dunlea used his considerable connections to find them a meeting place in an office block in the centre of Sydney, but after some months the caretaker found out who they were and, once again, they had to look elsewhere.

As time went on, enquiries about AA multiplied, so much so that a full-time secretary was thought desirable. However, there was no money to pay the salary, until a friend of Dunlea came to the rescue. Thus member Jack became the first full-time secretary of AA in Australia.

2GB radio personality Frank Sturge Harty gave good publicity to the AA group during those early struggling days. Another non-alcoholic, Jesuit priest Richard Murphy of North Sydney, had a profound and lasting influence on the early group and, indeed, on all Australian AA groups. An intellectual and noted theologian, he was a source of encouragement and a unifying force. Minogue, McKinnon and Dunlea, strong personalities with quite different approaches and ideas about the way forward, needed the reconciling, healing presence of Richard Murphy, who saw parallels between the twelve steps of AA and parts of the *Exercises of St Ignatius*, the basic source of Jesuit spirituality.

As spring dawned on a peaceful Australia in 1945, the group had many stable members, all known by their first names only. There was Rex, Ben, Norman, Wally, Vince, Russ, Dave, Ron, Victor and secretary Jack, some non-alcoholic wives, as well as the three founding fathers. When the Dunlea-provided money for the secretary was exhausted, Jack drowned his disappointment for a while, but quickly recovered. Instead of returning to the fold, however, he started a breakaway group of his own. Because he had difficulty in accepting the spiritual aspects of AA, he deleted all reference to a higher power and so he called his version, the Commonsense Group.

Meetings were held at the Hasty-Tasty Café in Kings Cross with some regular AA members present, but it didn't work. After a month it folded up.

> This was the first and only challenge to AA in Australia and its members, except Jack, returned to the original group because they had realised that their sobriety, even life itself, depended on sticking to the philosophy and traditions of AA as formulated at Akron twelve years before. The failure of the breakaway only succeeded in more firmly establishing the spiritual principles of AA in Australia. (McKinnon p24)

In January 1946, a pretty redhead, who had three daughters and an understanding husband, turned up at the meeting. She introduced herself in the usual way: "My name is Betty and I am an alcoholic". As this first-ever lady member told her story, she referred several times to Father Tom, her hero, who sat there beaming. The attention of beautiful women somehow did something for him. He and Betty had worked together eighteen months earlier when he had set up the tents for alcoholics at Sutherland. Although that had failed Dunlea still longed to provide a healing sanctuary for those men of the road to whom his heart went out.

13

Christmas House

On a hot steamy day in November 1945, Dunlea was feeling the worse for wear after several late fundraising nights. He had just finished reading an article about the town of Cowra in New South Wales, where Japanese prisoners were detained during the war. News of a disturbance there had been published the year before. It was only now, however, that he learned of the magnitude of the occurrence, which occasioned the death of two hundred and thirty-four Japanese and five guards in a mass suicidal attempt at escape. This deeply troubling news was on his mind when in walked a swagman from Victoria, a wire maker called Tommy, who for years had been addicted to methylated spirits. Although tired and weary himself, Dunlea welcomed him with the usual embrace. As he did so, he became aware of the Holy Face in a printing on the wall right behind Tommy's head:

A candle burning on the table showed up the deep furrows on the face of Jesus, which bore an incredible resemblance to Tommy's unshaven countenance, deeply lined with traces of many old sores.

It was not the first time this had happened, but this time he felt it was a call relating to people like Tommy. In the early post-war months they were becoming more numerous and he was becoming conscience-stricken that in his somewhat limited role at Boys Town, he was unable to put them up and look after them as he felt he should. After he had fed and shaved Tommy, in walked Ray, another, albeit younger, swagman, well known to Dunlea and his guest. Like Tommy, he was unwashed, unshaven and hungry! After Dunlea had attended to his needs, Ray sat at the table clothed in the only garment left in Dunlea's wardrobe, his old tattered dressing-gown. Then he dropped a remark that resonated with something that had been percolating in Dunlea's mind for some time. Ray had discovered an empty house in nearby Loftus, on the verandah of which he had squatted the last couple of nights. Dunlea remembered the place from his tent-city days. It was old but roomy enough to house a number of people.

It may fulfil his dream of making a new, better organised attempt at sharing, in his own area, his new and exciting treatment for alcoholism with the many alcoholics he knew and cared for. He thought of such a venture in his own special flamboyant way as a "Matt Talbot in the suburbs" catering for homeless alcoholic men in the bush, as the big institution of the same name did for those in the city.

After inspecting the place with Tommy and Ray and the dog Waffles, he was more convinced than ever that it was an answer to prayer. He lost no time in contacting the two people who could make the venture possible. One was Reuben F Scarf, the man most people associate with suits, but, who was also a very generous benefactor to charitable causes, especially those associated with alcohol rehabilitation. The other was Charles Cooper, his friend at Sutherland Shire Council whose help he sought to get the project listed on the next council meeting agenda.

In the meantime, he brought it up with Minogue and McKinnon at their AA meeting. They were quite surprised that he would venture into something like this so soon after getting his fingers burnt last time. Archie McKinnon especially was against it. He felt it didn't correspond with the philosophy of AA which works when people come along of their own accord, specifically to obtain sobriety. What Dunlea was proposing, he felt, was like bringing a horse to water. McKinnon knew the alcoholic mind and the cunning, deception and pilfering of which the addict is capable. His experience at the Reception House led him to believe that most hard-core alcoholics would exploit Dunlea, while paying lip service to AA.

Dunlea didn't think so. He saw people from a different perspective. He saw the waif, the derelict, the alcoholic, as it were, in technicolour:

> He saw in them some traces of a royal though long-forgotten genealogy. He just knew (or so he thought) that this derelict or that unfortunate was really a brilliant poet or philosopher or frustrated scientist from a family of geniuses who had never been given a chance to prove himself. This one must have had gypsy blood — there was a Romany air about her that was unmistakable. That one could surely have been a record-breaking Olympian if only his mentors had noticed his athletic gait, his eagle eye. This affirming positive outlook in life naturally brought out the best in all who met him. (Morrissey)

Minogue's experience in Rydalmere inclined him towards McKinnon's view of the addict mentality. Both men were realists, their feet securely planted in the seasoned ground of their own experience. And yet they knew that Dunlea had something special which they admired and found quite intriguing. His ability to embrace the down-and-outs, to convey a sense of value and worth to them, to convince them that in his eyes, and indeed in God's eyes, they were pearls of great price, was redolent of St Francis. And so, although they knew that provision and shelter, even with a dollop of AA, wasn't the answer to alcoholism, they went along with him, hoping the Dunlea charisma might make the difference.

A week later Dunlea learned from Charles Cooper that the Sutherland Council had turned down his application. A new housing development was being planned for the area, and they didn't want the place overrun by alcoholics. Also, Dunlea's failed rehabilitation project of a year and a half earlier was cited a couple of times at the meeting.

Never one to give up easily, Dunlea had another card to play, one that had stood him well in the past. He asked that he and Dr Minogue be allowed to address the aldermen at the next Council meeting, and surprisingly, ("unfortunately", Archie McKinnon would say) they agreed to this. At the meeting the Dunlea (and Minogue) humour, eloquence and feeling for the down-and-out won the day. The Councillors decided to reverse their previous decision.

On Christmas Day 1945, in typical Dunlea style, with flags flying and a brass band playing, with lots of speeches and ceremony, the new house was dedicated and opened as a home for alcoholics.

Anne Macinante with her fiancée Rowe Cuddy, was an early visitor. Dunlea arranged to pick them up at Sutherland station at 7 p.m.

> Imagine our confusion, writes Anne, when Father's little VW arrived with passengers virtually hanging on everywhere. We squeezed in and sat on top of those already seated, as we were whisked off to the newly opened house at Loftus. A meeting was in progress where an assorted group of men took it in turn to stand up and tell the story of their addiction. They came from various backgrounds but the one I most remember was an ex bank manager who, although still well-spoken, had suffered the loss of his position, his family and his home. He admitted to drinking methylated spirits laced with boot polish to satisfy his craving.

Although Anne learned that one of the men present that night recovered sufficiently to take a job Dunlea had found for him, the memory of that meeting remained a sad one in her mind for many years.

Dunlea insisted that it be known as Christmas House.

> He loved Christmas. For him life was a continuous Christmas, a celebration of Immanuel, God among us, humanity sharing with each other the Spirit God shared with us in his Son. He was, as someone said, a

man with a Christmas heart and would it be too much of a stretch of this Christmas mentality to add that he always had a sense of holiday. Life was to enjoy as if it were always holiday time. Not that he didn't work hard — very hard, but he did what he did without being crushed with any burden of compulsion or routine. He was always free. (Morrissey)

Problems began at Christmas House almost immediately. The money problems came first. For a little while in the beginning, Dunlea was able to finance the home from his own resources but that source petered out quickly. When the AA group had used up all its meagre resources, it became clear that some method of fundraising had to be undertaken. Application was made to the Chief Secretary, which resulted in The Alcoholic Foundation being set up as a charity. As well as Dunlea, the foundation comprised radioman Frank Surge Harty, Secretary of Boys Town Peter Ryan, Archie McKinnon and L Laurence, who operated a textile factory that generously employed reformed alcoholics recommended by Dunlea. The foundation attracted some wealthy sponsors, to such an extent that Christmas House was enlarged and furnished as well as maintained.

> Dunlea held AA meetings each day, and Frank Surge Harty gave talks, as did Richard Murphy SJ. However, sobriety wasn't being attained. The inmates were continually going on benders, bringing liquor into the house and, in general, were difficult to control.
>
> Father Tom worked out a system of treating the drinkers by isolating them in a small building adjacent to the home. This building was seldom without occupants and, as one would expect, was called the dog house. Whenever any of the inmates had money, they never seemed to think of contributing towards their own maintenance, and Father Tom was ruthlessly exploited. (McKinnon p28)

Towards the end of February 1946, Dunlea had a call from Pat, an alcoholic who was desperate to do something about his problem. Dunlea took him into Christmas House where he heard the AA philosophy, accepted it and went on the Programme. The story of his slide into alcoholism wasn't unusual. Like Dunlea himself, he had landed in Sydney from Ireland in the early 1920s. Being a qualified bookkeeper, he quickly got a job. He enjoyed the social scene, mostly centred in pubs like the Palisade Hotel near Darling Harbour of which, he was a regular patron. After many years as a social drinker he graduated to a new phase, where he found it more and more difficult to stop drinking. His work suffered, he lost his job, lost the next job and the next and eventually ended up as an inmate of the rather infamous Lidcombe State Hospital for homeless men. There, having hit rock bottom, as they say, he was fortunate enough to meet the local parish priest, Frank Lloyd, who was a friend and admirer of Dunlea.

Dunlea was delighted with Pat's progress in Christmas House and in the AA programme. Friendly and helpful, he got on well with everyone, was liked by the other men and gradually took on a responsible role. Eventually, when Dunlea appointed him as Home manager, the behaviour of the residents improved markedly.

After the Alcoholic Foundation was expanded to include George Nathan and other members of the racing fraternity, a Christmas House office with secretary was opened in Sydney, and finances began to flow in. So, too, did the clients.

Word soon passed down the grapevine to the tosspots along the Hungry Mile of Campbell and lower Elizabeth Streets about this new field ripe for exploitation, and business boomed. Some applicants for assistance indicated that they thought the sign on the door, Alcoholic Foundation, meant that free drinks were provided, as well as other handouts.

> The new members of the Board (of the Alcoholic Foundation) were energetic and outspoken, but

lacked any appreciation of the complexity and magnitude of chronic alcoholism, believing that free board at Christmas House, a new suit and a job would solve the problems of an alcoholic.
(McKinnon p29)

Unfortunately, the problems remained unsolved. No matter how Dunlea tried to deliver the AA philosophy, his pupils were continuing to lapse. Permanent sobriety wasn't catching on. The exception was Pat and a few others who came good at a later date.

Early in 1946, AA in Sydney was again forced to move on. They had to leave their rooms in Walker Street North Sydney and were desperately looking for a new location. While visiting his friends, the Boylans, in Surry Hills, in the February of that year, Dunlea ran into Helen Connolly, another old friend from his Surry Hills days. In telling her story, Helen mentioned how she had lost her hotel licence because she couldn't get the volume of liquor she needed during the war.

The de-licensed hotel was in Foveaux Street, Surry Hills, and was unoccupied except for a couple of upstairs rooms where two reclusive elderly sisters lived. When Dunlea looked it over as a possible AA place, he was amazed at the ironic fact that it was within sight of the smokestacks of Tooheys Brewery, and the air reeked of malt!

He discussed with Helen the possibility of giving it a new name. Helen mentioned that she had a sister, a nun whose religious name was Sister Vianney. Dunlea, as it happened, had great time for St John Mary Vianney, the Curé of Ars in France in the 1840s. The Curé's total detachment from worldly possessions greatly impressed Dunlea. He felt Vianney would be an ideal name. It might also help Helen to be patient with her new tenants.

The rooms, now known as Vianney House were just what AA needed. As Archie McKinnon and Dr Minogue pointed out, the house was capable of responding to the ever-growing stream of people who were showing interest in AA.

Dunlea made it a point to visit the two ladies in the top room to acquaint them with the new arrangements. At first he only got as far as the door and wouldn't have got any further only for suggesting they do the normal Aussie thing and invite him in for a cuppa. Somewhat flabbergasted, they looked at each other and reluctantly acquiesced. The rest, as they say, is history. The Dunlea charm worked, the connections were established. As Morrissey remarks:

> If he did not actually know everyone in Australia personally, he at least knew some relative or other of theirs, so phenomenal was his memory and the interest he took in everybody. In a cafe in Grong Grong, I once heard him ask the waitress her name and as soon as she mentioned it, sure enough, he could connect her with Duncans of Drummoyne or the Greens of Adaminaby. In a similar vein Anne Macinante (Cuddy) tells how Dunlea brought to her parent's home a large tome of Irish history to show them a passage relating to a famous fifth century Irish harpist named Macinanty, saying "you may be Italian but your roots are in Ireland".
>
> As Morrissey continues, this was his normal practice, because he really wanted to make friends with literally everybody, and he knew there was no better way to do this than by some familiar association.

When the connections were made and established, the two old ladies on the top floor opened up. They were really very lonely and desperately wanting to do something about it. They felt they had problems somewhat similar to the problems of alcoholics. The ladies couldn't stand the local residents, but somehow they thought they might get on well with the AA members, especially if they were anything like Dunlea.

Almost overnight it all changed as the building started to fill up with men, young and old, from every social level who wanted to talk and could talk to anyone willing to listen. Many brought attractive wives and girlfriends who also wanted to talk.

> Before they realised what was happening, the two old ladies were involved in the lives of dozens of people. They helped to prepare supper and took part in other activities; most important of all, they gave a touch of home to many lonely men, and they, too, began to live again. They cried over the ones who fell by the wayside and rejoiced for those who succeeded. There was always someone dropping in to see them, for the place had become a home and a club for AA, and members with time on their hands climbed the steep Foveaux Street hill to see the old ladies. AA enriched their lives and brought happiness to two dear women — such happiness, indeed, as they had not known for many years. (McKinnon p33)

Since there were several furnished rooms in Vianney House, Dunlea who, with Archie McKinnon and Pat, was still involved in Christmas House in Loftus, felt they should be used. Why not bring selected men from Christmas House to the safe AA environment of Vianney and get them work? Dr Minogue and Archie agreed, and the scheme operated smoothly for a little while. The men were comfortably lodged and boarded and sent to work. Work, however, meant pay, and that became a sticking point. The temptation proved too much for them and many landed back at Vianney intoxicated. Things came to a climax when two of them locked themselves into a room and refused to open the door for three days, and then only because the liquor supply had run out!

This led to the group having a long reflection on the principles contained in the American AA literature, now available for the first time in Sydney. They became convinced they should strictly uphold the twelve steps and the twelve traditions, which they were only now becoming fully acquainted with. They came to the conclusion that residential care didn't fully fit into the AA scheme of things. Moreover, from their own experience at

Christmas House and, in a small way, at Vianney, they could see that sobriety, as envisaged by AA, wasn't being attained.

Frank Harty and Archie McKinnon expressed their decision to withdraw their support for the Alcoholic Foundation, thereby making Christmas House impossible to maintain. Dunlea, being overseas at the time, was apprised by mail and reluctantly and sadly agreed to the winding down of his brainchild, Christmas House, just one year after it was opened.

During 1946 AA continued to grow, with many members maintaining sobriety. It was getting good publicity from journalists like Don Whittington and Brian Marien, Dunlea's friend from the *Daily Telegraph*, who himself joined the programme at Vianney House. Radio personality Frank Surge Harty was joined by Tom Jacobs of Radio 2SM in bringing the good news of AA to an ever-widening audience. As a result, Vianney House was bursting at the seams and some decisions regarding the future had to be faced. One of these was of great consequence, leading to an injection of new life into the AA movement. It was decided to branch out into the suburbs in all directions. Vianney House would remain the central headquarters and suburbs like Burwood, Manly, Mosman, Hurstville and others would have their own weekly meetings.

In time, the AA movement covered all of New South Wales as well as the other States and Territories. In addition to his involvement with AA and Christmas House and the Sutherland parish, Dunlea's main preoccupation in 1946 was still Boys Town. He discussed with the Archbishop in October 1945 the need to visit Omaha, Nebraska, to meet Father Flanagan and see for himself how Flanagan's Boys Town was doing. In January 1946 Gilroy wrote to the Customs Authorities in Sydney assuring them that "Dunlea's visit to the United States was for the purpose of studying problems (and their solutions) associated with youth and the victims of alcoholism. I am confident that Father Dunlea's visit to the United States will be of use and benefit to our country".

When he eventually got to Father Flanagan's Boys Town, he was just amazed at the quality and size of the buildings and the grounds, the variety of programmes and the capacity to accommodate and successfully train and form almost five times as many boys as he was dealing with in Sydney. He went to learn, and learn he did, but the smaller, more modest, operation in the Antipodes also had important snippets of wisdom to share with its bigger and wealthier American counterpart.

Archbishop Gilroy was reading Dunlea's enthusiastic report on Boys Town America when a beam wireless cable arrived, dated 23 January 1947:

> HAVING PRIVATE AUDIENCE WITH PRESIDENT TRUMAN TODAY.
>
> T DUNLEA.

When Dunlea returned from overseas in 1947, the Archbishop (now a Cardinal), concerned for his health and for the pastoral care of the rapidly growing Sutherland parish, recommended that he resign from Sutherland, reside at Boys Town and become priest in charge of Engadine, which thereby became a parochial district in its own right. As parish priest of Sutherland, he was irremovable and could only be changed if he himself agreed.

Being its founding father, the thought of breaking his ties with the parish of Sutherland and so many good and faithful people who had loved and supported him — and, indeed, put up with him for thirteen years — was daunting in the extreme. For Dunlea, however, the Cardinal's voice was the voice of God, so he readily complied with his wishes.

14

Riding into the silence of the bush

In 1946 Dunlea reported some exciting news to the Boys Town fundraising committee. It had to do with making Boys Town self-supporting. It was an ideal he had sought from the beginning, but never came close to attaining. Now at last it might be partially possible through a block of land south of Engadine in Heathcote. It wasn't a big block, just forty acres (henceforth to be called The Forty Acres), but he felt that with proper cultivation and care, it could be very productive. A farm of similar acreage in his native Tipperary certainly could be. Since it was a grant, the committee and the brothers felt it could be quite an asset.

Dunlea's efforts with Tommy, the erstwhile swagman, were now bearing fruit. Being a gifted handyman, Tommy was to play a big role in this new venture. There were two old cement buildings on The Forty Acres property which, with some difficulty, were converted into living quarters. One of these became home to former swagman, Ray, as well as wire-maker Tommy, who had now maintained sobriety for over a year and a half. Encouraged by Dunlea, Tommy had been using his wire-making skills. He had teamed up with Ray who, although seemingly backward and simple in appearance, had, in Dunlea's eyes, "the heart of a dreamer — the vision of a poet".

Dunlea was always highly amused at Tommy and Ray and himself and Brother Alban becoming a wire-making company, with Ray as door-to-door salesman! They had lightheartedly chosen JOG as the name of the company because of the story of St John of God which Dunlea had expounded with much flourish sometime before.

The wire-making had to take a back seat when they moved into The Forty Acres, and Tommy, by now, not only sober but scrupulously neat and tidy, plied his considerable handyman skills. Dunlea put Jackie, one of the early Boys Town boys, who worked on a farm in New Zealand, in charge of the farm, with some younger old-boys, who had failed to find employment, to help him. One of these, Irish Jim, whose parents lived in Queensland, was an epileptic, who never smiled and seemed to have a grudge against the world.

> He first smiled (John McRae relates) when Father found he had a lyric tenor voice of rare quality, a love for Irish singing and pride in his Irish ancestry. Father sent him to be trained by Bryson Taylor of the New South Wales Conservatorium of Music. This helped Jim's confidence tremendously when he sang for us at impromptu concerts. I used to be engrossed by Father's blue eyes as he listened to Jim singing the songs of his native land.

There was also Irish Kevin, who had a magnificent tenor voice and Mal, a Scotsman, who had a deep bass voice ... fiery rebel types, but very loyal and dedicated in trying to develop the farm as a working proposition.

Peter Morrissey sheds some interesting light on this aspect of Dunlea's character:

> He was in awe of artists of any ilk. Anyone who sang, recited, or played a musical instrument, to say nothing of the accomplished sculptor, painter or poet, was on another plane as far as Tom was concerned. They left him mystified as to their uncanny power. He himself could not sing or sketch or craft a poem, yet though he did not realise it himself, he embodied in his own way more poetry, music, power of communication, feeling and sheer giftedness than any half a dozen ordinary artists put together. For true artist he certainly was. He was

lucky to have been born with a most beautiful speaking voice, modulated to every nuance, liquid-clear as a bell and just enough strewn with original exotic metaphor, simile etc to mesmerise all listeners.

Respect was a quality he possessed in abundance, respect for everything, which manifested itself in the awe he had for all trades, "their gear and tackle and trim" — that is, he invested everyone with the full status of his calling. Not only did the medico possess an awesome unaccountable gift, but the policeman too was, as his uniform signified, possessed of a power that ordinary laymen could not share. As a matter of fact, there were, in his mind, no ordinary laymen. Everyone, the bus conductor, the accountant, the sailor, had a distinctive community role that was beyond the full appreciation of non-bus conductors, non-accountants and non-sailors. (Coleman p24)

At this time a report appeared in the Melbourne Age:

Mickey Rooney, one-time mayor of Sydney's Boy Town is in Melbourne. Not Hollywood Rooney from the Spencer Tracy film, but another with a genuine Boys Town background. He is in Melbourne to sing in the chorus of the Italian Grand Opera Company which opens next week at His Majesty's.

Michael Edward Rooney was 16 and the product of a hard unsympathetic Sydney environment when he happened to come under the influence of Father Dunlea. Later when the boys decided they needed a new mayor they elected Rooney just as the other Mickey Rooney became mayor in the film. He stayed two years at Boys Town and at 18 joined the RAAF.

Discharged, he followed his hearts desire — singing. He did well on radio programmes, won the ear of the conductor of the grand opera chorus and joined the tenors.

I know from experience, said Rooney yesterday, that the worst words in the English language are "institution" and "orphanage".

But whenever I went to a job or called on someone and said I was from Boys Town they accepted me. That is probably the greatest single thing about Father Dunlea's work — the boys take their place in society.

The news item carried a photo taken the night before of a smiling Rooney in a dress suit talking to a smiling Dunlea at the South Melbourne Town Hall.

Dunlea introduced a boy called Jim of Jewish origin to the Forty Acres. He was born in Shanghai, the son of a British army officer and a Jewish mother. During the Japanese occupation he had been held in a concentration camp, only to be released when the Allies took over at the end of World War II. After losing his father and mother, he was repatriated to Australia where he had a serious breakdown. The Jewish Community of Sydney, who were responsible for him, appealed to Dunlea and were very grateful when he gave him a place in Boys Town.

John McRae continues:

> Then there was Greg, a red-haired Scots Presbyterian, who loved farming life and had a passion for horses. He made the farm his home for a couple of years ...
>
> We added to the living quarters a large timber verandah, which served as a Mass Centre for ourselves and the local parishioners of Heathcote.
>
> It was here that I first learned and was privileged to serve Mass for a true saint of God. (Coleman p17)

John McRae was a member of the St Thomas More Students' Club, attached to the Sydney Teachers College. Club members visited Boys Town each Friday night to teach the boys hobbies, dramatics and debating, just as Joan Gortley and the Hurstville younger set gave them lessons on relating and socialising. John held a weekly campfire in the grounds with a real fire, folk singing and bush stories. When he graduated as a teacher and completed his country service, he offered his skills to Boys Town:

> I commenced duties under the guidance and inspiration of the shepherd who had followed humbly and faithfully in his Master's footsteps, searching the highways and byways for the lost and the stray, the unloved and the unwanted.

From their first meeting, Dunlea impressed him deeply and left him with the feeling of having encountered a truly great man:

> He dispelled all fear, his trust in God and in the goodness of people, even those who regarded themselves as failures (and I had such a complex) was tremendous. Talking of fear, he once said to me: "When a boy spits on you with hate it is because he is afraid and has been hurt. He has been looking for love and has not been given it".

Then John goes on to tell about Max, a spastic boy who slept in the Town hospital. He could only walk with the support of two other boys:

> One morning Max struggled out along to the hospital front door, looking for Father, as he was anxious about something. Father was talking to someone at the hospital gate, so Max tried to clamber down the steps and fell to the concrete pathway, a crumpled piece of misery, sobbing bitterly. Some boys rushed to help him. Father called out, "Leave him alone. Max, get up." Max called out, "Father, I can't".
>
> Father answered, "Yes you can". Max tried to struggle up and did. Father said, "Now, walk towards me". Again Max replied, "I can't". Father replied, "You can, walk to me". Max took slow, shaky steps, crying all the time but eventually reached Father. From then on he was able to walk unaided.

Inspired by Father, John entered St Columba's Seminary Springwood and was ordained priest and celebrated his first Mass "with Father kneeling at my side". "So", he goes on, "the old Forty Acres gave a priest to the world to minister to the poor and the afflicted as his Mentor did before him".

John McRae was a priest of the Sydney Archdiocese, who died in the 1980s as the much-loved Parish Priest of Enfield. He was a man of deep compassion and feeling for the underdog, like his mentor. Knowing Dunlea better than most, his fidelity to him and admiration of him never waned. They remained the best of friends.

* * * * * * * *

When Australia's wartime Prime Minister, John Curtin, died in office in July 1945, all Australia went into deep mourning. The war with Japan was coming to an end and did end within a month. Dunlea conducted a service for him in Boys Town and often expressed his regret that Curtin didn't live to experience the joy and relief that the Allies' victory in Japan brought to his fellow Australians on August 15th (VJ Day).

Ben Chifley succeeded John Curtin as Prime Minister, and Arthur Caldwell, became his Minister for Immigration. The perilous state of the nation during World War II convinced Caldwell that a country the size of Australia must have more people, must "populate or perish". He lost no time in introducing into Parliament an Immigration Bill that would eventually bring to Australia hundreds of thousands of immigrants, first Anglo-Celts and then Europeans.

Dunlea contacted Clareman Dan Minogue, Labor member for East Sydney, asking him to convey to Caldwell his congratulations for such a courageous and inspired initiative. Indeed, it was courageous in view of the fact that traditionally the Labor Party, as well as the Unions, were opposed to assisted immigration. It was felt the newcomers would take jobs from Australians, would be used by employers as cheap labour, would create unemployment and lower the living standard.

En route to visit Harry Truman, California, 1946

The march arrives at the Tent City

"Dublin Lad" a successful race horse who carried Boys Town's colours in the early 40s

ent City residents and helpers

)unlea always had time for the needy

Eric Green and Val Stannard at a fund raising dance at Hurstville

Dunlea and friend (Father John O'Connor)

Father Dunlea welcoming two aboriginal orphans to Boys' Town

Araluen pub where Dunlea spent R and R

Father Dunlea with two friends

Boys Town, Engadine 1942

The Hurstville 'live crib' was an attraction in the St George area of Sydney and beyond. The animals varied in number and species depending on Dunlea's remembering to make provision. At special times local people substituted for Mary and Joseph and the Child.

Father Dunlea, 1934

Thomas Vincent Dunlea

O.M., P.P., O.B.E.
Parish Priest of Burwood and the Metropolitan Area of Sydney,
Founder of Boys' Town, Engadine, and the Society for Lepers, N.S.W.
Australia

To our Most Beloved Priest and Friend the Reverend Father Thomas Vincent Dunlea, P.P., O.B.E., Born at Roman House, County Tipperary, Ireland, to Thomas Dunlea and Bridget Minogue on April 19, 1894, educated at Mt. St. Joseph, Roscrea, Mt. Melleray and St. Peter's College Wexford. Ordained by Bishop Coad at St. Peter's College Wexford on June 20, 1920 ———

Setting out from Ireland shortly after your Ordination, by the White Star Liner S.S. Olympic, you landed in Sydney, 91.5.28, Australia, on Friday, December 11, 1920, to say your first Mass under the Stars of the Southern Cross at the Church of the Sacred Heart, Darlinghurst, on Saturday December 12, 1920 ———

Charged with the care and responsibilities of many under privileged parishioners You set to work to bring into being, in the name of humanity, against overwhelming and almost impossible odds, the birth of the place you called Boys' Town, and in your own words, "Born of the Prayers of a Handicapped Boy and a Derelict Swagman"

Hurstville, where you had previously served as a Curate

Blessed was your work for the Parishioners of St. Patrick's, Sutherland
Blessed was your work for the Boys of Boys' Town, Engadine
Blessed is your work for the Parishioners of St. Michael's, Hurstville

And now in the twilight of a Holy and Priestly life ~ we join in a united voice in the
Bi-Centenary Year of Australia :
"Well Done Thou Good and Faithful Servant ~ May God Spare you ~
Ad Multos Anos"

This Councils of the Municipalities of Hurstville and Rockdale have resolved that this
tribute be executed under the Common Seal, and is presented as a lasting memorial
of your unsurpassed service to the Community

The Common Seal of the Council of the Municipality
of Hurstville was hereto affixed this Eighteenth
day of June in pursuance of a Resolution of the
Council passed at the Meeting
held on the 21st, May, 1970

_____
MAYOR
_____
TOWN CLERK

The Common Seal of the Council of the Municipality
of Rockdale was hereto affixed this Eighteenth
day of June in pursuance of a Resolution of the
Council passed at the Meeting
held on the 14th, May, 1970

_____
MAYOR
_____
TOWN CLERK

Cover of the American Boys Town magazine, 1946

The presbytery, Merton St, Sutherland

Boys Town, 2003

Reinternment at Boys Town, 197[?]

Father Dunlea's grave at Boys Town, Engadine

urstville, 1968

Father Dunlea with Mr Fenton Michell "Torrendorra", Inverell, 1952

Father Dunlea in a typical pose with his American cousin Bunny, San Francisco, California, 1947

Dunlea at Boys Town, America, 1947

ic Drew, Dunlea's friend and helper

Father Dunlea with Patricia Michell, 1969

ther Dunlea's funeral at St Mary's Cathedral

An early photo taken at St Peters, Wexford, 1918

These negative views not only echoed in the halls of Parliament House, they were carried on the radio airways and were strongly expressed in the print media. They became more shrill when Caldwell, having exhausted the Anglo element, turned to mainland Europe, north first and then south, and finally the refugee camps housing the thousands displaced by World War II.

An interesting survey was conducted at the time, seeking to ascertain how Australians felt about European immigrants. Strange to say, only a few short years after the war, people would have preferred Germans to Italians or Jews.

Although people felt Australia should take some small proportion of refugees, bringing reffos, as they were called, in the huge numbers Caldwell envisaged was seen to be very risky and not at all in Australia's national interest. Indeed, if a referendum had been held on the immigration question at that time, it would certainly have been defeated. Dunlea often expressed to Dr Minogue and to his friend Doc Tuomey, of Dulwich Hill, his admiration for the leaders of the Labor Party who stuck to their guns and pressed ahead with a plan that would bring new life and vitality to Australia, even though it could be electorally damaging for the Party.

There was one plank, however, in the political platform of both parties which many religious leaders at the time felt was at variance with the Gospel, but they didn't express their disagreement from the housetops, as it were. It had to do with immigration and colour, or the White Australia policy as it was called. As his good friend Eric Drew put it: "The love of Father Tom for people did not mean *some* people, it meant *all* people, irrespective of race, colour or creed".

Among his early Boys Town boys were several non-whites, including a number of Aborigines.

When his hero and fellow Catholic, Arthur Caldwell, declared at a press conference in 1947 that the White Australia policy remained a key plank in the Labor Party immigration platform, Dunlea was deeply hurt. On the following Sunday, he told his congregation at Engadine that a policy that discriminated against people because of the colour of their skin was not only unChristian, it was inimical to the egalitarianism he saw beginning to develop and take root in much of Australian society.

The White Australia policy, favoured by most Australians at the time, remained intact for over twenty years more, to be discarded by another Labor Government in 1972, two years after Dunlea's death.

Dunlea's health was deteriorating to such an extent that Eric Miles was adamant he had to slow down. At last, in April 1949, he informed the Cardinal that he was resigning from involvement in the organisation of AA, from public meetings, apart from those in Boys Town, and from lecturing to gatherings. The Cardinal replied by return post that he was all in favour.

During the years after World War II — from the mid-1940s — institutions, like Boys Town, that depended on charity were finding it difficult to balance their books. Dunlea was worried too about the growing tension in Boys Town occasioned by the system of dual control: the De La Salle Brothers and their staff on the one hand and the large enthusiastic committee on the other. Some of the committee's schemes and projects were felt by the brothers to be inimical to the internal management of the Town. Dunlea, found the resulting strain somewhat nerve-racking.

In June 1950, Dr Nicholas Larkin of Katoomba was so worried about Dunlea, who was having a short holiday in the Blue Mountains, that he wrote to his family friend, Cardinal Gilroy: "He is in a very run-down state of health — nervous exhaustion. He submitted with great cooperation to the rather severe restrictions I have imposed". Gilroy wrote a very caring note to Dunlea, telling him to take a couple of months of complete rest.

Dunlea returned to Engadine somewhat refreshed and ready to take up the lighter duties he had assigned himself.

By mid 1951, however, the old problems began to resurface to such an extent that he became aware things could not go on like this much longer.

Eric Miles left him in no doubt: "If you do not give up Boys Town, Boys Town will have to give you up". The brothers, too, who had completed ten years of service by 1951, decided to move on. In a tribute to them, Dunlea pointed out how Boys Town had prospered under the wise guidance of the De La Salle Brothers. During those golden years, it had grown to over a hundred boys and had sent forth an increasing number of citizens of whom every Australian could be justly proud.

After negotiations which included Cardinal Gilroy and his auxiliaries, as well as Dunlea, the Salesian Fathers agreed to take over the running of Boys Town, with Joseph Ciantar SDB as Director.

Dunlea's friend, John McRae, fills in some of the departure details:

> With the arrival of Joseph Ciantar SDB, the new director of Boys Town, Father left quietly in the evening, riding his horse and carrying only a few necessaries and set off down south, as the Cardinal had granted him twelve months' leave ... Probably he slept under the trees that first night, but early next morning Eric, the first boy he gave shelter to, asked me if I would drive him down to Helensburgh to find Father before he moved on, as there was an important letter from St Mary's Cathedral for him.
>
> We found Father at Helensburgh Convent, where he had just said Mass. The Sisters of St Joseph put on a fine breakfast for us — however, it was like a Last Supper, as our hearts were heavy having to bid farewell to one who had been such a wise and loving father to us.
>
> The letter, we found out later, was from the Cardinal: "To express our sincere thanks for the generous manner in which you have cooperated with Bishop Lyons during the past few months to

perpetuate the noble work you have established in Engadine.

"Father Dunlea's Boys Town will always be a memorial of your boundless charity and courage. It is an admirable work that owes its existence and progress, under God, to you.

"When you feel disposed to undertake duty you will do me a favour by discussing with me the task you wish to assume. Will you please accept the enclosed cheque as a token of my regard."

In the same strain, Dame Mary Gilmore (1865–1962), the grand old lady of Australian literature, wrote to the boys about Dunlea:

Whether you know it now or not, all your lives will be influenced by that man and through all of you at the farm as the years go on, a widening circle of others.

How far that little candle throws its beams, and like that too, a stone thrown in one side of the Pacific Ocean, affects the other side, infinitesimal though the effect may be. Father Dunlea has been that candle in a naughty world, and that stone in the Pacific. No prosperity and no adversity can take that from him or you. No matter who has helped his work and carried it on, it was Father Dunlea who began it and through him the help came. No other started it or would have done so. (Coleman p22)

So closed a most important chapter in the life of a man who had blazed a trail against prejudice and ignorance in the cause of the underprivileged of whatever colour or creed. John continues:

We watched the lone figure ride into the silence of the bush to discover new horizons and he found a warm response in that far outback.

Dunlea wandered to Broome in the north-western corner of the continent. Evidently he made firm friendships everywhere he went. He experienced the truth of

Banjo Paterson's poem, remembered from his Surry Hills days:
> And the bush has friends to meet him and their kindly voices greet him
> In the murmur of the breezes and the river on its bar.
> And he sees the vision splendid in the sunlit plains extended
> And at night, the wondrous glory of the everlasting stars.

15

Father Ciantar takes over

Joseph Ciantar, the man who became Director of Boys Town, was an outstanding member of the Salesian Order. Born in Malta, he spent twenty-five years travelling the length and breadth of Great Britain and Ireland as a one-man propaganda machine for the Salesians. In 1938 he became the fourth Director of Australian Salesians, based at Rupertswood near Melbourne, Victoria. More than anyone else, he was the one who put the small and faltering Australian foundation on its feet. As well as the many initiatives he spearheaded and completed in Victoria, he took on board Salesian responsibility for two small struggling Boys Towns, one in Tasmania and one in Adelaide.

In the spring of 1951, Cardinal Gilroy approached the Provincial of the Salesians, Father B M Fedrigotti, with a request that the Salesians take over the running of Boys Town Sydney. Although this was the type of work they were founded to do, Salesian personnel in Australia were thin on the ground at the time, and it was only after getting a very positive green-light from the Superior General in Turin that Fedrigotti concluded negotiations with Cardinal Gilroy. Ciantar, who felt that Boys Town offered the Salesians a new opportunity to work with needy boys, was the obvious choice to lead the foundation in Sydney. He was the one with the widest experience and the strength of character needed for a difficult assignment.

One of the difficulties had to do with finance. The proceeds from the Sydney Carnival had diminished unaccountably, creditors had not been paid for some time, the De La Salle Brothers hadn't received their stipend for some months and, according to Salesian historian Ted Cooper, Dunlea had lost all control.

This phase of the Boys Town saga could be said to begin with an unusual item that appeared in Granny's column in the *Sydney Morning Herald* on August 30, 1947. Granny's Column, or Column 8, as it was called later on, usually carried snippets of trivia, but now and again it aired something provocative that could lead to a public debate. This item was longer than usual and had some serious questions regarding George Nathan's running of the Sunday Carnival.

It may have been a public expression of rumours doing the rounds in Sydney at the time, rumours about some shady dealings involving the people who were raising funds for Boys Town. If this talk were to become public, it could become quite damaging to Boys Town and an embarrassment to the Sydney Church. The *Herald* item may have come from some group who had a hidden agenda, like securing the Sports Ground on Sundays for their own fundraising. It may even have had an anti-Catholic origin. Although Dunlea himself was known to be very ecumenical, the prevailing religious climate in Sydney wasn't at all ecumenical. Among other more subtle publications, there was, for example, a scurrilous little paper called *The Rock* which had a fairly large readership and which carried all sorts of extremely offensive allegations about all things Catholic.

The Sunday Carnival itself was a problem, in that it was seen as violating the Sabbath. For hardliners it was another indication of Catholic disregard for Scripture and the gradual infiltration of Rome into all aspects of Australian life!

The amazing thing was that Dunlea and Boys Town, who were bringing such favourable publicity to the Catholic Church, were allowed to keep such a high profile for so long in a society where bigotry was very much on the agenda. When the attack did come, the *Sydney*

Morning Herald directed its questioning not to the Church, but to the Jewish bookmaker, George Nathan:

> For more than four years a Mr George Nathan has been privileged to conduct organised sports meetings on Sunday afternoons at the Sydney Sports Ground. During peak periods attendance numbered up to 20,000. They are not so big now and vary between 5,000 and 10,000 according to the events. Profits are donated to Boys Town — and I thought it would be interesting in view of the privilege of being able to conduct Sunday sports, to be able to state how much Boys Town had received from it over the four years, how much had gone into expenses and so on. The head of Boys Town referred me to Mr Nathan. Mr Nathan said he wasn't going to tell and the head of Boys Town said he wasn't going to go over Mr Nathan's head. But I presume the State Government would be interested in these figures, because another organiser might be able to give more money to some other charity for the privilege — which seems to have become a monopoly of Mr Nathan's — of conducting Sunday sport on a publicly owned piece of land.

The Sunday Carnival at the Sports Ground had been the main financial support on which Boys Town depended. Being the only major Sunday entertainment in Sydney during the war, it was a great attraction.

With the ending of the war came some major changes. The dismantling of wartime price controls caused prices to rise dramatically. The cost of living and inflation kept rising, leaving far less money to spend on contributions to charities like Boys Town. The subsequent drive to increase wages in proportion to the cost of living led to a long period of industrial unrest. There were prolonged strikes, especially in the mines, the power plants and the waterfront, with striking workers losing their own pay packets and causing thousands of others to be stood down for lack of power. This resulted in money being in short supply.

Not only did the numbers attending the Sunday Carnival decrease, the amount available to spend on the various Carnival events was limited. It wasn't such big news then that the takings were down.

The fact that the *Herald* item wasn't followed up and investigated publicly by anyone else could be an indication that people weren't greatly shocked by it. If it were seen as pointing towards the possibility of a major scandal, the likelihood is that someone would have run with it, given the religious climate in Sydney at the time.

The next item to be reported in the print media was almost five years later, when the *Sydney Sun* in April 1952 reported the closure of the Sunday Carnival which was by then actually losing money. The article included some figures indicating receipts for a few Sundays in April/May 1950, with the amounts going to Boys Town being slightly less than fifty percent. Salesian historian Ted Cooper suspects these figures came from Ciantar himself, "who was making no secret of how shabbily Boys Town was treated. They (the figures) were most revealing and could have raised eyebrows but do not seem to have had any adverse repercussions". (p293). This again possibly indicates people were aware that an enterprise as big as the Sunday Carnival would have quite a lot of expenses to be attended to before Boys Town got its dividend.

Cooper heard from Ciantar that a wealthy and well-known Catholic businessman and entrepreneur, Bill Taylor, was the one who kept all the seamy rumours about Boys Town's shortcomings from becoming headline news. That was quite an achievement; rumours of scams and scandals that have to do with money and the Church are notoriously hard to keep under wraps.

That Dunlea had lost all control of the Sunday Carnival and other fundraising functions is true in the sense that he never did control these. Hurstville parishioner, Sheila Tearle, reports that, when someone complained to the Archbishop that he was not a businessman, Dunlea was quite hurt and explained rather passionately the following Sunday that he wasn't trained to be a businessman, his vocation lay elsewhere. He left the business side of things to those who were trained in this area and he didn't interfere. However, not everyone is trustworthy, especially in money matters, so maybe he should have interfered and insisted on more accountability. Certainly that's what his successor would have done.

The Church insists on financial accountability regarding parish finances, and a detailed financial report has to be furnished each year. Because Dunlea, as Parish Priest, was finding this somewhat beyond him, the Bishop authorised the curate to take responsibility in this area.

As regards fundraising activities, where people give of their time and effort free of charge, the demand for detailed accountability wasn't nearly as stringent. Although George Nathan, as a good businessman, would have kept detailed records of his bookmaking transactions, he would most certainly not have been asked by Dunlea to do the same regarding the proceeds of the Sunday Carnival. Even Cardinal Gilroy, who was rather meticulous regarding finance, didn't demand a strict accounting in regard to fundraising initiatives like fetes, bazaars, bingo etc. Bingo, in fact, provided most of the finances for building Catholic schools in the 1940s. Pastors, finding it very difficult to recruit the people needed to run bingo, had to presume they were honest and trustworthy. The Chief Secretary, however, did demand that a detailed account of each game be kept and forwarded to his office regularly. If something untoward was discovered, the licence to operate bingo was withdrawn. Presumably Nathan complied with this, and the fact that the permission continued must indicate that the Chief Secretary was satisfied it was being run properly.

Did Boys Town get its proper share of the proceeds of the Sunday Carnival, especially during the very lucrative war years? Joseph Ciantar and evidently others thought not. Ciantar felt the buildings he inherited, apart from those constructed by the meatmen and bakers, did not reflect the takings during those flourishing years. Although the boys were well fed and looked after and were comfortably accommodated, the fibro and weatherboard buildings were very basic and in some ways substandard. Ciantar, an experienced builder and a shrewd businessman as well as a very good priest, would not be likely to make allegations of this sort lightly.

George Nathan did not produce detailed financial accounts for the Sunday Carnival when asked to do so by Ciantar for the very good reason they probably did not exist. As well as being bad business, this practice has the innate danger of exposing people to suspicions. Dunlea himself never entertained such suspicions — "They are utter rubbish", he told Peter Morrissey. Ciantar and fellow Salesian Ted Cooper did not agree.

Ted Cooper came to Engadine in 1956 and was Headmaster of Boys Town until 1964. Although he didn't know Dunlea personally, he was very close to Ciantar, who convinced him that, long before the Salesians took over, large sums of Boys Town money were not reaching Boys Town. He became convinced, too, that Dunlea's entrusting the fundraising to a book maker without proper control was a disastrous decision. Lack of accountability for moneys raised at the Sydney Carnival in its heyday, he felt, deprived Boys Town of the capacity to build in the style needed. This resulted in Ciantar having to engage in a large, expensive rebuilding programme.

Cooper is of the opinion that there was a radical weakness in Dunlea that made him incapable of carrying a project through to its full development.

> "Boys Town," he writes, "began with tremendous publicity and support, but after a few years Dunlea was losing enthusiasm. His native charity and enthusiasm were only good for a certain distance. His was the smiling face of Boys Town, a great image of the battling priest doing so much good for deprived boys. It was great for publicity, but the reality was that the smiling face was beginning to look drawn and hollow. Nathan was the driving force behind the smiling face. Nathan, the entrepreneur, the bookie, was not a good public image for Boys Town. It was

his profession (if that is the correct word) that naturally made people suspicious of the man and to have him in such a position where he controlled the Boys Town finance was like putting the proverbial fox to look after the chickens. Granny's comments were a catalyst that set the alarm bells ringing and even though direct action did not take place for some years, the rumours, suspicions grew."

Catholic clergy are often one another's most severe critics. Some of his priest-contemporaries, feeling Dunlea was easy to exploit, would agree with Ted Cooper's assessment above. However, apart from two or three who expressed mild misgivings, all other correspondents, including many other priests and ministers who knew him well, would disagree.

Cardinal Gilroy remained on friendly terms with George Nathan for years after the Carnival ceased operating, giving the impression that, even if he did have some suspicions early on, he probably changed his mind.

In an operation involving as many people as the Sunday Carnival, some may indeed have been helping themselves to some of the funds. Unfortunately, that's the human condition and, even in the very best-controlled organisation, cannot be ruled out completely. Ciantar had first heard these rumours in Melbourne, but when he did come to Engadine in January 1952, he spent a day going through everything and concluded "first impression very good".

The rumours, evidently, weren't quite as bad as they sounded.

As everyone expected, Ciantar had his own ideas about the financing of Boys Town, and they didn't include George Nathan who had been linked with Dunlea for over a dozen years. Indeed, without him Boys Town would not have got off the ground. "We call him our miracle man", Dunlea had said in the late 1940s. He had also noted:

> Boys idolise him; whenever he calls he is soon the centre of a lively group. Many a punter collecting his

winnings from George has been induced to contribute some to the Town. He is always on the lookout for people with special knowledge who might be able to give us valuable advice.

* * * * * * * *

The Salesians were no strangers to Dunlea. He knew all about their founder, the nineteenth century John Bosco, who was so gifted in dealing with boys in the northern Italian city of Turin. He had started, as Dunlea himself did, with two boys and ended up with seven thousand. Dunlea regarded John Bosco as the real pioneer in the area and adopted him as his patron.

Although Dunlea had his own unique gifts, he would readily concur with Ted Cooper's assessment that he lacked the professionalism and training needed to rehabilitate delinquent boys. That is the special charism of the Salesians and so, although emotionally upset at having to give up Boys Town, Dunlea knew that the Salesian takeover was a blessing for the boys as well as for the Sydney Church.

Being a top fundraiser and financial manager, Ciantar started by dismantling what he thought was the weak link and a possible source of embarrassment to the Church — the Dunlea–Nathan fundraising arrangement. With the removal of these two pillars of the old Boys Town, he proceeded to build anew according to the very successful John Bosco–Salesian system.

Norman Thomas Gilroy, although a very pious and committed prelate, was a shrewd practical administrator, somewhat under pressure financially at that time. State Aid to religious schools wasn't yet operating. New schools had to be built and extra lay teachers employed to cater for the increasing influx of assisted immigrant families. With the departure of Dunlea and the imminent closure of the Sunday Carnival, responsibility for the financial support of Boys Town would be a serious drain on the already strapped diocesan finances. This was something to be avoided at all costs, and securing Father Ciantar and the Salesians seemed to be the only way to do so while still ensuring a very good outcome for the Town.

His senior auxiliary, James Carroll, an expert in canon law, was reluctant to make the extensive plant over to the Salesians in perpetuity; not so Cardinal Gilroy, so long as the Salesians took full financial responsibility for the boys and their future.

In this sense the Salesians did rescue Boys Town and the Sydney Church, which couldn't very well abandon something Dunlea and his myriad supporters had worked so hard to establish.

Ciantar noted in his diary that in January 1952, Dunlea gave him "the impression of a man suffering from a nervous breakdown. His conversation was very disconnected. He thinks he has been very much misunderstood and dealt with unjustly". (Cooper p290). That feeling of being misunderstood and treated unjustly were indications of a deep seated malaise that was beginning to be a real problem. The Cardinal and Bishop Lyons were convinced that the only way of saving Dunlea's life's work was by his letting go of it totally. To assuage the pain and the deep empty feeling of loneliness that this produced, Dunlea had recourse to a substance that had been very much part of his social life. This, sadly, he began to abuse.

16
Sobriety attained

Father Ciantar noted accurately in his diary on January 22nd 1952 that Dunlea was what one would refer to as a basket case. This was due to deteriorating health and the trauma of leaving Boys Town. It was also due to the demon drink. The one who had tried so hard to help others overcome the disease that was destroying their lives had now succumbed to that disease himself. He had become an addict. He tried to give it up, but the inner craving for alcohol was too much for him. This matter reached a crisis in January 1952 at a clergy social gathering in Sydney that got lots of publicity because one of those present, Father Chris Smithwick, had a fatal accident on his way home. He evidently dozed off and ran his car into the Harbour. Alcohol being deemed the cause, it became a great embarrassment to the Church. The fact that Father Smithwick was a non-drinker was not reported. Dunlea, however, did drink too much and, although not reported in the press, wrapped his car around a pole on his way home from the same party. Cardinal Gilroy was distraught. He suggested that Dunlea spend some weeks at Mount Eymard in the Southern Highlands under the care of Father McNevin of the Blessed Sacrament Fathers. Writes Pat Kenna:

> Need I add Tom Dunlea saw very little of Mount Eymard or Father McNevin, whom he described as having prismatic eyes. He spent his days in the company of Mittagong people, including at times John Purcell, and, in lashings of time, myself. This frustrated McNevin so much that I and a few others

witnessed him reprimanding Tom in a rather humiliating way. Those January/February weeks in Tom's company had a profound effect on me.

Then followed his outback journeying. His friends, including Cardinal Gilroy, felt the vast open spaces that he loved and the native tribes might help him beat his inner demons.

Perhaps that did happen to some extent because, on July 13, 1952 we find him back in Mount Eymard again, writing to Cardinal Gilroy:

> I am much rested and have entered upon a soul-restoring interval at Mount Eymard. Thank you tremendously for your cheque and letter of appreciation in regards to my Boys Town. After much consideration I beg permission to return your very munificent cheque as it is too much to expect when one considers the many calls of myriad responsibilities of your vast Archdiocese.

The Cardinal was not renowned for being generous, and yet he had given Dunlea one hundred pounds, which at that time was one year's salary for a curate — a compelling indication of his affection and esteem for his ailing friend.

A short time later, Dunlea is re-immersed into the Sydney scene and this spells disaster, indeed.

Eric Drew and Glad Rawlinson, his housekeeper, racked their brains trying to come up with the name of someone who might help. Strange as it may seem, the name that came to them wasn't that of Dr Minogue or Archie McKinnon or any other AA person. It was a woman, a Mary Michell from Inverell, who in her wisdom has recorded in some detail the long road he travelled to recovery.

Mary first met Dunlea at the Brigidine College in Randwick where she was a boarder. A curate in Hurstville at the time, he was invited by the Principal to give occasional talks to the senior girls. The Dunlea charisma worked so well that, as Mary says, "All the girls at the

College were in love with Father Tom, he was a good line in those days". His attractiveness to women and his attraction to them started when they were young! They flocked around him, confided in him and sought his counsel. Mary went on to do nursing at St Vincent's Hospital Sydney.

"Again I met Father Tom when he would visit patients. He was a great showman and could get people in." Years later they met again, when they were both patients at Lewisham Hospital. "I suspect he was drying out", writes Mary. She goes on:

> He claimed to remember me from school and St Vincent's but that could be a bit of blarney, of which he had plenty. Up to then I had only a passing acquaintance with him, he was more or less just a name to me. During that time I got to know Father better and we had long talks about horses and dogs, country life and so on. Father seemed interested in these simple things of life and expressed a desire to share them. Later he invited me to visit Boys Town and that's how I met Glad, who had some association with AA.

Mary returned to the farm she and husband Fenton conducted near Inverell in northern N.S.W.

Some years later, in mid-1952, Mary had an urgent call from Eric Drew and Glad. Among other things they told her of a letter Eric had from Jim Kelleher, Editor of the *Catholic Weekly*, in which was included a little one-line cutting from the *Mirror* newspaper, reporting that a T Dunlea, cleric, was fined five pounds for being drunk. It didn't elaborate and no-one seemed to notice it. Kelleher, having received a call from Katoomba a couple of days previously regarding Dunlea's drinking there, was alerting Eric Drew to the fact that something had to be done urgently. Eric intimated that he couldn't even bear to think of the furore that would have eventuated had the media discovered the identity of the T Dunlea, cleric.

He asked Mary if she would consider allowing Father and Glad to travel to Inverell and live at the Michell farm for a while. Mary talked it over with Fenton, and they both agreed to do all they could to help.

With Glad and Jim McGuire, a mentally retarded young man, in the back seat and Dunlea in the front with Eric Green, the driver, they headed north to the Central Coast, through the beautiful Hunter Valley, over the ranges and on to the city of Tamworth. There, they were met by Mary and Fenton. Eric returned to Sydney, while the Michells took Dunlea, Jim and Glad north through Manilla and Barraba, and on to Bingara, where they crossed the Gwyder River and headed north-east to Inverell.

In all, Dunlea and Glad and Jim had travelled over 700 kms over long stretches of dirt road and many rivers that were crossed only by car-ferry. Fortunately Mary had a large house and forty acres of land "to accommodate our many horses, cows, goats, dogs, fowls, turkeys and ducks". Torrendorra, as it was called, was about six kilometres from Inverell. The McIntyre River was close, which made it a great place for kids when they were home from boarding school.

"Father", as Mary put it, "was plagued by what he called 'the agonies of the mind'". She goes on:

> I am quite sure that no one except those who have lived with and nursed an alcoholic to health can possibly understand or realise the agony they suffer. The prayer "God grant me the grace to accept what I cannot change, courage to change what I can and the wisdom to know the difference" became well known to us and, for the first few weeks, Father lived from minute to minute instead of from day to day and we never left him on his own day or night. He was plagued by terrifying nightmares and his mental suffering was acute.
>
> At first insomnia was a problem. He was afraid to sleep because of the nightmares, but gradually Fenton indoctrinated him with his own system, which was to go to bed at 8 p.m. every night and

remain there even if sleep did not come. Gradually Father's restlessness decreased, as Fenton kept on expounding his cure theory and, in time, it worked. Father got so he couldn't stay awake after 8 p.m.

At this juncture, Mary and Glad thought it would be better for everyone if Jim, who at times thought he was John McCormack, returned to Sydney. As Mary said, "Father made arrangements and Glad went with Jim. I heard from Glad for years but eventually lost touch".

After a month or so, the patient was improved enough to assume a more normal routine. He was eating and sleeping well and didn't need the constant attention. He went on visits to Mary's parents, both of whom he had met before. Mary's father would delight him with anecdotes of life in the bush in the old days. He spent many relaxed happy hours thus engaged.

> Caring for a recovering alcoholic, writes Mary, is a humbling experience and I am glad Fenton and I were able to help Father when he needed it most, when he was at his lowest ebb. He was a very complex character. Behind all the showmanship and adulation bestowed on him, he was a very lonely man who knew his own faults more than anyone did and he saw only goodness in all people, the rich and powerful and the poor and disadvantaged, all races and colours. He was easily hurt but would never hurt anyone himself. He told me he thought what he witnessed during the Depression affected his brain.

He had no belongings except what he wore when he came to Torrendorra, so Mary fitted him out in countryman's clothes, which at that time consisted of moleskin trousers, blue cotton shirt, elastic side boots, wide-brimmed hat and sports jacket. She borrowed a big thoroughbred horse from a neighbour, Arthur Addison, and put it at his disposal. "And, by Jove," says Mary, "together they covered many miles".

After some time in Torrendorra, Mary and Fenton convinced Dunlea of the necessity of getting into good physical and mental shape. They set a very strict regimen, which Mary had found successful with a patient in a similar condition. It involved a regular daily swim and lots of horseback riding.

On freezing mornings, everywhere white as snow, Father would get up at daybreak, jog in shorts to the Macintyre River a mile away, have a long swim and jog back to the house. (A swim in the river in mid-winter? "Yes," said Mary, "I bullied him to do it".) Having arrived back at the house and showered and dressed in clerical gear, he had to catch and saddle his horse and gallop the four miles into Inverell to celebrate mass in the convent chapel. After breakfast with the Sisters who conducted the school there, he was on his horse again for the gallop back to Torrendorra.

He thoroughly enjoyed being on the horse and, in Mary's opinion, was a better-than-average rider, absolutely fearless. He told them about his thoroughbred grey, Bill Sykes, which he used in Sutherland to visit the sick and needy during the Depression. When once visiting Dalby in Queensland "he met the horsey crowd", he said. Predictably he was presented with a racehorse, which he named Dalby, and the race club had it delivered to Boys Town for his use.

He loved to talk about all sorts of things, like his overseas visit in 1932 and participation in the greatest international event ever hosted in Ireland up to then — the Eucharistic Congress in Dublin in the June of that year. When overseas travel became possible after World War II, he had made another epic trip abroad in 1947, staying with his brother Jim at Roran House in Tipperary. Although his parents were deceased, he loved to recount his many visits to the McKeoghs of Ballyvalley; the O'Briens of Amanish-Ogonnelloe; his sister Ailbe, a Sister of Mercy in Thurles; Anna (Mrs Ryan) in Limerick; another sister Margaret, a Holy Faith nun in Dublin; Kathleen, a Daughter of Charity at Kensal Green London, and Maria (Mrs Condon) in County Clare.

The children had delighted him, as had the music and singing for which that part of Tipperary/Clare is famous. He had revisited all those places that meant so much to him, even walking all the way to his old school in Killaloe. He had been feted by the Ballina Gaelic Football team, who presented him with the trophy won the year before. It had been good to meet so many of his friends of yesteryear, whose families were now quite grown-up.

His return to Australia had been through America, where he had spent some time with his idol, the founding director of Boys Town Nebraska. He had learned much and shared much, although Father Flanagan's health had been deteriorating rapidly. Flanagan happened to have a pipeline to the White House and arranged for Dunlea to meet the President of the United States. He told Mary and Fenton that he had found Harry S Truman a delight to be with, informal and humorous and laid-back.

The President didn't give private interviews and, indeed, during his five years at the White House, Dunlea was one of only three people to whom Truman did give an interview. "Father, before I was made President", the Chief Executive told him, "I had worn a path between my home and Boys Town Nebraska. Father Flanagan has stolen all the laurels of social work in America".

Even though the aides were knocking on the door to indicate the end of the interview, Truman had taken no notice. He loved Dunlea's accent and wanted to hear all the details about the founding and running of Boys Town Australia.

Dunlea waxed eloquent about his recent 1952 trip to the outback and the reception he got from the Aboriginal and other communities he visited. He even got as far as the Kimberleys, visiting Kalumburu and Lombadina Missions in the far north-west. He stayed at the Beagle Bay Mission, where Daisy Bates spent some time. He was delighted to learn that Bates was a Dublin woman sent to Australia as a reporter for *The Times*. As the colonial authorities were about to cut back on the funds allocated to run the mission, Bishop Matthew Gibney of Perth contacted Daisy Bates, inviting her to visit the Kimberley Mission with him.

She came dressed in all her elaborate finery, intriguing and amusing the native women, who loved to watch her robe and disrobe. The fact that she stayed on at Beagle Bay for several weeks during the steamy uncomfortable rainy season impressed him very much. She penned several telling articles for *The Times* (as the Bishop hoped she would), thus embarrassing the Government into continuing to fund the Aboriginal missions.

Inspired in part by the Bates story, Dunlea decided to start a Boys Town for Aborigine boys whom he had got to know well. He wrote to his good friend, Dame Mary Gilmore, to inform her about it and seek her advice. Dame Mary, probably aware of Dunlea's problems at the time, strongly advised against any such project and recommended a quick return to Sydney.

During his eight months with the Michells, Dunlea never once had a drink of alcohol. Some of his friends, including George Nathan, travelled all the way from Sydney to visit him. George was so pleased with his friend's progress that, on returning to Sydney, he couldn't wait to tell the Cardinal the good news. On August 2, 1952 the Cardinal wrote to Dunlea:

> In a visit Mr Nathan recently paid to me he mentioned that you were very well and looking better than ever before. This news gave me great pleasure. I would like to have confirmed by yourself that the reality corresponds to appearances. If you could let me know the date on which you would be prepared to resume duty.

The mail Dunlea received was phenomenal, some of it very helpful and encouraging. He asked Mary to reply to some items. One letter so impressed her and meant so much to Dunlea that she kept a copy. It was from Jimmy R in Ireland:

> I feel I must put pen to paper to express my deep gratitude for what you did when you visited Dublin

back in 1946. Little did you realise that when you were interviewed by *The Evening Mail* about Boys Town in Australia and mentioning the good work AA was doing there, that you were being used by God to sow the seed of AA which was to grow in Ireland and Britain and spread to Europe. At the time you gave that interview, there was in Dublin on vacation a Conor Flynn, a member of AA in Philadelphia. Seeing the report in *The Evening Mail* his wife spurred Conor on to do something about getting a group started in Dublin. After a lot of disappointment and much humiliation he met, at his last port of call, St Patrick's Hospital, a Dr Moore, who had an alcoholic patient called Richard P, to whom he allowed Conor to talk. When Richard heard what he had to say the penny dropped, he had found a way out of his dilemma and as Conor was shortly to return to America, they decided to try to start a group in Dublin, the first meeting being held in the Country shop on November 25th 1946.

I went to that meeting drunk. I didn't want to stop drinking, I couldn't see myself living without drink. I wasn't an alcoholic, how could I be when I didn't know what an alcoholic was. Conor was, he said, dry for three years. He explained how AA worked but it was the two speakers who followed that made me sit up and take notice. They told their stories and I was able to identify with them. If they were alcoholics so was I.

After the meeting Conor asked me if I believed in a Power greater than myself. I knew what he meant and I am glad he didn't ask me if I believed in God, if he did I mightn't be writing this to you today. He told me to ask that Power to help me get through one day without a drink. This I have done since that first meeting and contented sobriety has been my reward.

It took eleven years and many thousands of miles for AA to get from America via Australia to Dublin and I for one am convinced that the Programme is divinely inspired. I cannot see any body of men formulating the twelve steps in the way they are set down, without help from a divine Power. God works in strange ways: a priest on a visit to Dublin from Australia, Conor on vacation from America, Richard in a Dublin hospital (his home was in Belfast), this cannot be coincidental. It was God working through these good men, who started AA in Dublin from whence it spread to the rest of Europe. I shall always be eternally grateful for what you did for me and if I have helped someone since I joined AA I have been well rewarded. I would appreciate it very much if you would let me have a photo of yourself to hang along with Bill and Lois, Dr Bob and Anne and my good friend Sackville, who were instrumental in putting AA on the map.

Yours very sincerely
Jimmy R.

During the time Dunlea was with Mary and Fenton, Mary marvelled at the number of feeble and bedridden people he located around the area. Some she had taken him to see, but others he had learned about from the many people he had visited. In fact, Mary felt sure he knew more folk (and all about them) than she did. He had an uncanny ability to sniff out the local dead beats and down-and-outs and had no hesitation in bringing them to her place. Some were not so easy to get rid of after he left!

In the same vein, his niece, Maura Hannan, and nephew, John McKeogh, recently remembering his last holiday in Ireland over half a century ago, made a similar comment. News of his homecoming would leak out, bringing people down on their luck from all directions, to Roran House. So much so that (as Mary experienced) it became quite a problem to deal with them when he returned to Australia.

Winter changed into spring and summer at Torrendorra, and the Michell children came home from boarding schools for holidays. "They went riding with

Father", Mary writes, "and they still laugh about those rides":

> Father, like a general leading his troops, giving out the Rosary at the top of his voice, with the kids yelling the responses in between the dancing and prancing of their horses.

(Eric Drew, who was Dunlea's long-distance driver, reported on Dunlea's habit of starting on the Rosary beads when the trip began. Bruce Aley, his city driver, noticed the Rosary beads came out whenever Bruce pressed the accelerator more than he should!)

Mary presented Dunlea with a stock-whip and taught him how to use it. He practised and persevered until he became a good whip-cracker and was able to delight the children with his skill.

> On one occasion, dressed only in shorts, sandals and scapular, things got out of hand. He cracked off his scapular and very nearly cut off his head! Another day he was out practising when two Jehovah's Witnesses approached him. Father told them politely he wasn't interested, but they pursued their pestering, so he said, "I'm a Catholic priest" and cracked the whip. They ran up our hill in record time, every now and again looking over their shoulders as they ran. Would be interesting to know how they described that visit to their friends! They never came to our place again.

Although Cardinal Gilroy was fond of Dunlea, he himself was a total abstainer and couldn't understand people, especially priests, being addicted. It was said that there were problems in his own family caused by his father's drinking habits. Once he got to know of Dunlea's problems in that regard, he virtually suspended him from ministry. He allowed him to celebrate Mass, but not to preach or minister Sacraments. Dunlea sometimes celebrated Mass in the parish Church at Inverell. Many people, writes Mary, were keen to hear him preach and wondered why he didn't. She reflects:

My own thoughts were that the hierarchy were severe and lacking in understanding and charity and Father suffered much humiliation. Could be tantamount to kicking a dog when he is down. The local clerics ignored him. When he was well enough, he took the car and went to Armidale to visit Bishop Doody. He never spoke about that visit, but was obviously disappointed. We can draw our own conclusions?

His health improved dramatically at Torrendorra. Mary's programme worked wonderfully for him. After conveying this news to Cardinal Gilroy, he was called back to Sydney and appointed Chaplain to the Matthew Talbot Hostel for homeless men in Woolloomooloo. Mary and Fenton left Torrendorra in 1956, to be near their family in Queensland, but Dunlea kept in touch by letter or phone. Mary tells us:

> When our daughter Patricia was married in Brisbane in 1969, we were delighted that Father and his wonderful friend Mr Eric Drew were able to be present and Father spoke very beautifully about the parents of the bride. He had a profound effect on those who heard him. Because of his ailing health he was unable to perform the marriage. On this occasion Father renewed acquaintance with my family — in a way, he was one of my family. Last year on August 15, Father phoned to say he couldn't make the trip to our son's wedding.
>
> That was the last time we heard from him. One week later at almost the same hour, Eric phoned to say Father had, to use one of his own sayings, "gone to God".

Commenting on the gone to God way of putting it, Mary summed up her own appraisal of him: "Where else could he go, this very human man of God?"

17

Matt Talbot Hostel

It was early spring 1953 when Dr Minogue and Archie McKinnon took Dunlea to an AA meeting, his first since his return to the city. They were delighted to see him in such good health. There was a radiant glow about him. Although they had had some communiques from him, they hadn't seen him in person for a couple of years.

The meeting was late getting going because everyone wanted to meet him. When it came to his turn to speak, he was fidgety and a little nervous. As a member of the leadership group, he was expected to tease out some aspect of the AA philosophy which, of course, would be interspersed with interesting anecdotes and humorous experiences.

This time it was very different. He got to his feet slowly and almost with a certain strained awkwardness. The words didn't come for a while. Then, into the tense silence they echoed. "My name is Father Tom and I'm an alcoholic..."

All eyes in the smoke-filled room were fixed on him. All hearts went out to him in a brotherhood of love and support. As he told his story, he was subdued and reflective and sometimes quite emotional. In time, the story would be embellished and drawn in technicolour, in typical Dunlea style. Strange to say, he didn't embroider a truth that didn't sit well with this audience, namely, that it wasn't the twelve steps of AA which worked so well for so many of his friends, that brought him to sobriety. No, in his case it was, in fact, a good woman.

Only a few short weeks before that, the letter of appointment had arrived at Inverell. There was an air of excitement in the Michell family. Although they could see that their treatment had worked splendidly and that he was ready for ministry, Mary and Fenton had got used to the presence of this unusually warm person and would miss him. Dunlea himself deeply loved and appreciated the family, and the thought of leaving and perhaps not seeing them again pained him greatly. As he opened Cardinal Gilroy's letter, he knew his next posting would be a testing one entailing punishment and probation, as he put it.

The Cardinal put it much more benignly. Dunlea's next appointment would be one "without heavy responsibility. After the strain you have had and the ill health you have suffered, a gradual return to full responsibility would seem to be the best way of promoting your welfare".

If punishment was to be the focus, as Dunlea feared, then the parish of Burragorang was a possibility; it was small, isolated and, although dreaded by the clergy, Dunlea and other clergy enjoyed their short stays there. It is now under the placid waters of Warragamba Dam. A softer option, which the Cardinal seemed to have in mind, would be a residential chaplaincy to some monastery or large convent.

Chaplaincy it was, one that was created specially for him, one that most clergy would like to avoid, but one that uniquely appealed to Dunlea. He was to be Chaplain to the Matt Talbot Hostel for homeless men in Young Street, Sydney. Cardinal Gilroy had asked the St Vincent de Paul Society, who manage the hostel, to make a room available there for Dunlea who would become the first-ever resident Chaplain. The Society would pay an annual salary of two hundred and four pounds and, wrote Gilroy, in a caring fatherly way: "After you have settled down in your quarters in the hostel, you will call in and tell me your impressions of the work".

Not only did the homeless have a special place in Dunlea's heart, but the person after whom the hostel was named likewise appealed greatly to him.

While in Dublin in 1932, he had found out some details about a man who had died on his way to St Saviour's Dominican Church on Sunday June 7, 1925 at about 9.30 am. As the corpse was being prepared for burial, he was found to be wearing a light chain around his waist, attached to which were several medals. His body was scrupulously clean and well looked after. His name was Matt Talbot, and like Dunlea, for part of his life he had become an alcoholic. He would often come home without some of his possessions, like shoes, not because he had given them away as Dunlea did, but because he had sold them so that he could purchase more drink. He was a good worker but spent most of his wages on drink. Most nights he came home hopelessly drunk.

Then, all of a sudden, at the age of twenty-five, when he lost his job and was penniless, he decided to take the pledge and remained sober till his death over forty years later. The pledge didn't just mean no more drinking; it entailed a complete transformation of his life.

During those sober years, modelling his life on that of the old Irish monks, he vowed to follow their way of poverty, prayer and good works. He was a good reliable worker and, although his weekly wage as a labourer wasn't great, he managed to live on the smell of an oil rag, as Dunlea put it, so that he could share as much as possible with the poor of Dublin.

Dunlea had confided in Mary and Fenton that he was most impressed by the efforts Talbot made to hide his extraordinary life from the people around him. Apart from some fellow worshippers in Dublin's inner-city churches, where he spent hours and hours on his bare knees, he was known as a smiling pleasant man who took great care of people in the margins, especially alcoholics. He was always afraid of lapsing himself, and the chain he wore was a reminder of his pledge. It also led to the discovery of the extraordinary piety, devotion, prayerfulness, God-centredness of his life.

Although not at all moved to imitate the sheer volume of Talbot's pious practices, Dunlea was quite convinced he could feel that distinctive whiff of sainthood as he walked in his footsteps around Dublin. In his asceticism, Matt Talbot was practising a tradition of sanctity that appeals greatly to something in the Celtic mentality.

Dunlea experienced it at what is called St Patrick's Purgatory, on the tiny island of Lough Derg in County Donegal, where three days of prayer, fasting and deprivation of sleep attracts countless thousands of people each year. He also experienced it on the slopes of a bleak rough stone-littered mountain in County Mayo called Croagh Patrick, which thousands of people climb even in their bare feet.

The kingdom of heaven, he would say, is not promised to the sensible and the educated, but to such as have the spirit of little children.

This spirit that distinguished the extraordinary life of Dublin's holy man also coloured, in a notable way, the extraordinary life of his Australian admirer, who was now becoming part of a group giving the name of Dublin's Matt Talbot such a high profile in downtown Sydney.

The Sydney hostel had been located in several other places before the Society of St Vincent de Paul bought and renamed the rather spacious building in Young Street. It provided an evening meal, bed and breakfast for sixty homeless men. It was closed during the day. It encouraged its clientele to seek work and accommodated them until their first pay packet arrived.

The Marists at St Patrick's, Church Hill, had filled the role of chaplain with distinction for many years. Now that he was residing in the hostel itself as chaplain, Dunlea began to see his role as a sort of mini-parish priest. The homeless men, as everyone expected, got his undivided attention in the evening as they arrived and in the morning before they left.

Being listened to is a luxury few destitute people enjoy. They have stories, real and imaginary, but no-one has time to listen to them. Dunlea had the time and the interest and so, as Ed Campion put it, "his listening kindness was put to its full stretch".

The hostel, being also the headquarters of the St Vincent de Paul Society, was the meeting place for all members in leadership positions in Sydney and New South Wales. Not only did they have the benefit of Dunlea's always entertaining, often inspiring, if somewhat long-winded talks, but they were able to call on him to celebrate Mass at a time convenient to them. When people staying in the local hotels or working in them and other people living in the area became aware that Dunlea was the Chaplain, they frequented his midday and evening Masses. He became a very popular confessor and, as John Monahan who was on the staff at the time, points out, his presence lifted the profile of the hostel and was a great asset to the Society. The men felt honoured that such a cultured man, with a beautiful speaking voice, would have meals with them and regard them as his friends.

Yvonne Marien, a friend from Sutherland days, recounts part of a conversation Dunlea had, towards the end of 1954, with one of the men at breakfast:

> The man was once a quite famous and successful boxer called Bobby Delaney, now in AA and homeless. Father told Bobby, he had a bad dream in which he saw a very dear friend walking in the gutter with no shoes. "What do you think it means, Bobby?"
>
> "I think he needs help, Father."
>
> Father Tom rang me and asked for my husband, Brian. I told him he'd been missing for three days. "I'll find him" and he hung up. He did find him and Brian went to his first AA meeting in Kingsgrove. We lived in Bexley North and each Wednesday night he walked to Kingsgrove.

At an AA meeting one night at Kingsgrove, Father reported that Bill Wilson's wife, Lois, had started in America, a group called Al-anon to help the families of alcoholics. I was asked to contact Lois with a view to establishing Al-anon in Australia. We had our first meeting in a hall in St Jude's at Randwick ... about 1958.

Dunlea was delighted with the changes Arthur Caldwell's "New Australians" were making in areas like The Rocks and Woolloomooloo which were both within walking distance of Young Street. The air was redolent with strange cooking smells that were quite new and, at first, somewhat offputting. Still wondering how anyone could eat such odd-smelling food, he and John Monaghan decided to try it out. It wasn't just curiosity, it was an impulse, "it was part of him. He just couldn't let anything that was new or interesting pass him by without enquiring into it and sampling it; his mind was ever awake to the infinite possibilities of things" (Morrissey).

In fact, the smells of cooking that attracted and in some ways repelled him in the inner city in the mid-1950s, were to signal the beginning of a culinary revolution that would drastically change his own eating habits and, in time, those of his fellow Australians.

Father John McRae, who visited the Matt Talbot regularly, loved to listen to the short pep talks Dunlea sometimes gave to the men as they ate their meal. He had the words and the phrases and the earthy way that they related to and understood. They could see in his eyes and in the ease with which he moved among them that destitution and rags and the unwashed smells weren't in any way offputting for him. They were, they felt, truly his brothers.

McRae noted how they flocked around him, seeming to get consolation from touching his hand or his coat.

One day, when John was standing at the entrance with Dunlea, an old Scotsman came up, grabbed Father's hand and in great emotion sobbed: "I am not one of your faith but I want to say a heartfelt thank you. You have given me the hope to keep going".

Among the many strange and interesting characters at the hostel, one stood out. Father Tom introduced him as a friend of the poet and scholar Christopher Brennan (1870–1932). The man would quote Brennan's poetry with tears in his eyes and tell many interesting stories about the poet and his life. Brennan, like Dunlea, was a man who knew acute loneliness and suffering through alcoholism. Once a university professor, he died in obscurity and poverty, befriended only by the Marist Brothers at Darlinghurst. His old friend loved to quote a very poignant verse from the poem, *The Land I Came Thro' Last*, the opening line of which is on Brennan's headstone in the Macquarie Park Cemetery.

> I know I am the wanderer of the ways of all the worlds
> To whom the sunshine and the rain are one.
> Not one to stay or hasten because he knows
> No ending of the way — no home, no goal.
> (Coleman p21)

One night John was delighted to hear Eric Baume, a very high-profile 2GB radio presenter, read a poem about Dunlea over the air. The poem wasn't a masterpiece, it was actually composed by Dorothy Coleman, but it echoed the general perception of Dunlea in the minds of most people who knew him. Dunlea was amazed that so many people had heard it and took the trouble to let him know. Even Mary and Fenton in far-away Inverell rang to tell him they heard it relayed through their local station. One verse gives the general theme and poetic standard:

> A dreamer and a pioneer,
> He lived the Golden Rule.
> A helping hand for everyone,
> The sinner and the fool.

> His way was stony, long and hard
> At times he met disaster.
> With faith and trust he followed in
> The footsteps of the Master.

Apart from that mention on radio, the media didn't bother with Dunlea and, actually, this suited him at the time. He just wanted to do his work at the hostel, to go to AA meetings and get on with his life in a low-key, normal, run-of-the-mill kind of way. He was on probation, and the last thing he wanted to do was to make headlines. However, there was something in the Dunlea psyche that made it well-nigh impossible for him to remain unnoticed.

On August 24, 1954, the Cardinal had a rather terse note from Joseph Ciantar. He had been informed that a concert was being organised in the city in aid of what was called Dunlea's charities. Even Dunlea himself was actively selling tickets at one pound each. Ciantar had been asked to explain what Dunlea's charities were. It made him fearful that the ghosts of a few years back were on the scene once again: "It would not do to see Father in the hands of the old crowd who only run these charities for their own ends".

Gilroy forthwith wrote to Dunlea to find out the true story. "As it is difficult for me to believe this information, I shall be grateful for your advice on the matter".

Dunlea replied:

> The concert was donated by the Bracey family to
> help my helping of men and boys who come or are
> sent to the hostel. When I received the concert offer I
> approached Mr J B Meagher, our Metropolitan
> President, who directed me as I have acted. Owing to
> the number of calls from men and boys (some ex-
> Boys Town), calls to provide fares, meals at
> inopportune times, jobs etc, this concert has been a
> God-send.

The unusual hostel hours afforded Dunlea a good opportunity to indulge his flair for socialising. He was welcomed at many tables especially those of his contemporaries Barney Hudson of Maroubra and Jim O'Donovan of Cronulla. By way of acknowledgment of their open-house hospitality, he invited Fathers Barney and Jim to make the almost 700 km VW trip north to South Grafton to see their mutual friend, Charlie Maguire, parish priest of St Josephs. They accepted with some misgivings and arrived safely after a tedious journey on mostly unsealed roads, with ferry crossings over the Hunter, the Manning and the Hastings Rivers and a driver and vehicle subject to fits and starts.

Discovering that a mission was being conducted at St Marys the Grafton parish on the other side of the Clarence River, Dunlea couldn't wait to go over and investigate. A parish mission was a high-powered renewal programme lasting a couple of weeks and generally conducted by the Redemptionist Fathers. Dunlea loved the heightened atmosphere of excitement and fellowship generated by the missioners.

While attending one of the sessions an idea burst on his consciousness — why not have a parish-style mission for the homeless men at Matt Talbot. So aroused was he that at the end of the session he rushed to discuss it with the missioners. They were not very encouraging at all, nor were his confrères back at the presbytery. "It just wouldn't work, there's no way these men would attend" they told him. It continued to excite him however, so much so that as soon as he got back to Sydney he took it up with the hostel staff and the men themselves. The idea of making history, of doing something that hadn't been tried before, appealed to them as it did to Dunlea.

They felt a twenty minute talk each day for one week would be feasible if the hostel doors opened a half-hour earlier each evening and closed a half-hour later each morning for the week. In that way attendance would be quite voluntary.

Dunlea was surprised when one of them suggested that a Father Francis Clune, a Passionist from Marrickville and a distant relative of his, be asked to conduct the mission.

Father Clune, a famous World War I military chaplain and prisoner of war, was revered and loved by ex-servicemen and women. Indeed, he was regarded by many people as a living saint. Like Dunlea's, Father Francis' name would resonate with people of every creed and none. A small spare man, nearly blind, with a grey beard and an appealing husky voice, he made a huge impression on the retreatants and even on those who didn't join in the formal (mostly informal) sessions. Although for many of the men, alcohol was a big problem and would remain so, they insisted on lining up for a prayer or a blessing.

When Dunlea visited the Cardinal to share the good news of the mission with him, in his enthusiasm he suggested that the Cardinal visit the hostel from time to time to meet the men. Gilroy readily took to the idea and, in dialogue with the staff, it was decided that at an evening meal each year, the Cardinal would don a suitable apron and help wait on the men. It worked well and gave a strong message.

Dunlea dropped a hint to some reporters he knew, and they gave some good reportage in the media. The Cardinal, who was forever opening and blessing schools and churches and appealing for funds, was very pleased to be seen donning an apron. It was so different and so obviously in tune with the Gospel.

He mentioned to Dunlea at the end of his 1955 visit that he was happy with his progress at Matt Talbot and would consider promoting him to a parish when a suitable one became vacant.

Dunlea was somewhat taken aback. He liked what he was doing and had made up his mind that chaplaincy work, with no responsibility for organisation or finance, gave him the freedom to spend time with the people who most needed a hand-up in life, as he put it. But now, with the Cardinal's little bombshell, he wasn't so sure any more. The gremlins of ambition and prestige became active once more. They began to play another tune on his heart-strings.

Two priest friends in the country — Monsignor McGuire of South Grafton and John Purcell of Nowra whom he consulted, played the same tune. John Purcell had been one of his curates in Sutherland during the early days of Boys Town. He was an assertive determined County Clareman, who disagreed strongly with the Dunlea outlook and general softness towards strays. Since he had no hesitation in telling Dunlea what he thought, the presbytery had seen many flare-ups between the fiery curate and the relaxed rather easygoing pastor. After some months with Dunlea, Purcell was changed, eventually in 1948 becoming priest in charge of Nowra, on the South Coast of N.S.W. Strange to say, after that, the two became the best of friends. In 1952, however, the South Coast was cut off from Sydney to become the new diocese of Wollongong. At that time the Coast was somewhat of a backwater, and Purcell was utterly disgusted and very angry at being cut off from the city, where everything was happening. Then he got a letter from his new bishop, Tom McCabe, which had an amazing effect on him; miraculously, it pacified him.

Dunlea was astonished and delighted with his friend's incredible change of mood. Describing it to Pat Kenna, he said he had seen the impossible happen. "I saw, in front of my eyes, a miracle: the cedars of Lebanon began to bend!" Nowra grew to become a city itself, and Monsignor John Purcell became the respected and much loved Dean of the Coast.

The encouragement of his friends, McGuire and Purcell, didn't move him to write to the Cardinal to indicate a willingness to assume parish responsibilities again. It did, however, dispose him to be open to the possibility of being drafted into that role in the future.

18

The concursus

Norman Thomas Gilroy sat at the head of the big table, surrounded by his board of consultors. On his right sat the tall, lean, ascetic-looking Vicar General, Richard Collender; on his left, the Auxiliary Archbishop, James Carroll. The others were senior clergy chosen personally by Gilroy. This was an important and interesting meeting because several vacant parishes were to be filled. The clergy of the diocese had been notified and invited to indicate to the Archbishop a desire to be considered as parish priest of one or other of the parishes concerned. They were also invited to give their reasons for thinking they would be suitable pastors for that parish.

If Gilroy felt the applicant would be suitable, he asked him to front up to a concursus, that is, a small group of former seminary professors who would enquire into his knowledge of church law and his preaching ability. Although the clergy, especially the senior clergy, didn't take the concursus very seriously, it could play a part at the consultors' meeting.

Among the places to be filled at the April 1955 meeting was that of St Michael's Hurstville, an important parish in the St George area of Southern Sydney. The former pastor, Monsignor John Sherin, had gone to a nursing home and Pat O'Rourke, his curate, was acting pastor. In fact, it transpired, as the Cardinal produced his short list of applicants for the vacant parish, the same Pat O'Rourke was among them and, although not quite as senior as some of the others, he looked like being a front runner.

After the group discussed the merits and suitability of each one, some were eliminated, either because they were inexperienced or lacking in seniority or deemed to be unstable for one reason or another. Of the remaining names, O'Rourke looked like the one to get the nod. Collender, the VG, and Carroll, the Bishop, had some misgivings, however. O'Rourke wasn't yet twenty years ordained, and his health wasn't good. Although Gilroy had given O'Rourke a qualified undertaking that his application would be given favourable treatment, he too had similar reservations.

Suggesting a way out of the impasse, Gilroy dropped a veritable bombshell by mentioning a name that wasn't on any list, hadn't even applied or gone through the normal process. The name, Thomas Vincent Dunlea, produced quite a hubbub around the table and even a modicum of light relief.

At the mention of the name, Harry Kennedy, the Cardinal's secretary, threw up his hands almost in horror. "Tom Dunlea!" he exclaimed. "Last time round he could never get his parish returns in on time!" Michael Cronin, the diocesan Master of Ceremonies, felt his free and easy attitude to ceremonies and his tendency to extemporise and adapt the Sacred Rites to suit a particular congregation or situation made him unsuitable for a major appointment like Hurstville. Ted O'Donnell, the Chancellor, drew a chuckle by declaring that Dunlea's past performance had shown that parish properties and parish finances might be in some danger if another depression eventuated!

When Paddy Flanagan, the Dean of the Cathedral, who had been sent by the Cardinal to sound out Dunlea, returned to report that Dunlea would be happy to do whatever the Cardinal decided, the meeting was brought to a close. Dick Collender knew that this wasn't the first time his boss had introduced an outsider and handed him the baton, with or without the consensus of the Board of Consultors.

"No-one else would have given me a second chance," declared Dunlea gratefully, on receiving his letter of appointment.

****

His little VW eased into the driveway of his new home in Hurstville on May 15, 1955 with all his earthly possessions, including his books. Sitting on the back seat were the two young whippets. He was met by Pat O'Rourke, whose feelings at being passed over for the job were still raw. Although this was his first visit as parish priest, Dunlea knew the place well from his two short stints there as assistant priest.

O'Rourke experienced a certain perverse satisfaction in looking Dunlea in the eye and painting an overtly dismal picture of the parish and its needs, emphasising all the changes that had to be made and all the work that had to be done to bring the plant up to scratch — and, of course, all had to be attended to as a matter of urgency. To O'Rourke's frustration, this didn't in the least faze Dunlea, who wanted only to talk about the providence of God, the goodness of the people and the need to look after the poor and the marginalised. As any young aspiring pastor would, Father Pat wondered why this old fool, as he called him with a smile, was chosen for a position that he himself or one of his young colleagues could fill so much more efficiently.

The visit to Our Lady Star of the Sea primary school was an eye-opener for O'Rourke, who himself was quite skilled at entertaining and relating to children. They took to Dunlea straight away as if they had heard all about him from the Sisters of Charity or their parents, many of whom would have had contact with him when they themselves were at school. One cute little girl in third grade read a story her mother had given her about growing up in Rose Bay during Dunlea's time there:

> We as small children were always delighted to have a visit from Father because his question to my mother when he left was "May I give the children a medal?"

Whereupon the medal turned out to be a sixpence!
... so much from one who had so little.

Several weeks after his arrival in Hurstville Dunlea had a ring from Neil McKinnon, a helicopter pilot who had married Pauline, a member of the Moclair family who were dear friends of Dunlea's in Sutherland. On learning that Neil was a helicoper pilot he organised a big surprise for the children. On the following Wednesday, Dunlea went to Bankstown airport, was picked up by Neil and exactly play-lunch time, the helicopter hovered over the school. It descended slowly and noisily as the children watched transfixed and fascinated. As the helicopter touched down in a cloud of dust, the new pastor alighted like superman, to the applause and delight of the children and the distress of many of the Sisters of Charity who wondered what kind of pastor they had.

The official welcome to the new pastor on Sunday, May 28 was, as might be expected, a gala affair. Not only was Dunlea an expert impresario, so also was O'Rourke. Among the star-studded line-up of entertainers were singers and musicians from Boys Town under the baton of Joseph Ciantar himself. There were old Boys Town boys and some of his most loyal Boys Town helpers, including George Nathan, June Russell, Eric Drew, Eric Miles, Sheila Tearle, Anne Cuddy, Bruce Aley, Olive Fletcher, Mary Rose and a host of others, as well as AA members and a large gathering of Hurstville parishioners. Dunlea was at his sparkling best, expansive, theatrical and obviously enjoying the great welcome he was receiving.

He sounded one warning bell, however. He cited George Nathan and June Russell as having been given by God an extra gene marked business. When God came to sorting out the gifts to give to himself, He got distracted and forgot to include that one. And so he would need a lot of help in that area of parish life.

The Hurstville curate, Kevin Spillane, and the parish tennis club members were surprised to find the new pastor was interested in tennis. He loved to have the occasional game with them and provided reasonable competition on the court.

Teaching Christian doctrine to adults who wanted to enter the Church was a large preoccupation of the clergy at that time. Those who wanted Dunlea to instruct them were not always run-of-the-mill kind of people. He asked Kevin, for example, to take care of one man who spoke with a low-key American accent. Kevin was unable to do so for some reason, and how "fortunate I was", notes Kevin, "for that man turned out to be a woman, masquerading as a man — causing much consternation and not a little amusement as the news came to the notice of the local clergy".

Another interesting character receiving instruction from the new parish priest was a man called Happy who was prominent in the advertising world. He used his not inconsiderable expertise to keep Dunlea and St Michael's before the public. He even had Father Tom featured using a lawn mower in the back page of one of the dailies. It was an advertisement for the famous Australian icon, the Victa mower.

Hearing Dunlea reminisce about the proliferation of bonfires in the hills of Tipperary on the Vigil of the Feast of the Birthday of John the Baptist, Happy suggested that Dunlea's first great fundraising function should be colourful, unusual and newsworthy.

As an extravaganza of huge proportions that could be seen all over the St George district, what could be better than a great Australian bonfire!? Volunteers were rounded up from all walks of life, including AA and former Boys Town boys. Happy made sure the publicity was extensive. Even Coca Cola was somehow inveigled into donating two thousand bottles of the precious beverage. Two fire brigades, with firemen in full uniform and sirens blaring, descended on St Michael's from different directions. At the dramatic moment, Happy gave the nod and Dunlea ignited the great pile, which burst into flame almost like a mountain erupting.

Among the huge crowd of children and adults were many of Dunlea's old friends, including George Nathan, who was one of the speakers; the former boxer, Bobby Delaney, now a member of AA; and three special clerical friends: Joe Giles, Pat Kenna and Tony Newman. Of all his colleagues, these three best understood and admired Dunlea and shared his more mystical qualities and his great concern and rapport with the down-and-outs. They also enjoyed the unexpected, the unpredictable, the novel that seemed to accompany Dunlea and made him exciting to be with.

With Dunlea now in residence, St Michael's was fast becoming a Mecca for those on whom fortune didn't seem to smile. Anne Cuddy, who kept in touch with Dunlea through her brother Tory, a school teacher, who once a week helped to bathe and clean up the men at Matt Talbot. Although the coming of Dunlea to Hurstville was for her an answer to prayer, she acknowledges the problem of his entourage:

> Typically, his coming brought with it an assortment of his previous contacts. Although Father Byrne, a soft-spoken Wexfordman who succeeded Father O'Rourke, had a little success in dispatching big George and some of the other characters who continually called at the presbytery to see him, the problem did not go away.
>
> One night a fundraising function was being held in the grounds with a couple of reformed jailbirds waiting behind the church to assist in the counting of the takings. Somehow, the tent was set on fire. I never knew what happened to the money.

Appearing out of nowhere, they rang the doorbell or had a catnap in some sheltered spot in the grounds or savoured the last precious drop of the empty bottle. Presbytery doors are normally well patronised by people in need, but what made St Michael's unique was the fact that they were welcomed, brought in, sat down, listened to, provided for and entertained, no matter how disreputable or unkempt they appeared.

> He was absolutely tolerant. In fact, it seems that this tolerance boiled down to the simple fact that he failed completely to see any difference between any group of human beings and he seemed to lack altogether any critical perception of their religious, national, political or other differences. (Morrissey)

Eric Drew felt that Dunlea recognised in their faces the face of Christ infusing them with new life and the will to belong. Their presence in the presbytery must have been somewhat of an annoyance to Mrs Falvey, the housekeeper, who left Hurstville to join O'Rourke in Richmond after he returned from a holiday in Ireland. The senior curate, Jim Byrne, took the precaution of attaching a padlock to his bedroom door! Parishioners came to accept these uninvited guests as an inconvenience and nuisance they couldn't do much about. Dunlea himself regarded welcoming them as an essential response to the Gospel and hoped his people would come to see them in the same light.

When the St Vincent de Paul Society was having a gathering in St Michael's Church in the spring of 1955, Dunlea suggested his friend, Doctor Tuomey, be the occasional speaker. A fiery orator with an imposing presence, Tuomey was in very poor health and this, in fact, was his last outing. He took his text from Matthew's Gospel Chapter 25, verse 40: "As long as you did it to one of these you did it to me". The packed church was all ears as The Doc, with drama and flair much like Dunlea himself, had Jesus identifying himself with the down-and-outs: I was hungry ... I was a stranger ... I was homeless ... I was cold and naked ... I was in gaol ... and you fed me, welcomed me, clothed me, came to see me.

As he concluded, he told them he expected the final Judgment Day described in Matthew 25 would be enacted in his regard very soon (he actually died that same year). His only hope, he told them, was that St Patrick might smuggle him in! When that day arrives, however, for the Pastor of Hurstville, Tuomey declared, he will have a multitude of little people whom he helped here on earth, rolling out the red carpet and putting on the best ticker-tape reception ever recorded in heaven!

Dunlea's ability to see Christ in the poor and the needy worked as well by night as by day. As Bruce Aley notes, if woken up by a hobo, he would give him food, drink, money — whatever was needed. "If some complete stranger rang him at 3 a.m.," notes Morrissey, "he would answer with all the gentleness and concern in the world, just the same as he would have done had they an official appointment at some reasonable hour".

A Hurstville man, whose wife and family were members of St Michael's parish, was having a quiet drink with some friends at the Grove Inn Hotel in nearby Kingsgrove. They were watching a tramp sitting on the sidewalk opposite, near the steps leading to the railway bridge. Just then Dunlea drove along Shaw Street, probably after a visit to his friend Ned Clune, parish priest of Kingsgrove.

He pulled up and had a talk with the tramp, without getting out of the car. Afterwards he drove off a short distance, stopped for a moment and reversed back to the tramp. The car door opened and Dunlea threw a pair of shoes (apparently his own) to the man before driving off again. The tramp looked at the shoes, took his own off, put on the priest's shoes and stumbled away. The observers were not noticed by either the priest or the tramp.

That incident had a profound effect on the man from Hurstville. It led him to re-examine his wife's religion and seek to be received into the Church by Dunlea. His story survives through the good offices of a priest in Tamworth who had a good friend, a Christian Brother, on the staff of St Patrick's College Strathfield who happened to be the son of the man in question.

Notwithstanding what Ted O'Donnell had said at the Consultors' meeting about Dunlea's deficiencies in financial matters, he did something in Hurstville that revolutionised fundraising in Australian parishes. To raise money for schools and churches in Sydney, indirect methods were used! These entailed all sorts of labour-intensive events, the success of which, to some extent, depended on the entrepreneurial skills of the Pastor. Being aware of his absence of gifts in this area, Dunlea sought to solve his problem by introducing a completely new and untried method that had scarcely been heard of in Australia.

His imagination, as Morrissey notes, was ever dancing. ... He could never bear to hear of any new idea or invention criticised. *Give it a go. Just do it* — no matter how unplanned it seemed or how few turned up to the meeting. For this enthusiasm, he was often ridiculed by his timid colleagues. Not that he didn't do his best to order things as well as his teeming imagination would permit.

Fundraising had been a headache for him as long as he could remember. It worried him greatly. Parishioners were frequently singing the praises of other pastors who were having great success in building schools and churches. His near neighbour, in Kingsgrove, Ned Clune, was particularly gifted and setting a challenging pace in parish development in the St George area. Clune's sudden death in 1956 saddened Dunlea greatly and left him wondering at the extent to which money worries were leading to stress and burnout in a pastor's life. His good friend and confessor, Dick Funcheon, Pastor of Gosford, had much the same problem as Dunlea: he was into mysticism rather than building. But he had an American parishioner who told him about a direct-giving method that had achieved great results in the United States. Called The Wells System after the firm that promoted it there, it appealed to Dunlea straight away. He tracked down a Don Clover and invited him to Australia.

When Clover arrived and explained to parishioners how the system worked, Dunlea was amazed at the heat and anger it generated, especially among the better-paid professionals. Clover explained that the pastor would need to know how much he was going to receive in the

Sunday envelopes in order to make building plans and to service debts. This would involve envelope-users making a promise or a commitment to give a certain proportion of their income each week. Tithing was even mentioned. This caused an uproar; it was unCatholic, even unAustralian.

The other sticking point was what was called The Loyalty Dinner, to which all parishioners would be invited. At the dinner the system would be explained by leading parishioners, who would also disclose the amount they were willing to pledge.

Dunlea was quite out of his depth. Unwittingly, he had touched the very sensitive hip-pocket nerve of some well-to-do people. The less well-off, who formed the majority at the meeting, were not so fearful of the new system. Fortunately, Clune's successor at Kingsgrove, Brian McGinley, was present and spoke. A larger-than-life ex-army chaplain, McGinley was very much in favour of this direct system and would introduce it to Kingsgrove as soon as possible. Dunlea followed with an impassioned plea to give it a go.

More out of loyalty to him, and with some reluctance, they accepted the Wells System and volunteered to work for its implementation. It brought amazing results. Parish income quadrupled, parishioners were delighted and other pastors were flocking to St Michael's to study the new system. Before too long, just about all parishes in Australia, of whatever denomination, were involved in some form of direct planned giving.

Ironically enough, the one who lacked business expertise was the one who introduced the plan responsible for putting Australian churches on a sound business foundation!

It's an irony, too, that community-orientated Dunlea was more or less responsible for the almost total demise of the community-building, indirect methods of fundraising.

The fetes, bazaars, dances, house parties, etc, were no longer necessary. Apart from Sunday church, people didn't meet each other, interact and work together as they once had. This was missed. And, to a great extent, it is still missed in parish community life.

19
All God's creatures

Early in the summer of 1956, a news flash from Radio 2GB related a little incident that listeners found intriguing and somewhat comical. It was about a kangaroo hopping along the busy shopping area in Forest Road, Bexley. Such a sight way out on a country road wouldn't surprise anyone. In the city, however, it was causing a sizeable traffic jam. The kangaroo itself was only indirectly to blame. The real culprits were the motorists who insisted on stopping their vehicles so they could focus on this unusual scene. The shoppers, too, got involved and, of course, the children.

The children chased the intruder, who evaded them by doing some U-turns and hopping over obstacles like car bonnets and bicycles. The police, who were trying to unravel the traffic chaos, appealed for information about the animal and how on earth it got from the wild outback to a sedate suburban street in Southern Sydney.

Frances Massey, who later entered the Little Company of Mary (LCM), heard the news flash and rang to say the 'roo hadn't actually come from the wild outback, at least not directly. It had come merely from the neighbouring suburb of Hurstville which had a very unusual pastor. As well as caring for people, especially broken people, he had great love for all God's creatures from dogs to kangaroos.

> At the back of the presbytery was a newly-fenced yard in which were penned a kangaroo, a goat, a wallaby, guinea pigs, doves, rabbits, two dogs and some cats, all living in harmony as in a second Garden of Paradise. These were the non-human

strays collected by the parish priest in his vision of the precious miracle of life, in whatever form God bestowed it. (Lea Scarlett p31)

It wasn't the first time the 'roo had jumped over the fence, especially around Christmas. Sheila Tearle witnessed the rather interesting spectacle of Skippy careering down Croydon Road with a bevy of boys of all ages and sizes in hot pursuit. They never caught up with it. How it got back she doesn't know, except that from time to time a rather exasperated policeman would ring St Michael's to say he was being driven to distraction by a kangaroo, which his small station wasn't equipped to house.

Dunlea's frequent forays into the country with Eric Drew, Bruce Aley, Eric Green and others weren't just to view the wild life from a distance, but to bring some back, especially the wounded, to his menagerie in Hurstville. Although Dunlea and driver might start off with a couple of overnight bags, on the return trip the small car would be crowded with, among other things, a dog or two, galahs of various kinds, a speckle-back and other varieties of lizards, as well as pieces of Gidgee timber and the flora and fauna needed to provide an authentic setting for his mini-zoo.

The laundry of the presbytery housed the dogs, stray or otherwise. In an emergency, the wardrobe in the pastor's own bedroom could be home to a pup or two. When a friend who collected exotic birds brought him some samples, he kept them in cages in his room, much to the distraction of his housekeeper.

The animals and birds came into their own in a very special way at Christmas. Ray Green, a former Boys Town boy, who had grown to over two metres and weighed over one hundred kilos, was commissioned to augment the regulars with a donkey, a calf, a sheep, a goat, some ducks and even an Irish Wolfhound. A friend, a retired farmer from Robertson in the Southern Highlands, volunteered to take care of the animals that were to appear live in the outdoor Christmas crib.

Dunlea's love for St Francis of Assisi didn't just entail a certain Franciscan-like embracing of Lady Poverty, as Francis euphemistically called a life of radical simplicity. He was delighted with Francis' attitude to Christmas; it resonated deeply with his own. He loved the way Francis dramatised the Christmas event, even to the extent of creating a stable and manger containing real live people and animals and birds and, of course, a real live baby.

Francis and Dunlea felt that seeing real live beings would help people to come to terms with the great mystery of God among us. Seeing a flesh-and-blood baby and flesh-and-blood creatures around him would help people come to rejoice in the mystery of the Word becoming flesh. And just as it worked for Francis for the first time in the Christmas of 1223, so it worked for Dunlea in Hurstville nearly seven hundred and fifty years later.

The large framework for the crib was set up on the vacant lot in front of the presbytery, a parishioner painting the background scenery in full colour. Into it were led the donkey, the goat, the pig, the sheep, and the kangaroo, as well as some doves, white fantail pigeons, a galah, a chook and a rooster. That was the full complement, but the full complement would only appear when Dunlea remembered to begin preparations on time. If Christmas crept up on him and he found out at the last minute that the backyard menagerie did not have an essential item, such as a sheep, there would ensue a wide hurried search for someone who had a sheep to spare. Once found, the said animal would be ferried back to the presbytery in the parish priest's little VW.

News of the live crib spread quickly. It became a talking point all over the St George area and beyond. The local paper chipped in, as did talk-back radio and other Sydney media.

> The crib was a great success. People in cars pulled up at all hours of the day and night to visit it, and bring their children in night attire to see it — and to listen to the music relayed from the radiogram at the

presbytery. On the Feast of the Epiphany, Father Tom had a special celebration. The visit of the three Wise Men was the occasion for giving of gifts to the children. Parishioners were invited to bring small gifts and sweets for this purpose. On one or two occasions, Father had Indian students for his Wise Men. (Sheila Tearle)

A real live baby was featured for special occasions when public prayers were recited at the crib, the baby's mum and dad taking the place of Mary and Joseph. On one such occasion, when baby began to cry, the young mother, a Filipina, sat on a small stool near the cradle, undid her shoulder strap and fed the baby there and then. Although only witnessed by a small group of people, it was evidently a deeply moving scene, giving a new existential dimension to the human reality of the God among us.

As could be expected, not everyone approved of the live crib. For one thing, the braying of the donkey resounding in the night air brought some complaints from the neighbours. A newly resident priest declared he "couldn't get to sleep for things maaing and baaing all night". Another worry was the expense entailed in feeding the Christmas animals. People did leave some money at the crib, which sometimes disappeared and, even when it survived, would hardly suffice to feed plaster animals! The pulpit notices for Christmas 1959 indicate that Dunlea solved that one by announcing "a special Christmas livestock collection".

Livestock confined in a small space can be quite messy. The fact that it was a very special holy space doesn't inhibit the normal natural processes. When Arthur Maher pointed out that this could scandalise people if it wasn't cleaned up constantly, Dunlea chided him, a country man, for being too squeamish. Arthur, like most Catholics, felt that the divine and the holy should be protected from the crude and the smelly. He was expressing an aspect of the widely accepted dualism that separates the supernatural from the natural, the divine from the human, the sacred from the profane. The profane — the mess, the smells, the filth — must never be seen to be near or touch holy people like Mary and Joseph and their baby. Religious correctness demands that the Christmas Crib be sanitised, uncontaminated and spotlessly clean.

Dunlea, like St Francis, didn't subscribe to this at all. His friend, the Presbyterian Minister Neil McLeod, assured him that the Christmas scene scandalised sophisticated people in the early Christian centuries. Dunlea felt the crib is actually meant to shock people, himself included, into dealing with this new, rather scandalous coupling of the divine and the human. He saw the live crib doing this so much better than the spotless, unsoiled, neat plaster figures that normally feature in Christmas cribs. Benevolence and sentimentality in most Christmas cards and carols, as well as in the traditional crib, didn't fully proclaim the good news that the sacred and the holy need no longer be protected from the profane and the indecent. Incredibly and happily, the Word which the Father so wonderfully uttered at Christmas must no longer be shut out from the coarseness and vulgarity of the world in which that Word became flesh and dwelt.

Although Cardinal Gilroy subscribed to this in theory, he could also see that, if the idea spread, it could lead to expensive insurance claims. Consequently, he asked the *Catholic Weekly* to play down the live-baby/animal aspect of the Hurstville crib, while making sure not to hurt Father Dunlea. The clergy in general were somewhat amused and a bit miffed by the Hurstville Christmas special. It was, many felt, a typical attention-seeking Dunlea stunt! And so it was, but with an underlay of Franciscan depth.

* * * * * * * *

Most bishops and priests were convinced that Dunlea would not make a good pastor, because pastoring just one parish would fence him in too much. In Sutherland and Engadine, he had had Boys Town to absorb his energies and claim his attention. In a way the clerics were right.

Being limited to one area didn't suit his expansive personality and dancing imagination. "Although, technically, he was Parish Priest of Hurstville", Ed Campion remarks, "his parish was Australia-wide, for he felt called wherever there were broken people".

As pastor, he had two great advantages: his *joie de vivre* and his rapport with people.

> Every aspect of his goodness can probably be traced to and summed up in his great joy to be alive. For despite his spasmodic depressions, when conversation was lost in a sort of mist of remote distraction, this joy generated an incredible magnetism that precluded mere casual acquaintance and made the most fleeting contact memorable.
>
> People who met him in a queue or going into a shop would enquire most concernedly about him years later, recalling the words he'd used or the interest he'd taken. He had become something of a point of reference in the life of some.
>
> His joy jumped all gaps in human relationships like the bushfires breached the creeks round the Sutherland hills. Young drop-outs and rebels used to sit at his feet, as it were, because of his Assisian optimism.
>
> It was likewise this joy, and not so much a desire to be kind, that was behind his extravagant generosity. It was as if he did not think of a gift as a help to someone, but rather as a token of the fun everyone was having, as an overflow from God's abundant providing. "Ah, fun", he would say, "wasn't it fun?" in describing the light or serious drama of other days. For even the sad events of life were to be taken only in the context of the delight that God was planning for us in the Kingdom.
>
> That is why his funerals were a speciality, when tears and laughter mixed round the gravesides. (Coleman p25, quoting Morrissey)

As well as that *joie de vivre* which so attracted people to him, he had that pastoral attitude that saw something special in people. He never met any ordinary people or situation as others do.

> Every housewife was, apart from the irrelevancies of washing, cooking and shopping, a poetess, or an incomparable intellect or an undiscovered visionary ... He had no eye for externals; the Kingdom of God was within — his perception was limited to the unseen. That was true of every tramp who came to the door. We should say *his* door, because for him there was no such thing as an impersonal door, it was his or yours or mine. Things had no existence except in relation to human persons or, truer still, to that Divine Person whom he recognised in everyone.
>
> Every homeless caller was an artist or a scholar of some sort. There was no down-and-out whom I heard him speak of but could lay claim to some world-stopping talent, and it is amazing how often this proved to be literally true. For Father Tom had such an uncanny range of mind and memory that, together with the Irish bent for family trees, he could piece together a background with a cross reference to relate today's derelict to yesterday's prince. He induced in everyone he met the very qualities his mind imputed to them. (Coleman p23–24, quoting Morrissey)

Anne Cuddy noticed his uncanny memory too:

> He could be meeting someone for the first time but by the end of the conversation that person would have been locked for ever in his memory bank. He never forgot a name or a face, however long the span between meetings.

As well as being thus endowed with gifts of memory, as well as humour and mysticism, Dunlea surprised and, to some extent, embarrassed his fellow pastors by the practical way he went about leading and guiding his people. The vitality of a parish and the numbers attending the services depend to a great extent on the enthusiasm and imagination of the pastor. Dunlea began with himself, taking a course which was much in vogue at that time, a course, however, which would seem entirely unnecessary in his case. In fact, it was one which he himself could well create and deliver. But no, he bowed to Dale Carnegie who knew "how to win friends and influence people". He is listed in the Sydney class 22 starting at 6.30 p.m. (to 10.30 p.m.) on Tuesday September 3, 1957 and continuing each Tuesday till December 10. He was the only cleric among three women and thirty-nine men, several of whom were company directors. They had to promise to read three times ten pages of Carnegie's book (*How to Win Friends and influence people*) each week during the weeks of the course. Also on the fourth week they had to report on some highlights experienced in keeping with the three rules:

> Don't criticize, condemn or complain;
> Give honest sincere appreciation;
> Arouse in the other person an eager want.

Dunlea didn't fill in his score card on the fourth week so there could be some question about how seriously he took it all.

It would have been interesting to monitor the pupil/teacher exchanges during that course!

Being convinced of the importance of preaching well and at some length, he got together a list of successful and inspirational preachers. These he invited on a regular basis to address various groups; it might be the sodalities, the Novena and even the Sunday congregations. They inspired people to open their minds to savour the bigger questions which so excited him at a summer school he attended in January 1958. It was open to all priests Australia-wide and held at St Patrick's College Manly. Called "The Living Parish Week", its keynote speaker was an English Jesuit, Clifford Howell, whose *The Work of Our Redemption* had become a best-selling piece of popular theology. Although Howell was a gifted and high-profile communicator and writer, Pat Kenna remembers that many regarded him with suspicion and even a little hostility. Kenna writes:

> The man around whom The Living Parish Week revolved, who had invited Howell to Sydney and who had headed the organising team, was University Chaplain, Roger Pryke.
>
> What he and Howell and their speakers were doing was to expose ordinary, everyday clergy to some of the insights of liturgists and scripture scholars of Europe and North America. As it turned out, they were — unknowingly — setting the scene for Vatican II. At an open forum one afternoon towards the end of the week, Cardinal Gilroy was in attendance. His presence was, as far as Roger Pryke and the organisers were concerned, important indeed: his imprimatur. Something else, however, seemed to be needed beyond officialdom giving its blessing and going on its way. That something was provided by Dunlea. He seized the moment (*carpe diem* could well have been his life's motto). Standing among the troops and no more than an arm's length from the Cardinal, Dunlea gazed around at the assembly, ensuring that he had total attention. He then proceeded to remind us, to challenge us, as only he could do, to a realisation that the week now concluding must not be thought of as a passing entertainment. It had been not only informative, but energising. We had been participants in a history-making event. His head thrown back and arms extended full length, Dunlea proclaimed, "I see Australia at the crossroads".
>
> The enthusiastic applause that followed was not so much for what he had spoken as for the speaker himself. Then into his sixties, when the overwhelming majority of those present were in their twenties or thirties — Roger Pryke himself was yet to celebrate his thirty-seventh birthday — Tom Dunlea was an elder who had borne the heat of the day. That such a man, universally known and loved, should be

embracing The Living Parish Week and all it stood for, signalled a blessing upon the whole enterprise, not from above but from within.

Dunlea followed the progress of the Council through the Melbourne *Advocate* (now defunct). Through its Roman reporter, Michael Costigan, it gave excellent weekly summaries of the issues discussed, the personalities involved and the changes being floated. This was quite different from other Catholic papers and reports coming from Australian Bishops, whose bottom line seemed to be: nothing has changed, it's business as usual.

Dunlea was excited to learn that many of the changes mentioned in the liturgy discussions were already part of his own practice of integrating religion and life.

> For example, the Church's tendency today to humanise and localise parts of the Baptismal Rite, to emphasise the priority of the couple and their families in the Marriage Rite and to relate ritual more directly to everyday living — all these things he had done naturally since his ordination in 1920.
>
> He always welcomed and congratulated the parents at the font and made the wedding party feel at home in the Lord's House and often, at a party, beautifully related the prevailing conviviality to the joy of sharing the Eucharistic banquet. (Morrissey)

At a clergy conference in the early 1960s, the Dialogue Mass was proposed as a way of making the Sunday Eucharist more participatory. This meant the people, as well as the altar servers, would join in the responses. Dunlea was impressed. This, he felt, would really brighten up the silent quiet Latin Mass. So he dialogued with his curate about setting aside time each Sunday to train people in Latin, the Mass being still in the old language. Latin was a subject in Catholic schools at the time and the Latin responses weren't that difficult to learn.

Eventually, as many as three of the four Sunday Masses were dialogued. This was quite unusual for the Sydney of his time.

When visiting Toowoomba he noticed that the parish church of Warwick was open for worship all night. This impressed him to such an extent that he felt St Michael's should follow suit.

> Scores of projects, succeeding or failing, blossomed from his lively mind, even in old age, and he would try any new experience. A helicopter trip, a night in a field or under a tree, a midwinter swim, a rigid fast, an exotic feast — anything he hadn't tried before. (Morrissey)

As well as the Dialogue Mass and good singing, which Dunlea strongly encouraged, he added practices like public Rosaries, Benediction, Holy Hours, May devotions, Fatima devotions. The Hurstville Mass Notice Book of that time bears witness to his own devotional enthusiasm, especially for the Holy Hour:

> If you have never spent even a little time entirely alone with the Blessed Sacrament, you have never known real peace and the overwhelming feeling of wellbeing which comes from just the act of kneeling there.

The Bishops of South America made headlines around the world in the late 1960s by introducing the Basic Christian Community structure into their dioceses. Parishes were divided into small geographical units, each of which functioned like a little church, responsible for ministering to the needs of the families in that small area. Dunlea, in the early 1960s, had seen the need to do something like this to build a sense of community, centred on the Eucharist. With a team of parishioners, he divided the parish into ten zones, with a leader and deputy leader who got to know the families in the zone by regularly visiting them and attending to any special needs that surfaced. Each zone was asked to attend St Michael's on a specific weekday, when Mass would be offered for the people in that zone. The invitation to the Mass gave the home visits of the leaders a non-threatening practical orientation.

Some clergy were convinced that to foster community realistically the parish needed to be divided into smaller units or cells. Dunlea was among the very few who had the enthusiasm and courage to try it out. "By the end of the year the zone organisation was an accepted feature of parish life." (Lea Scarlett p139)

20
Australiana — Arthur Maher

A tall lanky priest from the Bathurst Diocese with a boy in tow had arrived at the tent City set up in Loftus in 1940. He had wanted to see Dunlea about the possibility of enrolling the boy, only to find that Dunlea was sick in the Sutherland Presbytery. When he eventually caught up with him, he had noticed that even on the horizontal, Dunlea had a certain flair about him, giving audience from his bed ... like a King from his bunk. That was the first meeting between two very different people, Arthur Maher and Dunlea. They were to become mates together in Hurstville for many years.

After the 1940 incident, they didn't meet again till the late 1950s, when an urgent communique arrived for Dunlea from Mudgee, where Arthur Maher was curate.

In his excitement Dunlea dropped in on his friends, Katie Brady and Margaret Pulbrook, who were working in the sacristy on the Saturday afternoon. Katie reports:

> Ladies, he said, I've got an invitation to Mudgee. Father Maher wants me to go up to receive the Debs. I said, "I'd love to go", and do you know, he booked me in before I could turn around! So I went to Mudgee with Margaret and Mrs Gibson, who was president of our Parish Ball Committee that year. We had a most marvellous time with him. As soon as we got into the car, of course, he said, "Please start the Rosary", so we said the Rosary all the way up and all the way back.

Subsequently, Arthur spent some time in the St John of God Hospital in Richmond. Towards the end of his stay there, he went to see Cardinal Gilroy at St Mary's Cathedral. It so happened that Dunlea was visiting the Cathedral on the very same day and came on the scene as the Cardinal and the priest were saying good-bye.

Seeing Dunlea the Cardinal pleaded, "Can you do something for this poor man? He had a breakdown and is very fragile". Dunlea, looking on the broken hurting priest, responded with alacrity: "You have a home with me in Hurstville as long as you like to stay". (Flora Wickham)

Having obtained the necessary permission from the Bathurst Diocese, Arthur stayed with Father Tom, to use his own words, "till death us do part". (Coleman p29)

They became best of friends. Dunlea patiently nurtured Arthur back to health, restored his self-esteem and whetted his appetite for life.

Arthur had travelled extensively throughout the country, and was well versed in and enthusiastic about all things Australian. Dunlea, too, was no stranger to the bitumen and dirt roads. As Eric Drew points out, he had travelled from east to west, from north to south, from the centre to the sea.

> For whereas many travellers might come and go unnoticed in a township, he would seek no privacy at all, but would be at the complete disposal of everyone he met and no exclusive connections or groups could reserve him. Sharing was instinctive with him. He shared his means, his time, his personality with everyone. Again, not so much due to any virtue, but rather as a result of his natural desire to be with people. His passion for people overwhelmed all else. (Coleman p25–26, quoting Morrissey)

Retelling the travel stories delighted him as did Arthur's knowledge of the variety and the beauty of the wild flowers of the outback deserts and the details of the native flora and fauna. But most of all he loved to hear Arthur recite and explain the poems of Banjo Paterson, the tales of Henry Lawson, the lyrics of Henry Kendall and other Australian artists — all this recalling the beautifully scented memories of his own dreamtime wanderings in the bush. He encouraged Arthur to devote at least one night a week to sharing his extensive repertoire of Australiana with young people, whetting their appetite to discover outback Australia for themselves. Dunlea seldom missed attending and contributing to these sessions.

Fathers Tom and Arthur made many trips to the Tavern of Araluen (southwest of Braidwood in Southern N.S.W.) where Molly Collins never failed to make them welcome.

> Here Father Tom would sleep straight through for twenty-four hours, for when he was exhausted, he would head for the Valley of Peace. He was greatly interested in the history of this once-thriving goldmining town ... Molly's gift of rest "refreshed his spirit", as he would say. The Tavern was the last of forty-two hotels (sic) once in Araluen. As he strolled by the river in the beautiful Valley of Peace, he would ask Arthur to quote snippets of the poem, *Araluen*, by Henry Kendall:
> Cities soil the life with rust
> Water banks are cool and sweet
> River tired of noise and dust
> Here I come to rest my feet.
>
> (Coleman p29–30)

While resting his feet in Araluen after Easter 1963, Dunlea was delighted that a fellow Sydney priest, Ted Kennedy was having an Easter break there, too. Although Kennedy was a much younger man, in their love for the poor and marginalised they had much in common. En route from Sydney, Ted had been listening to Question Time in Federal Parliament and, to his amazement, heard Tom Uren, a left-wing controversial Labor parliamentarian from Western Sydney, asking a very unusual question. Uren had picked up, in the Parliament Library, a commentary on Pope John XXIII's 1963 Easter message called *Pacem in Terris*, which had impressed him greatly. The question Uren subsequently addressed to the Prime Minister, Bob Menzies, so amazed Ted that he was able to repeat it verbatim to Dunlea:

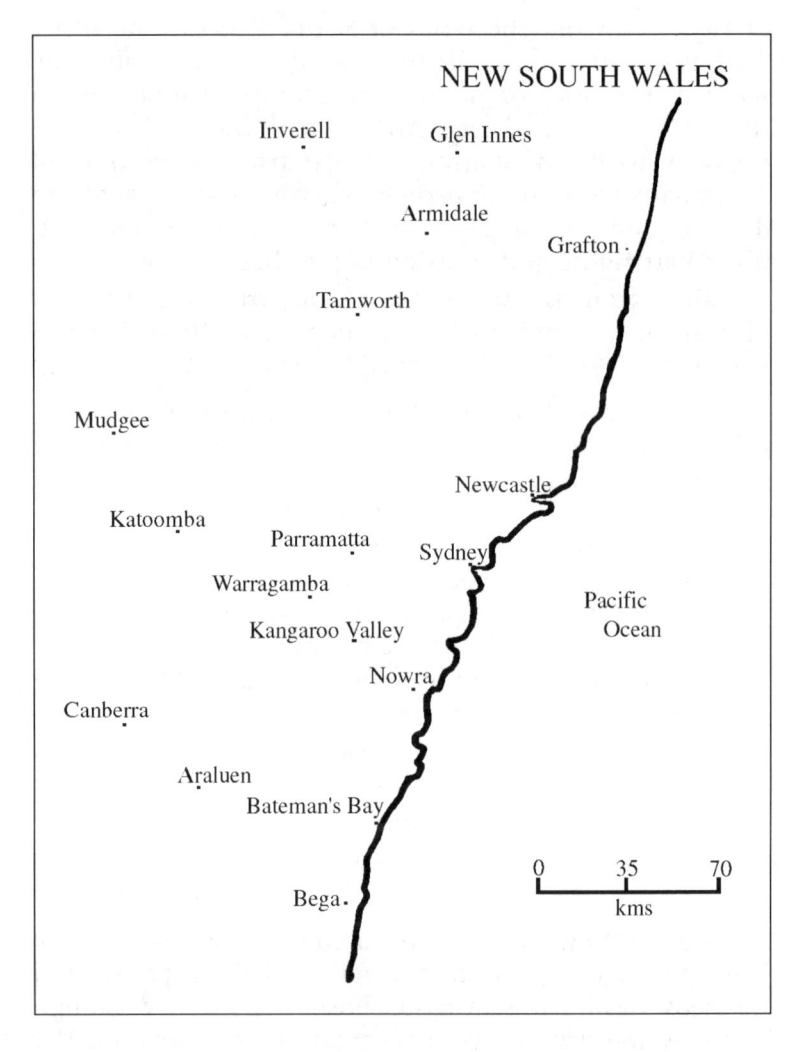

> Has the Prime Minister read the text of Pope John's Easter message and, if so, does he agree that it is one of the outstanding statements of our time in regard to world peace, disarmament, tolerance and goodwill to all men? Will the Prime Minister send a message

of congratulations to Pope John on behalf of the Australian people?

Menzies, somewhat perplexed at such a question coming from Uren, replied that although a Presbyterian himself, he had the greatest admiration for Pope John and, although he hadn't yet received the text in question, he felt it would be full of deep wisdom and he looked forward to reading it.

Ted Kennedy and Tom Dunlea were both well-versed in and intrigued by the Aborigine attitude to the environment and creation in general. They were convinced that it was akin to that of Francis of Assisi and, indeed, to that of their own Celtic ancestors. One of Dunlea's favourite Canticles in the Breviary was that of Daniel, where the sun, the moon, the stars, mountains, trees and rivers, birds, animals and fish are seen as continually offering praise and adoration to their Creating God.

When discussing this with some Aborigine elders in the desert camps he visited back in 1952, noting their utter reverence and rapport with the earth, he wondered if they actually identified the earth with the earth's Creator, which would amount to pantheism. He discussed this with Ted Kennedy who had in his pocket an apt quote from the Scottish theologian, John Macquarrie, about Celtic spirituality and pantheism which he shared with Dunlea:

> At the very centre of Celtic-type spirituality was an intense sense of presence. The Celt was very much a God-intoxicated person whose life was embraced on all sides by the Divine Being. But this presence was always mediated through some finite, this-world reality, so that it would be difficult to imagine a spirituality more down to earth than this one. The sense of God's immanence in his creation was so strong in Celtic spirituality as to amount sometimes almost to pantheism. (*Paths in Spirituality*)

He liked this. It more or less expressed his own spirituality and, he felt, that of the Aborigine elders.

His interest in the Aborigines went back a long way. Among his early Boys Town boys were several Aborigines, and that trend continued during all his time at Boys Town. His proposal to open a Boys Town for Aboriginal boys in Beagle Bay in 1952 was a serious one and probably would have eventuated only for his own personal problems at the time.

When he was as yet a curate in Hurstville in 1928, Yvonne Marien reports that he helped to establish a settlement for Aborigines in the Peakhurst–Lugarno area. He was maybe the only clergyman who offered help and advice to Hazel Wilson, who ran the Kirinari Hostel for Aboriginal students at Sylvania.

His friend John McRae testifies that:

> He had visions and hopes of a better deal for Aborigines and was behind everyone who promised to give them their proper dignity and at least equal opportunities and basic civil rights. He lived to see the beginnings of a breakthrough that same wall of prejudice, as Aboriginal poets and artists began to emerge who could speak for their people and demand their heritage.

Among the down-and-outs, the alcoholics and other homeless people he reached out to, there were many Aborigines. The fact that they were hugely disadvantaged made it natural for him to be their champion:

> For this reason he was an energetic crusader for Aboriginal rights long before it became fashionable. His efforts on their behalf, however, were never published for several reasons: his ideas were not specific enough to convince the media or the public at large and he was not adept at political lobbying and that whole area of influence so natural to the late Archbishop James Carroll. This struggle for the disenfranchised came from his own sensitivity to the cruelties and injustices suffered by his own people in Ireland at the hands of a senseless overlordship by a foreign power. (Morrissey)

His occasional trips to the valley of peace at Araluen were especially appreciated in the late 1950s, when he was experiencing some hassles with his new curate at St Michael's. Pat Archbold, a short rotund young priest with a cherubic face and bright blue eyes, had some responsibility regarding a new building project to enlarge Our Lady Star of the Sea High School. He shared with the Pastor control over the parish purse strings. Coming from a high-profile, very wealthy family, he was a quietly-spoken, no-nonsense person who was efficient, direct and intelligent.

He had the disadvantage, however, of lacking a support base in Hurstville because he was perceived to be somewhat upper-class and not fully blessed with the common touch. His tight grip on the purse strings was sometimes irritating for Dunlea and off-putting for many parishioners, leaving him in a more or less no-win situation. And not only that, he had no empathy with the Dunlea way of being pastor. He regarded most of the things going on at Hurstville as quite crazy and not at all in the interests of the Church.

Archbold had his own ideas about how a parish should function; they were also somewhat unorthodox and untried. Fortunately for all concerned, before the end of 1959, the Cardinal decided to give Father Pat a stamping ground of his own at the newly developing public housing suburb of Mount Druitt in outer Western Sydney. There he pitched his tent and started on a centre which deliberately omitted provision for a parish school — a school being considered at that time a *sine qua non* for a viable parish. Pat envisaged the money saved going into services for adults and children. It was a bold and courageous direction to take and evidently led to the development of a fine community, although the precedent wasn't followed elsewhere.

Archbold was succeeded in Hurstville by Peter Farrelly, a more flexible, less dogmatic man, who had experienced the rigours of a five-year stint of missionary work in post-war Japan. In his patient and wily way, Farrelly managed to keep a fairly low profile, which posed no threat to the parish priest. He admired and lauded Dunlea's pastoral skills, his amazing rapport with people and enjoyed and shared in his whimsical sense of humour. Although, like other clergymen, he felt for the poor and the needy, he questioned, as indeed his predecessors had, the need to have an open-door policy for all and sundry, especially the homeless, at St Michael's.

At lunch one day, Dunlea explained to his nephew, Gerard, who was visiting from Brisbane, some details about people that gave Farrelly a new insight into the plight of the homeless, aspects that hadn't occurred to him before. Homeless people, Dunlea was saying, are just that, people — people who can be hurt like other people. Only they are hurt much more than most people. To experience being uncared for, being unwanted, being a reject, being thought of as a no-hoper, hurts deeply. Most of them are not thick-skinned. It hurts to know that your life has no significance for anyone else, that you could disappear off the face of the earth and no-one would miss you.

When stretched on a park bench, it hurts when people pass by without even looking in your direction because you embarrass them. It hurts, too, when their eyes express contempt. In fact, hurting is a permanent condition of homeless people. The external circumstance, the hunger and thirst which gnaw continually, the heat and cold, the sleeplessness, the vermin and the smells are readily recognisable. The emptiness, the loneliness, the hurts are just as real to the homeless, but are not generally recognised by others.

Helping the homeless begins by recognising this internal condition and recognising the dignity that is theirs as people; as well as seeing Christ in them, seeing oneself in them. Turning to Farrelly, he would purse his lips and with a grin, declare: even Father Peter here, who experienced such loving care from his beautiful family in County Cavan, if his circumstances were vastly different, even he, could be the man on the park bench!

After that very interesting conversation, Dunlea agreed that one could go to extremes in helping the homeless, but did not think what he himself was doing in any way extreme for him. He couldn't live with himself if he did less.

Farrelly was amused by parishioners like Kath Ryan who had some vacant rooms in her house after her family had dispersed. Kath would appeal to Farrelly not to mention her vacant rooms when he saw Dunlea worrying about finding a place for someone, because he'd be sure to fill them. And, of course, he did. Kath's place, in fact, became a second home for former Boys Town boys for whom she was a very caring mother.

> Another parishioner Kate Brady was one of those very efficient and generous women who could cater for a number of people at short notice. She warned Farrelly not to ever mention her name when he saw the kitchen table piling up with unexpected guests. However, Dunlea would remember, and Kate would find herself cooking dinner for twenty men, encouraged by the silver compliments which tripped so lightly from his tongue! (Lea Scarlett)

Among the many interesting characters encountered by Farrelly during his time with Dunlea was one Alex Brown. While staying at the Matt Talbot Hostel in 1952, Brown made his confession to Dunlea who, on discovering that he was an alcoholic, did something most unusual. He flaunted all the recognised rules of the confessional and those dealing with addicts by giving him money — a pound note, actually. That note had an extraordinary effect on Alex Brown, according to Farrelly. He folded it, put it into his pocket, took it out again, looked at it, but didn't spend it. It became almost synonymous with Dunlea in Alex's mind. It carried his graciousness and interest and eventually motivated Alex to seek out AA and go to a meeting.

After attaining sobriety, he went interstate, still carrying Dunlea's note. Five years later saw him back in Sydney on a business trip, looking up his former confessor. He still didn't part with Dunlea's note, but gave him a substantial donation — Farrelly didn't quite know how much, probably fifty or one hundred pounds — in thanksgiving for saving his life! It could so easily have gone the other way; somehow, once again, the Dunlea intuition, or one could even call it the Dunlea magic, won the day.

> Altogether too common to single out were his daily points of contact with the strange unseen world of coincidence and intuition. He was preternaturally tuned in to things mystical and other-worldly. One night he told me he might be going to die because his pet whippet dog had given him a sign: it did what it would never have normally done — it came upstairs and lay on Tom's bed. Sure enough, next day it was the dog that died, killed when the wall of a shed fell on it during demolition work in the school yard.
>
> I was present when Jim Morris showed Tom his new car and asked him what colour he reckoned it was. Tom said he had seen a finch in Ireland the very same colour. Jim said, "Well, what a strange coincidence! That is the precise colour given to it in the official label, Finch Green".
>
> Tom would consistently dial a telephone number to make one contact, only to find he had dialled the wrong number, which put him in touch with another person in some need or other.
>
> All life's daily little pictures were transparencies to him, behind which he could always see, sometimes clearly, the mysterious presence of God.
>
> His gift was no doubt partly natural, partly ingrained by a childhood atmosphere of beautiful harmony and happiness at home and partly won on the battlefield of a specially hard later life.
> (Morrissey)

21

GROW is born

Late at night in April 1957, a distraught young man in pyjamas and slippers knocked on St Michael's Presbytery door. Dunlea was used to this and so had no hesitation in opening up and inviting him in. The visitor was fit-looking, fair-haired, with piercing blue eyes and a bright intelligent face. Although obviously distraught, there was a buoyancy and alacrity in his movements and a certain warmth and cheerfulness in his attitude. Even though the hour was late, Dunlea insisted on making him a welcoming mug of tea. This turned out to be an historic and providential meeting between the youthful Father Con Keogh and the veteran Father Tom Dunlea. Dunlea knew Keogh to be a young priest in the Archdiocese and was vaguely aware of his rather tragic health problems. He even had discussed with Dr Minogue the possibility of group therapy, à la Alcoholics Anonymous, helping someone like this.

The young man told his story without inhibition. After completing his studies in Rome during the turbulent years of World War II, he had gone on to Louvain, where he had acquired a double doctorate in Theology and Philosophy. After returning to Sydney in 1954, he was appointed to Springwood Seminary as a lecturer. He had immersed himself in the controversial social issues of the day, as well as in the stimulating world of academia. As a result he had had a nervous breakdown from working at night without sleep and taking Benzedrine, thus becoming hyperactive.

Admitted to the St John of God Hospital in Richmond, Keogh had had a lot of shock therapy. Being deluded, hallucinating and violent, the nursing staff at Richmond, unable to control him, had sent him to the Reception House in Darlinghurst, where he had been certified and sent to the State Mental Hospital at Parramatta. There he had received a good deal of the coercive treatment — the solitary cell and the straitjacket — that was still common then. There he was also one of the first patients to benefit from the new wonder drug, Chlorpromazine (Largactil), which had come into use at the time.

Still very disturbed, unable to remember and mortally afraid, Father Con had been discharged from hospital and allowed to resume light parish duties. Feeling the need for group support, he had looked everywhere, and the only group he could find was Alcoholics Anonymous; there was, in fact, no other group therapy available (even in hospitals) at that time. He had found the warm welcoming fellowship of AA a truly therapeutic experience; without any feeling of stigma or shame, he felt one with them. Each had a problem like himself, a problem that had thrown his life into disorder.

He told Dunlea about people he had met at the AA meetings who, like himself, were not alcoholics, but former patients of mental hospitals who had had a breakdown and were trying to get better. He felt they had special needs not fully addressed by AA and wondered if they should become a group by themselves. Keogh had heard the name Father Tom mentioned again and again at the AA meetings, and some months previously, Archie McKinnon at the Reception House had strongly recommended he consult Father Tom. Dunlea had discussed the matter with McKinnon, as well as with Minogue, and thus it had been at the back of his mind for some time. Keogh was greatly relieved to hear this, for it provided the kind of confirmation he was seeking and, in Dunlea, the support he was hoping for. With Dunlea's encouragement, a gathering was arranged and a room at the back of the Hurstville Presbytery was set aside for future use.

On Easter week 1957, the first of several weekly meetings took place at St Michael's, with a girl called Irene in the chair. First names only were used, as at AA meetings. Various aspects of their illness were discussed, how it had started, and how they might beat their nervous condition. Dunlea just listened and encouraged. He was a valuable resource regarding the twelve steps of AA and how they could be adapted or changed or added to as needed, in this new grouping. Con was the leading inspiration of the group and the scribe who faithfully reported what was discussed.

The brilliance of Keogh amazed Dunlea. In the Seminary and after ordination he was said to be one of the most intellectually gifted men the Church in Australia had produced. He was also said to be almost incapable of living a normal orderly life. Stories about him were rife: being found asleep at his desk after a night of writing, missing the last train home, sleeping on a railway station bench, catching the milk train and walking miles to be on time for the 7 am Mass. Dunlea, aware that this was a unique human being, noticed the alertness, the wit and the almost uncanny capacity to analyse the consequences of decisions. He shared with Dunlea and the others his conviction that much of the work done in mental homes and by psychiatrists ended in sheer waste. When patients returned to their old surroundings, they lost most of what they had gained. A way must be found in which patients could help themselves while helping others.

As they were groping for a way forward, one of the members showed Dunlea a small green booklet she had picked up in her local church pamphlet rack. Called Recovery Incorporated, it revealed the existence in America of groups of sufferers who were helping themselves as the Hurstville groups were hoping to do. From the booklet they learned that Recovery Inc was started in Chicago in the mid-1930s by a Polish Jew trained in Vienna, Dr Abraham Low. Disillusioned with

Freudian psychoanalytic methods, he pioneered the then revolutionary idea that patients could and should be actively responsible for regaining their mental health.

The Hurstville group were delighted to hear that there were hundreds of groups of Recovery Incorporated scattered over the United States and Canada. They liked also the name Recovery and decided adopt it in place of the AA style names: Neurotics Anonymous or Mental Sufferers Anonymous, which had been mooted. They knew from the booklet that Recovery Inc followed a textbook called *Mental Health through Will Training* by Dr Low which hadn't yet arrived in Australia.

The early meetings in Hurstville saw Keogh and the group studying the two models: Alcoholics Anonymous and Recovery Inc. How much of each would they adapt and how much discard? It was in this area especially that Keogh shone. The temptation was to adopt fully the American model, which had such a proven and successful track record. Why reinvent the wheel when they had one that worked or thought they had? Keogh wasn't so sure; he felt they didn't have enough information about it initially and, when they did get more reading matter, he had some doubts. He wrote:

> By the time we had access to Dr Low's material, we were well and truly launched on self-activation and mutual help methods of our own, which not only differed from, but seemed to be considerably in advance of the strictly guided self-help technique taught by Dr Low. In fact, much of what we were doing — sharing experiences and recording what we sufferers found to work — was forbidden in Recovery Inc groups.
>
> The overall impression we had, in comparing the two Recoveries, was of something like two different sets of rules for the same sport. Our Recovery seemed to be as different from Recovery Inc as a game of Rugby League or Aussie Rules differs from a game of American football — what was damn good play in

one put you offside or got you penalised, in the other. (Grow p14)

Recovery Australia was born of the creative and imaginative skills of Keogh and the early members, aided and abetted by Dunlea, AA, Dr Low and Recovery Inc.

It was an essentially Australian creation. As an American professional writer states:

> Where else could it have sprung from except Australia? It seems to me that it needed a country like this, with its easygoing egalitarianism, its pioneer give-it-a-go spirit, its earthiness and its still unspoilt idealism, to make this inspiration viable and to launch this restorative movement on its way. It is no hazard at all to predict that it will spread around the world. But as it does, I believe and I hope it will continue to live and breathe with the spirit and the tang of its birthplace down-under. (Grow p137)

Spread around the world it did. Twenty-one years later, Con was able to record that out of that first group had come hundreds of groups scattered throughout Australia and several other countries, making it the largest and most rapidly expanding voluntary work in mental health in Australia and overseas.

It had touched and restored countless thousands of lives, for many of whom it was the light at the end of the tunnel, the dawn of a new exciting day. Like Dunlea's Boys Town and Alcoholics Anonymous, it restored to the wider community people whose lives had been broken and put together again, people aware of their gifts and resources, which they were now free enough to use for the benefit of others in need.

Their experience in finding mental health together produced an elaborate program of personal growth, a carefully structured group method and a vigorous caring and sharing community. The secret of its success was in making the maximum use of each one's personal resources. The principle that animated the groups was friendship and friendly help. The primary common aim was understanding — understanding of what mental health is, how to get it and how to keep it.

Unlike Boys Town, their financial needs weren't great, but the fact that their enthusiastic supporter was Dunlea's great friend, the well-known and respected businessman, Reuben F Scarf, won them influence and affirmation which carried the good news of Recovery into all states and territories of Australia.

Two Americans, W Clement Stone, Chairman of the American Foundation of Psychiatry, and a Hobart Mowrer, Professor of Psychology, University of Illinois, discovered Recovery and Con Keogh through Reuben F Scarf. Committed to getting self-help methods and spiritual values back into mental health, both found Recovery tailor-made for their needs. Through them and their considerable influence and the tireless organising work of Con and his helpers, groups began to form in all States of the Union, spreading into Hawaii and Canada, and thence to Ireland, Great Britain and Europe.

In 1970, the year of Dunlea's death, the name Recovery was changed to GROW; thus, Recovery Groups became GROW Groups, as they are today. The change reflected a change in membership. As they became well known, they began to attract people who hadn't suffered breakdowns but had problems coping and needed help. The result was that roughly half the people attending were there for what might be called preventative reasons, rather than for rehabilitation. The common goal of all members is growth to personal maturity.

GROW, like AA, is open to persons of any faith or, indeed, of no faith. It's amazing, however, how it reflects Gospel insights into the power of love. It defines itself as people helping people to live and grow:

    — to love one another back to health
    — to summon one another forth to be the true persons we're meant to be,
    — to share the wisdom, love and strength of true friendship, this beautiful and essential human

relationship which makes life meaningful and growth possible,
—to grow to mental health and happiness together by learning the natural rules for healthy living,
— to take the proven steps to personal maturity which Growers have found successful,
— to spread the healing relationship of true friendship and this sound program of healthy living out to our families, community and the whole world. (GROW p6)

The retaining of the AA God step in Grow was motivated by practical experience. Benefit, often of an altogether remarkable kind, was reported by members as resulting from prayer for God's help, Surrendering to a higher power was seen by many as the key to getting well and remaining well. It seemed, too, that those who had that firm faith in a higher power had a strong influence on the motivation of others towards recovery.

Progress was reported on a range of crucial problems with the aid of the spiritual step, as it was called, and very little of note without it. These problems ranged from guilt over real or imagined wrongs, compulsions, hopes and fears, to permanent handicaps, intractable illnesses, and other grave ills. Problems which had no temporal solutions were surrendered to the Supreme Healer, with surprising results. (GROW p93)

What most struck the famous English author and publisher, Maisie Ward, about the movement was that it took seriously the Gospel words about prostitutes and publicans entering the Kingdom of Heaven before the self-righteous.

> Its literature reinforces something I felt strongly after attending three or four meetings: human beings are all made of the same stuff, and which of us has not experienced depression, self-disgust, escapism and all the ills that converge in neurosis? It is in degree, not in kind, that our reactions differ from those of the

neurotic — we may all fall over the edge and need what this program offers. (GROW p57)

One of the people whom Dunlea introduced to the first Recovery Group was his friend from Matthew Talbot days, Bobby Delaney, former Australian Lightweight Champion boxer. Bobby was an alcoholic who, at the time, was putting his life together again as a ship's painter on the docks and, in his spare time, conducting boxing classes for young lads at St Michael's. Like Dunlea he went somewhat to extremes to identify with the ex-mental patients at the meetings: he would sum up his years of drinking in a great outburst of new insight.

> "And I was schizophrenic!" he would exclaim, roaring it out for emphasis. "I was a split personality. I was split from stem to stern!!" All this would be accompanied by a mighty gesture of his right arm, as if he were ripping himself in two with a knife from his head to his toes. The conclusion he would almost frighten us into accepting was this: "If truth and friendship can fix up a drongo like me, it can do the same for any of you!" (GROW p12)

Dunlea had his own homespun way of putting them at ease: "I am just like an old beer mug that's been broken and put together again. I'm all right so long as you handle me gently". Keogh refers to Dunlea as "a real friend to humanity, our beloved, fragile but fearless friend...".

> Father Tom was by no means a perfect performer or a great organiser but, from weakness and suffering, he had learned compassion. And as a result, he had the remarkable distinction of being the inspirer of others — resulting in his being involved in the beginnings of three important movements for mutual help and human restoration:
> — He was the founder of Boys Town (Engadine);
> — He was one of the first members of the first Alcoholics Anonymous groups in Australia, and finally

— He sponsored and gave a home to the first Recovery group. (GROW p12)

On July 28, 1970 a beautifully scripted scroll was among those received and published at an important milestone in his life:

Father Thomas Dunlea

In this year of your Golden Jubilee of Priestly Ordination, Recovery wishes to honour you and to express its affection and gratitude for the important part you had in its origin by your friendship and personal inspiration and kindly providing its first meeting place.

22

The Bell

The Bell is forever linked with the Dunlea name in the minds of countless people who knew him in Hurstville. For them, his name evokes amusing memories and lively stories of the tinkling bell. For many of them the bell is the best remembered and maybe most unique aspect of a man who had many unique aspects. It had to do with his ministry of preaching. He was what could be termed a flowery preacher. He sought to entertain as well as teach. His message was couched in expressions that were flamboyant and poetic.

> He was obviously a man of very great memory, a very widely read man and high in appreciation of the melodic virtues of the English tongue. It would be very rarely that we would have the privilege of listening to a sermon from Father and not hearing a verse of a poem echoing forth in his deep, rich, melodious voice. (Lea Scarlett p131–132)

Journalist Ken Scully, a perceptive and witty reporter not given to hyperbole, writes: "Did you ever hear Father Tom preach or give a charity address? The stream of love and faith and hope and all that was great and good flowed from his lips and heart like the water pouring over Victoria (not the deafening Niagara) Falls!"

Though he could be classed as an orator, even "a great orator" (Lea Scarlett), he had the greatest difficulty in keeping to the point. He was brimful and overflowing with life's interesting happenings and remembered quotes which, while illustrating the point he wanted to make, also concealed it, to some extent. The exciting illustrations and anecdotes made for easy relaxed listening, but they tended to ramble on and on.

Aware of the problem, Dunlea devised some strategies to deal with it. In Surry Hills he had one of the church wardens, sitting in the back seat, give him a signal. The warden, more or less at his own discretion, was to raise his hand when he thought it was time to stop. Although the problem of time wasn't so bad in his curate days when his fluency and eloquence hadn't fully developed, the stratagem helped, depending on the courage of the warden. In Sutherland he tried an alarm clock, but with limited success. In Hurstville he opted for a different approach. Noticing that his senior altar boys, Bill Tearle and team, were generally equipped with watches, he appointed one of them to time the sermon and signal the end by a stroke on a brass gong.

> Needless to say, gonging Father off made every sermon exciting for the boys, particularly as there was no limit imposed on the muscle power which they used. Sympathetic to St Paul's horror of becoming sounding brass, Father stopped abruptly on the sound, even in mid-sentence or even in the middle of a word. One day, in the midst of a rhetorical declamation, he left the pulpit and returned to the altar for the Creed with his hand still held high. (Lea Scarlett p136)

This had an amazing effect on the congregation. It seemed to focus people's attention, to keep them alert and listening and determined not to miss the dramatic moment. In some curious way, it turned on some unused psychological switch. As Dunlea was coming towards the point in time when the boy began to rummage around for the striker, all the coughing and wheezing stopped. An eerie silence seemed to float over the congregation, as all eyes focused on the preacher and on the boy at the altar. People seemed to hold their breath as they watched the boy being nudged by his companions. This is it. Now!

And lo and behold! the ringing echoes through the church loud and clear!

Dunlea had been announcing: "The second point I'd like to explain is ..." when he was gonged and there it stayed. The second point was never made. The people relaxed, with the usual noises, distractions and movement returning.

Once the news of this phenomenon got out, which it did with great alacrity, people from other parishes came to St Michael's just to experience it. Some evidently looked on it as a sort of a retribution for the long, sometimes boring homilies they had to endure in their own parish.

In general the gonging enhanced Dunlea's stature and popularity and became another much-acclaimed first among his many initiatives. The media found it newsworthy and gave it somewhat exaggerated headlines.

The neighbouring clergy, however, more bemused than enamoured of it, mostly regarded it as yet another attention-seeking Dunlea gimmick. They predicted it wouldn't last and, although it did last for quite a while, he didn't always stop dead. It was unusual for him to be so caught up that he ignored the gong, but once in a while when given a second hint by the altar boy, he'd retort with "I heard you the first time", or, "end of round one", and keep going.

More often, if he failed to make his point clearly enough before the dramatic end, he would waive the strict liturgical norms of the time by slotting into the second part of the Mass the points he felt he hadn't got to in the sermon. That could happen more than once during the same service. However, stopping even in the middle of a word was his more usual practice. On one occasion a visiting priest was gonged! The pained look of surprise on his face was worth seeing. (Tearle)

The reasons the time factor became urgent pertained to most city churches, as well as St Michael's. Many people travelled to Mass by public transport, which tended to run on schedule and could be missed if the celebrant went overtime. Many others came by car and, with Masses on the hour and parking spaces limited, going overtime could result in parking chaos.

Things came to a head one Sunday in Lent 1959 when Father Tom White, of the Catholic Enquiry Centre in Maroubra, came to the parish to appeal for sponsors. Dunlea, an enthusiastic supporter of good causes like the Enquiry Centre, invited White to St Michael's many times. On this occasion Dunlea celebrated the Mass, Father White con-celebrating with him and preaching. Towards the end of the Mass, Dunlea mounted the pulpit to thank the visitor and elaborate on his noble family origins in County Tipperary. Getting into full flight, he didn't realise the clock had struck, indicating the time for the next Mass to begin.

Pat Archbold, however, a stickler for punctuality, decided to confront the problem head on. With his troop of altar boys in the lead, he marched out to the altar to begin the next Mass while the pastor was concluding his Mass at the same altar! In his strong vibrant voice, Archbold began intoning the prayers at the foot of the altar as Dunlea, in an even more vibrant voice, was intoning the final prayer! The normally serene prayerful atmosphere of St Michael's suddenly gave way to audible sighs, gasps and wonderment at the confusing confrontation being played out in the sanctuary.

Dunlea didn't seem to understand what was happening until he saw Archbold ascending the steps of the altar. Quick as a flash, he responded by adding an extra prayer to thank God for giving Father Pat such an abundance of the gift of punctuality and to forgive God for giving himself so little of that same gift!

On the following Thursday night, which was Holy Thursday, Dunlea and Archbold were conducting a Holy Hour in the church. The *Novus Ordo* hadn't yet come, so the Liturgy of the Last Supper was conducted in the early morning with a small congregation. Many more gathered for the evening Holy Hour and the reflection on the institution of the Eucharist. There was still some tension between the two priests when Archbold got to his feet and, going through the Gospels of Matthew, Mark and Luke, described how Jesus took the bread and wine at the Last Supper, saying "This is my Body, this is my Blood, do this in memory of me". Having given a fairly scholarly reflection on those words, he graciously asked the Pastor if he wanted to add anything.

Dunlea complimented Pat and, borrowing his New Testament, opened St John's Gospel and read the account of the washing of the feet. He then went on to tell those present that this is John's way of referring to the institution of the Eucharist. John doesn't say anything about bread and wine in his lengthy Last Supper discourse. He just describes how Jesus washed his disciples' feet and cautioned: "If I, the Lord and Master, have washed your feet, you should wash each other's feet". (John 13:14)

By replacing the words of institution with this simple act of service, Dunlea commented, John is telling us that the Eucharist is meant to lead us from the church into a relationship of humble service of others, especially the poor and the homeless. The Eucharist sends us forth to serve, to wash feet. Nourished by the Eucharist, we're called to express Jesus' love and compassion for people, especially the people whom society looks down on as unimportant, as nobodies.

To make his point, Dunlea even sang a verse of an old hymn:

> Called from worship into service
> Forth, in his great name we go
> To the child, the youth, the aged
> Love, in loving deeds to show.

He concluded by explaining that, having partaken of the food and drink and the divine love and peace, we bring it with us into the nitty-gritty of daily life, where it becomes translated directly and immediately into loving service. The Eucharist invites us to change the world's way wherein the poor serve the rich and, instead, don the apron and the towel and kiss the feet of the hungry and the hurting, the lonely and the homeless, in our midst.

After a period of prayerful silence, Archbold turned his small bright face towards the people present and admitted that he and his pastor had to agree to disagree about many things. However, having heard this interpretation of the washing of the feet, he felt he had a lot to learn from the experience and wisdom of the older man. Dunlea responded by giving him a warm sign of peace. *Pax tecum, Patricius*, he said in Latin.

Archbold commented on this years later when the *Novus Ordo* came out. To the surprise of many, the Gospel chosen for the Solemn Mass of the Last Supper on Holy Thursday night, which commemorates the institution of the Eucharist, was the Washing of the Feet from St John. The man whom, for a while, he had loved to hate was, in many ways, a man before his time.

This came home to him on Friday afternoons, which Dunlea reserved for the young priests in the area to come together to talk about the homily for the following Sunday. It was a special time for Dunlea, a kind of sacred time, not to be missed. Having read the Scripture reading set down for the Sunday, each one shared his reflections on how it related to his own life and that of his people. Dunlea's role was that of encouraging, affirming, reassuring, more than inputting. But now and again, Archbold noticed a flash of deep inspiration coming from the Pastor. He remembered the day they were sharing on the passion of Christ and the power of the Cross. Dunlea compared the power of the Cross to the power of a little baby he had encountered in a home he had just visited. Every one in the room had focused on the baby, drawn towards it; no-one could resist as the baby invited, beckoned, smiled. Its powerlessness, its vulnerability is a baby's great attraction.

"That's the power that the Gospel calls *exousia*", Dunlea had continued. It's not energy or *dynamis* (dynamism), it's a different kind of power, with no reference to force or muscle or fire and brimstone. It's the power of a newborn baby. That's the power of the Cross, the power of powerlessness, the power of vulnerability.

On the Cross God becomes totally powerless, vulnerable, helpless, fragile. The Cross is the great sign of God's solidarity with human beings, with all human beings, of whatever colour or creed or culture. The Cross reveals a God who is non-violent, non-coercive, non-threatening, non-punishing, a God who gently invites, attracts, even coaxes, as a mother who is teaching her child to walk coaxes it to take one more step.

As they talked about this together, Archbold remembered concluding that when they themselves experienced helplessness or powerlessness, or when dealing with people who are helpless and powerless, they are touching the divine power, the divine *exousia* of the Cross. That's the power that leads to Resurrection.

Dunlea was absolutely convinced that God was in solidarity with all people. As Peter Morrissey remarks, "He failed completely to see any difference between any group of human beings". Before ever the word *ecumenism* became part of popular religious parlance, Dunlea was a deeply convinced ecumenist.

> He spontaneously recognised God's grace in the lives of all sincere seekers after truth, even in the days when bigotry was normal and pagans damned. He needed no modern psychiatry to teach him that alcoholism and other weaknesses were true physical and personality failures, and not simply depravity and wickedness. (Coleman p26, quoting Morrissey)

The conditions for entry into Boys Town or participating in AA or GROW were never religious or national or ethnic. Humanity was always his starting point. Men and women, made in the image and likeness of God, deserved respect and esteem and love as human beings, before any considerations of religious, national or political affiliations.

One of his best friends in Hurstville was the local Presbyterian minister, Rev Neil MacLeod. These two men formed a deep friendship.

> They were both steeped in literature, and both were Gaelic scholars of considerable merit. Their Celtic blood gave them a common bond, and they had the same love of life, with an underlying deep spirituality. The Rev Neil was at the first ecumenical service to be held at St Michael's, and these two men of diverse faiths prayed, talked and laughed together. There was no barrier between them. (Coleman p23)

After Vatican II, the great ecumenical Council, they shared pulpits and, to some extent, shared congregations. Even after MacLeod became the Presbyterian Moderator of New South Wales, the friendship continued, and so did his interest in and support for Boys Town.

For this fellowship Neil MacLeod received one of the finest compliments ever paid by Father Dunlea. It happened during the Church Unity Octave, when there was a combined service at St Michael's, and Father Dunlea gave the occasional sermon. He drew on the examples of great people down through the ages — one of his favourite themes. He sketched Betsy Fry for the Quakers, Florence Nightingale for Anglicans and John Wesley for Methodists. "Coming to the Presbyterians," he said, "I couldn't think of anybody, so I'll settle for Saint Neil MacLeod".

Another friend and admirer was Dick, aged thirty, a Protestant from Belfast who lived in Penrith and was a recovering alcoholic. They met at the AA meeting in Arncliffe, where Dick would listen to Father Tom share his wisdom in his gentle brogue, in a way that was never judgmental. Writes Dick:

> By then, I had left teaching, and taken a job as a youth director with the YMCA. This job involved working at night, and I could not attend evening meetings. As a result I used to visit Father Tom in his presbytery at Hurstville, along with other alkies, wounded animals, ex-students from Boys Town and graduates from the University of Life. These were special times where Father Tom would quietly

> encourage many who were going through troubled waters. As Father Tom's illness caused him to slow down, he did not go out at night, and the afternoons at the presbytery became very special in learning about unconditional love. On one of my last visits, Father Tom gave me his copy of *The Confessions of St Augustine*, which is one of my prized possessions. I am sure that many others can trace their recovery to the quiet, encouraging influence of Father Tom Dunlea, and I give thanks to God for his life.

News of AA friends like Dick who went on to better things gave him a great lift. Ray was another such friend whose letter to Dunlea explaining the leading role he played at some big rally in New Zealand attended by the Prime Minister, was responded to with enthusiasm.

> Your letter was a Godsend. It has filled me with such optimism in regard to the human person that has made me feel as if I was only twenty. I can really say that it has verified the saying "hope springs eternal ..." and it has made my interest in the future beam illuminatingly like the voyagers in the Bay of Naples when, in the darkness of night, they viewed Stromboli.
>
> Your winning through, your instance (sic) of reorientation has been a beacon light on the hillside, one of my future signposts.

He then goes on to wax eloquent about Ray's countryman Hillary, Edmund Hillary the famous mountaineer who had climbed Mt Everest:

> Should you ever meet him and have the honour to shake his hand put my name in with that handshake and tell him in our schools and from my pulpit I have taught him and preached him as a historian to the future success of my listeners.

To make sure that the graduates from the University of Life, as he called them, weren't the only ones who gathered and were entertained at the presbytery, Dunlea held regular parties for groups of St Michael's parishioners. Sometimes the invited would bring a plate, and sometimes the housekeeper and her many helpers would cater. The conversation, much more important than the food, went on and on after the meal finished. Although, as Ted Scanlon noted, Dunlea could talk on all subjects, he was also able to listen. He went to some pains to encourage shy ones to have their say.

Arthur Maher and the curate loved the parties, but weren't always able to stay the distance like the Pastor. He was happy to sit at the table for hours as the guests shared their life stories. If he thought they were getting too serious, he would toss in some funny anecdote or maybe a poem or quote from some book he had read. This brightened things up while enabling him to reveal some insight into his own attitude to life. He loved to hum "Look for the Silver Lining", a song in vogue at the time. He felt that was the way to keep a positive attitude when dealing with the clouds that kept sweeping across the horizons of life.

23
Hands can speak

Thomas Dunlea, parish priest of the needy, citizen of the world, might easily have failed as pastor of Hurstville in all his concern for wider issues. That he did not do so is explained by his concern for scriptural studies, good liturgies and intensification of prayer and devotional life. All these demands were best attended to at the local level and, through them, his parishioners were made coadjutors in the adventure of doing God's work. (Lea Scarlett p135)

Among the many wider issues he was concerned about, one had to do with clergy who had drink problems. He was the specialist to whom they were referred by Bishops and fellow clergy. He was very successful in this role, and his ministry to the clergy was recognised, applauded and deeply appreciated. He helped to rehabilitate Michael Kennedy and Gerard Wallington, two gifted priests who were to become well known and respected as Dunlea's successors in this ministry.

After the death of his good friend and confidant, Monsignor Joe Giles, Joe's protégé Pat Kenna, along with Peter Morrissey and Tony Newman, were regular visitors to Hurstville. Although a generation after Dunlea, they shared his mysticism and much of his nature-centred Celtic spirituality.

Joseph Ciantar and the Salesians at Boys Town also kept in touch, informing him about progress at Engadine and inviting him back on special occasions.

John McRae, by now parish priest, often had Dunlea over to the Enfield Presbytery for lunch. A friend of a friend of John's, Anna Barry, a journalist with a country paper called *The Land*, was doing a series entitled, People You'd Like to Meet. The paper was getting many enquiries about delinquency among country boys and how to deal with it. Anna Barry had got Dunlea's name and was hoping her city friend could, through John, arrange an interview for her. Dunlea was hesitant, because it was now eight years since 1952, the year he had left the Boys Town scene. McRae, however, knew quite well that Father Tom's heart was still grappling with the problems boys were experiencing and felt this would be a great opportunity to tap into some remaining wisdom in that regard. Also, in a recent talk to the Hurstville Presbyterian Church Fellowship, he had shown that the Boys Town experience was still etched vividly in his memory.

Strange to say, the rendezvous with Anna Barry took place in the press box in the Members Stand at the 1960 Royal Easter Show. As it happened, Anna was covering the Show for her paper, and Dunlea never missed this annual opportunity to sample and savour the big country-come-to-the-city event. He told her how he just loved the carnival atmosphere, the excitement, the colour. He normally joined the children in the huge slippery-dip, but of late years, the odd stab of pain in the joints was indicating the proximity of arthritis, and so he had to settle for encouraging and cheering from ground level.

He was running a bit late for his appointment because of a Grand Final at the woodchopping that he couldn't miss. As it happened, Anna turned out to be an attractive young woman, one of those in whose presence Dunlea sparkled and who seemed to bring out the best in him. With enthusiasm he began to tell her about himself, but she gently re-directed his thoughts to the specific matter she wanted to explore with him: the subject of bad boys. This he responded to with fluency and passion.

He began with the waif he had heard in Surry Hills singing the popular song about wishing he had someone to love him. That song, he felt, expressed the core of all delinquent problems.

The young mind, he told her, is a clear slate. What are we writing on it? Sex, in its most uncreative and negative aspects ... and brutality, in its most sordid form of excitement. The young, ardent and rushing, cannot discriminate. Neither can we. They watch us and find us wanting. The adult world, which so many of them watch in movies ... the press ... advertising — the stuff of daily life — is shallow and empty.

Anna asked if broken homes played a part. It is not only broken homes and alcohol and poverty that cause the trouble, he told her. There are parents who never fail in their duties, but show neither love nor affection.

This results in children feeling lost and being driven into the company of others as lost as themselves. Danger and excitement, he felt, are the two substitutes that make up for lack of parental love. The child whose parents have:

> A harmonious relationship, especially a harmonious and mutually satisfying sexual relationship, is sure of himself and better fitted to face life. If one of the parents is failing, the child's emotional life is frustrated. There may be poverty, even illiteracy — these are small things where there is mutual love. It gives the child an armour against temptation and an assurance that grows with him.

You've got to know what the child is, he told her, not what he's been made by bad handling. You've got to give up surface judgments, for if the truth were known, we wouldn't stand much judging ourselves.

Then he went on to tell her the story of a boy brought to him from the far west of New South Wales, an incorrigible thief and bag-snatcher:

> No-one could do anything with him — no one wanted him anywhere. He was against society and he resented it. He thieved and he was silent. He'd done with us all.
>
> I watched him. He was a fine little fellow, but he didn't want anyone around him. He wouldn't speak,

not even to boys of his own age. What was the use in talking? He had locked himself away from the world for, in his few years, he had learned that people don't listen to a child. They think they do, but they're only listening to themselves! It was a waste of time to speak. He was the product of a broken home, and there was mistrust from the beginning.

I noticed his hands. They were beautiful sensitive hands always reaching out to touch things, to hold them. I noticed that particularly — the reaching out for things, the clutching. You couldn't leave anything lying around. He took it. He wouldn't speak but, all the time, his hands were busy speaking for him, grasping, holding, with a life of their own I couldn't follow.

It was hard trying to get near him. What can you do with a child who won't speak and thieves all the time? But I couldn't let him go. Those hands were trying to tell me something that his tongue couldn't or wouldn't — they were expressing a terrible inner need.

Then one day I was watching him, as we had to — and it dawned on me. Here was the poor child ignorant of his needs and going blindly through an equally ignorant world. But the hands couldn't stay still, because they wanted to be used. I took him to our carpentry shop and let him loose. He walked round and grabbed a plane. Instinctively he knew how to use it. You couldn't break through the absorption.

Dunlea told Anna that at first the boy ignored the teacher. He didn't want interference, but gradually that broke down. Within a month the teacher told Dunlea he was a genius at woodwork. In all his long experience, he had never come across such talent. They couldn't get him away from the woodwork school. He learned so fast. His hands had found an outlet at last and, although he still spoke very little, the thieving had ceased.

Dunlea was still worried about him because silence in a boy is a bad thing. He wanted him to laugh. The lad did everything with such intensity that Dunlea knew there were still barriers to break down. He could trust Dunlea and his helpers because they were not placed over him as judges or masters, keeping him in a routine, expecting him to behave like a well-trained animal. He had never known love, and they knew that deprivation can make a child so psychologically ill that it can hurt and maim him for life.

"Then it happened," continued Dunlea, with some drama.

> One day I was passing by a room where there was a piano. I heard great chords crashing out — harmonious, powerful and true. I was so astounded that I turned back.
>
> It was the youngster. I stood watching him. He'd never heard much music, but he was making his own and it wasn't discord. Whatever was in him was playing it out of his system.
>
> I wanted him taught music, but he was too quick, too nervy to take tuition. He felt he didn't need it, for once he heard a piece of music, he could play it.
>
> After that he began to laugh, to talk, to be a real boy. Loveable, bubbling over with life.

"Where is he now?" asked Anna.

"You'd be surprised if you knew his name. He is well known as a pianist and as a creator of beautiful works of art in wood. Even the Governor has congratulated him on his brilliant creations."

Just as Dunlea warmed to Anna Barry, so did she to him. She described him as broad-shouldered, with a noble head and beautiful speaking voice, who had saved thousands of the underprivileged young for good and creative lives.

Even in 1960 he still didn't use the word delinquent in connection with a child or teenager. He used the word underprivileged. "Even if they come from good and comfortable homes, and many of them do, a child who finds itself on the wrong side of the law or society is to me an underprivileged human being!" he would say. He would reserve the word delinquent for adults who make and tolerate the conditions that foster delinquency.

"We're able to absolve ourselves of guilt because at heart we find it difficult, ourselves, to cope with the kind of world we've made." In that world, from the time the child can see or read, he or she is surrounded by the cheap and vulgar in reading matter, movies, television, advertising. It's not only salacious, but it's brutal also, and no-one, either child or adult, can escape its influence. "We reel off a moral code to our young. We say ... 'This is how you must behave', and then go our way allowing the very opposite to penetrate our world."

The article brought a flood of mail. Dunlea had already informed Anna that Father Ciantar and the Salesians at Engadine were the ones to whom correspondence arising from the article should be directed. Many of the correspondents, however, wanted to contact no-one but Dunlea. So much so that his secretary, unknown to Dunlea, had to do some screening and dissuading. Even so, he was preoccupied with the topic, until midwinter, when he was due to pack up and leave for an important appointment overseas.

On August 15, the Feast of the Assumption of Our Lady, he was welcomed by the Holy Faith Sisters at their Glasnevin Headhouse in Dublin. He was there to celebrate the Golden Jubilee of his elder sister, whose name in the Congregation was Augustine. It was a great happy gathering of two families, that of the Holy Faith Sisters and the Dunleas. As well as three of his sisters and two brothers, many nieces and nephews and other relatives had travelled to Dublin, his brother Dan travelling with Father Tom. The McKeoghs (including Father Albert OCD) of Ballyvalley and the O'Briens of Ahanish-Ogonnelloe were there in strength.

At the homily of the Mass with no bell to gong him out, and afterwards at the reception, he regaled them with memories of the weird and wonderful happenings at Roran House when the Dunleas, all eleven of them, were growing up. His prodigious recall of those far-away days surprised even Sister Augustine, who was herself blessed with a good memory. As he was speaking, she began to see that absence makes the heart grow fonder. The sober black and white of those days had become beautiful technicolour, through being remembered with affection in the far-away antipodes.

After a couple of wonderful family days in and around Dublin, Dunlea met with Mary Monica McSherry, the Superior General of the Holy Faith Sisters, and discussed the possibility of the Sisters opening a house in Sydney. At the behest of Eris O'Brien, the Archbishop, they were already committed to establishing a foundation in Canberra. Cardinal Gilroy had asked Dunlea to point out how advantageous it would be for the Sisters in Canberra to have a place on the coast. The astute Gilroy thought the Dunlea charm just might make the necessary impact, thus procuring another teaching Order for his schools.

With great eloquence and all his considerable powers of persuasion, Dunlea painted a glowing picture of Sydney: its mild temperature, its ready access to beautiful beaches and other recreational activities, its intellectual and artistic outlets, its first-rate medical amenities — features the inland Sisters would need if they were to cope with the extreme Canberra climate.

Having heard from Sister McSherry that the influential John Charles McQuaid, Archbishop of Dublin, a good friend of Archbishop O'Brien of Canberra, was the one who had twisted their arm regarding Canberra, Dunlea began to realise that it would take a lot more influence than he could muster, to turn Sister McSherry's eyes towards Sydney. And indeed that seems to have been so. The Sisters came to Canberra in 1961, but didn't open a house in Sydney 'till 1973.

He was successful, however, in convincing Mother McSherry that a short holiday would be good for Sister Augustine. They headed north from Dublin and ended up at St Patrick's Purgatory in Lough Derg — a place of rigorous penance, fasting and prayer. Augustine coped with it with some difficulty, Dunlea just loved it. The fasting and the all-night vigil didn't worry him; only the walking in his bare feet over jagged stones was painful penance for him, even more so than for Augustine.

In between the penitential exercises (the rounds as they called them) which went on throughout the day and the night and the next day, there was ample time for whispered conversation. He noted the levelling effect of the penitential exercises, especially the friendship, even egalitarianism, that developed between strangers, as the rich and the poor, the great and the small, grappled side by side with the pangs of hunger and lack of sleep. The movers and shakers of Irish life, as well as labourers and people on the land, listened with great interest to his seemingly unending repertoire of Australiana. The good-humoured way he managed to connect their names with some Irish person of note or some Irish-Australian who was a dear friend of his, delighted them.

* * * * * * * *

As the beautiful autumn colours were giving way to the dull grey of winter, he was happy to head for the warmth of the Southern Hemisphere. He was very grateful to be returning in one piece, with no major health problems and, above all, no accidents of any kind, even though he had travelled extensively, encountered so many different people and experienced much that was beautiful and awe-inspiring.

24

Striking a balance

One of the great characters of Sydney in Dunlea's early days was the parish priest of Darlinghurst, Monsignor Tommy Hayden, much acclaimed former professor at St Patrick's College Manly. He had for many years been involved in training students for the priesthood. He felt that celibacy was of great value in making the priests' commitment focused and total and, for parishes, it had quite substantial financial advantages. To be life-giving, however, it had to be embraced freely and deliberately. After many years of working with students and priests, he was aware that, for many clergy, priesthood was embraced freely and deliberately, but celibacy was accepted as a *sine qua non* for entering priesthood in the Catholic Church. If priesthood could be attained without celibacy, it would be the preferred option for many clerics.

Because celibacy wasn't the big issue, therefore, it was more taken for granted and not fully explored theologically or spiritually. Its eschatological and mystical aspects weren't seen by the priest to be as enriching and transforming as they should be.

Hayden was an ecclesiastical stirrer who frequently expressed ideas that were somewhat radical for his time, although not quite so radical in the post-Vatican II Church. He felt celibacy and community should go together. With members living together in a committed community of faith and love, celibacy could thrive and blossom. Hence, for religious orders celibacy is an essential ingredient. For secular priests, who have no community commitment to each other, even when they live in the same house, it is a different matter. For them, Hayden felt, celibacy could be optional.

He arrived at that rather radical position after encountering so many priests who were feeling lonely and somewhat isolated, often living alone in large presbyteries. There is no record of Dunlea and Hayden discussing the pros and cons of celibacy, but the presumption is that Dunlea would have been on Hayden's side.

A woman who was married by Dunlea in Hurstville in the mid-1960s wrote to say she became good friends with Dunlea and visited him as a teenager when she was a student at Our Lady Star of the Sea school. She found him to be a lonely man, without any close relationships. He hungered for closeness and the human touch. "I felt sorry for him," she went on to say, "well known even then, but still lonely ... a nice human being in a very restricting profession".

Frances Massey LCM remarks that it was almost impossible to be annoyed with Father. "With his smiling Irish eyes and lilting laughter, he gave the impression of being the happiest man in the world. I think the reality was different, that was between himself and the Lord." She is probably, in that last sentence, referring to his drinking as a pick-me-up in his down times.

Joe Walsh, one of his early curates at Sutherland, intimated to his classmate, Pat O'Rourke, that his pastor's moods caused some tension in the presbytery. Peter Morrissey, the curate perhaps who knew and loved him more than anyone, speaks of his spasmodic depressions, when communicating — which was his special gift — became almost impossible: "When conversation was lost in a sort of mist of remote distraction".

These and a number of other correspondents refer to his loneliness and down days, not as a main feature, but as one small yet noted exception to his normal *joie de vivre*.

Although it might be true in exceptional cases that flamboyant high achievers like Dunlea are subject to the blues more than their ordinary run-of-the-mill colleagues, it would also be true to surmise, as Hayden did, that the blues feature to a greater degree in the life of priests whom he felt had the vocation to priesthood, but not necessarily to celibacy. For them celibacy is more a burden than a transforming richness.

The correspondent above perceptively mentioned that Dunlea hungered for closeness and the human touch. But, as Hayden sometimes pointed out, closeness and the human touch, which are so essential to emotional and spiritual maturity, would be inimical to celibacy if yielded to inappropriately.

There were a couple of facile Latin rules of thumb that Hayden liked to keep before the clergy. He did so with a certain amount of whimsy, for he was witty as well as intelligent. They were seriously accepted, but with a modicum of good-humoured clerical teasing. The rules were *noli tangere* (do not touch) and *nunquam solus cum sola* (never alone with a member of the opposite sex [in a car or other confined space]). They were looked on as prudent ways of circumventing the occasions of sin. If they were observed strictly, which indeed they mostly were, women were kept at arm's length.

This tended to make growth in closeness and the human touch somewhat daunting. Women, especially if they were young and attractive, were regarded as hazardous, and any feelings of desire in one's self or signs of such in the other would call for a polite but speedy escape. This situation resulted in the celibate having lots of friends who loved him dearly, but no-one to whom he could bare his soul except perhaps a priest friend.

It seems that Dunlea's yearning for closeness and the human touch was too passionate to be confined within these logical but debilitating constraints. Most clergy would give women, whom they felt were a bit dodgy, a wide berth. Not so Dunlea. He luxuriated in their company, he trusted them and, indeed, blossomed when they were around. He mostly observed the safety in numbers configuration, but wasn't unduly afraid of the *solus cum sola* setting — although not noticeably the same *sola*. Although he was romantic and amorous and women found him somewhat flirtatious, Cupid doesn't seem to have entered into any of his relationships.

Beryl Ferris, a teacher at Frensham, a rather up-market girls' school in Mittagong, got to know Dunlea in the early 1950s through John Purcell, who was curate at Mittagong and Helena Kenna, Father Pat's mother. She describes how the close relationship of a young attractive woman in her twenties and a celibate in his fifties, worked out:

> Some weeks after he returned to Sydney he invited me to help him continue fund-raising for whatever project might emerge. He had an office in Martin Place and during the long holidays I spent much time there, talking a lot, and not being very sure of the final outcome. We often went for a meal together, sometimes where he was well-known and offered hospitality. Wherever we went he invited others to share the conversation, which mostly they gladly did.
>
> What I particularly liked was his sense of humour, anecdotes, ready response to any situation — but I suppose most of all, his great compassion and his determination to keep going in spite of everything.
>
> One night, Beryl continues, he suggested a visit to some old friends in Paddington. I was then always ready to accept! On the way he said, "I have to tell you, these people sell a bit of alcohol". This was still the time of early closing. I understood clearly what he meant and when we arrived at the home we were warmly welcomed. A couple of well-dressed attractive girls appeared from upstairs and joined us for dinner, then disappeared. No trade in alcohol was apparent and he entertained everyone, as usual, with his stories. The host drove us home — I think he was then staying at Newtown.

She goes on to describe a celebration of Epiphany at Tempe under the direction of Dunlea's friend Joe Giles, the Parish Priest:

> The plan was that we go to the presbytery, from where a procession was to make its way to the banks of the Cooks River. As we set off Father Tom was, as usual, welcomed by all. When we got to the river, paper boats, with lighted candles inside, were launched from the mud-lined banks — their destination was a little island not far from the shore, which, I think, had been designated a Marian Shrine. After prayers were recited, we stood in silence, marking the progress of the little boats, none of which were seaworthy enough to reach the island. Then we returned to the presbytery where I was introduced as a recent release from Long Bay prison. No one found that at all unusual but I was somewhat dismayed at their ready acceptance! The night passed happily with a large cake and much frivolity.
>
> On my way home as we stopped for a cup of coffee at Tempe Station, the waitress was clearly curious about us. I heard her remark: "He looks like a priest but he can't be, because he's with her".
>
> On another day he asked me to join him in Centennial Park where he was going horse-riding. When I arrived the ride was over, so we sat under a tree and talked. His energy seemed unfailing but I do recall visiting him (perhaps at Tempe where he was staying) and finding him in bed. He then invited me to stay and talk by his bedside.

He sometimes asked Beryl to socialise with men-friends, including George Nathen, whom he felt needed a little cheering-up. Beryl obliged but after a couple of encounters desisted because she had doubts about their intentions. She didn't seem to have any doubts about Dunlea and retains very pleasant memories of him to this day.

When Pat Kenna was gathering material on Dunlea, a woman and her son travelled to Kiama to see him. Kenna writes:

> She had known Tom from her girlhood and was now married, and financially struggling, in another part of Sydney. When she came into his office in Hurstville, Tom came forward and warmly embraced her, kissing her gently on the lips. As she explained to me, a woman can tell at once if a kiss is a prelude to further intimacy or not. In this case she knew it was affection, pure and simple. Nothing more. But it was just what she needed there and then. The fact that she could relate the incident in front of her adult son told me of her sincerity — and Tom's.
>
> He was possessed by the Holy Spirit, at least at such moments — where else did his gentleness, kindness and compassion have its origin?

Did he ever transgress that rather nebulous borderline leading to a form of closeness inappropriate for a celibate? All the indications are that he didn't, which is a fine compliment to him and to the many good women associated with him. As a celibate, he entered into situations where even angels fear to tread and came out unscathed — or so it seems. Among the voluminous correspondence, all but two were enthusiastically affirming. One of the latter letters is from the correspondent above who noted he hungered for closeness and the human touch. "I got to know Father Dunlea well in my teenage years", she writes. "I was a very naive person in those days, but even then I felt if I had allowed it, the relationship would have become more than friendship." Interestingly, the relationship did survive, with Dunlea being the celebrant at her marriage, perhaps in her mid-twenties or later.

The other correspondent is one of those very pious women for whom Dunlea's liberated way with the ladies would always be a worry. He would even, as a joke, create a situation for the sole purpose of shocking someone.

When visiting patients at Lewisham Hospital, for example, he was often greeted by Frances Massey, a young Blue Nun from Hurstville parish, who writes: "If he saw the Superior in the distance, he would immediately give me a big hug and kiss (prior to Vatican II!). 'Oh Father!' — 'Yes, I can see her.' Once again, a tinkle of laughter — all forgiven!"

Mary Cooney was for some years his devout and loyal housekeeper in Sutherland. In April 1944, when Dunlea was still parish priest of Sutherland and at the same time Director of a rapidly growing and developing Boys Town, Mary was so concerned that she felt she had to get in touch with the Archbishop, whom she seemed to know personally. She wrote:

> One case worried me so much, that I spoke to the girl's mother. I am a terrible girl, God forgive me, but I felt it was my duty somehow. He has to mix with all classes and types, as you know, in the work he is doing, and it is not easy for him to keep in the narrow path. He has told me that a certain woman who counts the collection for him upset him one day. I don't know if that is true, but I have known him to go to his room and rest; he leaves things lying about, he doesn't seem to care. And when I saw him that day lying in the bed saying the Rosary, so tired-looking, I felt if only I could talk to you about him, I'd be doing my duty. He has said to me "Don't be too hard on me, I can't get anyone to do the work...". He tries hard, but he is only human. He has often told me he thinks he should go to a Monastery. However, God knows best, where he will do most good and where there will be less temptation for himself and others.

Mary finishes with a great fervent invocation of the passion of Jesus and the Sorrows of Mary as a protection on her friend, the Archbishop. From the general tone of the letter, the path envisaged for a celibate by Mary would be very narrow, indeed, even too narrow for the most traditional clergyman. The fact that the classes and types he had to mix with were not at all up to Mary's standards concerned her greatly because, like many other good housekeepers of those days, she felt she had to protect Father from rambling off the narrow path. And of course even the most pious of housekeepers weren't fully resistant to slight traces of jealousy, when they noticed the classes and types he had to mix with getting into that free and easy relationship with him that they themselves might secretly aspire to.

Among the correspondents, including some former Boys Town boys, several have asserted that they never heard anyone say anything bad about Dunlea. This is a grass-roots assertion; it is, in a way, what could be called the *sensus fidelium* (the voice of the people), and it is a consistent theme running through just about all the correspondence. The word *saint* with a small "s" is used frequently. It is a title that can be used in a fairly superficial way to indicate a good, holy, wise person, or it can have deeper connotations, indicating a very good, very holy person. With a capital "S", it can refer to an extraordinarily good and holy person worthy of being recognised by the Church. The context would often give the key to what people had in mind: He was the nearest to a saint that I will ever know or, as far as we are concerned, he was a saint on earth or, a true socialist and a saint, and so on. The word *saint*, for many religious people, indicates the highest affirmation they can envisage.

Once when Arthur Maher referred to a very pious but rather unpleasant parishioner as a saint, Dunlea rather perceptively responded:

> To live with the saints in heaven is peace and glory,
> To live with the saints on earth is another story.

One Sunday morning after Mass, recounts Sheila Tearle, we were talking to one of the locals whom we knew. Father came and joined us. Our friend asked Father, "Do you know S?" His reply: "Yes, I'm S's pinup boy". Then turning to me, he said, "And I'm Mrs C's nail-up boy".

As well as from the grass-roots, there was affirmation from what could be called the big end of town. Much to the surprise and joy of his friends, Queen Elizabeth II included him in her 1965 Queen's Birthday honours list. Year after year people go through the list in the mostly vain hope of finding someone they know. If they do succeed in coming across someone, it gives them quite a lift. For the multitude of Dunlea's fans on that fateful early winter day, it was a great thrill to see him made a Commander of the Order of the British Empire, an OBE. For Dunlea it was great news — even though not every Irishman would thus regard it. He was thrilled to be so recognised, and thrilled, too, with the fan mail that followed.

> Like the Australian Aborigines, who fascinated and mystified him, he lived only for the day. So giving and receiving the good things of life was his daily exercise: easy come, easy go. He never refused to take a gift, as if he had already acquired the grace — only talked about by modern psychologists — of allowing others the more blessed experience of giving. Thus, the chain reaction of giving and enjoying and receiving meant he always had enough money on hand to give to others and to expand continuously his own experience of life. (Morrissey)

With gratitude and joy and good humour, he accepted the letters and telegrams and phone calls bringing him the congratulations and felicitations of people of all walks of life, including the Governor-General of Australia, the Premier of New South Wales and a host of others, all of whom were VIPs in his eyes. Cardinal Gilroy mentioned how pleased he was that the Queen had recognised Dunlea's special contribution to the welfare of his fellow citizens and indeed to the whole Australian nation.

> Boys Town presented its unique form of tribute the morning after the honours list was published by

sending a truck-load of boys, complete with band, who gave three rousing cheers for Father outside St Michael's Presbytery. Later he was welcomed back to Boys Town in a very moving ceremony.
(Coleman p22)

To the conferring ceremony at Government House in Sydney, he was allowed to take only two companions. The conferring wasn't high in his priorities because he was hoping to receive the honour from the Queen herself at Buckingham Palace when visiting England the following year. His faithful helper and driver, Bruce Aley, and Peter Morrissey, his second-time curate and good friend, were the ones who accompanied him to what he intended as a low-key ceremony, in lieu of the more official one coming up in London in 1966.

Dunlea was among a very select group of non-Jews to whom the Sydney Jews presented the Jewish Cross of Honour. His association with George Nathan and his generous ecumenical attitude to all religions endeared him to the many Jews he met through George. So did his presence at George's funeral service, probably a first for a Catholic priest, where he was afforded a very cordial welcome and asked to give a blessing.

At a special ceremony at the Illawarra Catholic Club in Hurstville, the Sydney Church presented him with The Papal Cross, which he much appreciated and, with the Jewish Cross and the Queen's Medals, was proud to display at all times. They were an indication of his universal outlook.

25

He Loved his Bishop

In July 1965 the Convention Centre in Scarborough, Ontario, Canada, was decked out in gala fashion. Flags and banners from around the world were fluttering in the gentle breeze, which was bringing much appreciated relief from the stifling Toronto heat. Visitors from all parts of the Western world, mostly men in jubilant mood and colourful gear, were pouring into the Centre for the much-proclaimed Alcoholics Anonymous Convention, the first ever held outside the United States. Representatives from just about every country of the free world were among the ten thousand registered. "From all arts and crafts, from Cape Horn to Alaska", as Dunlea colourfully put it, they came from every State in the Union, as well as from Finland, Norway, Sweden, Great Britain, Ireland, Australia and New Zealand

When the registrations were finalised and the delegates formally welcomed, Bill Wilson addressed the gathering. This was the father-figure of AA, the revered and much-loved co-founder. As Wilson stood on the dais, Dunlea could feel the hushed air of reverence and affection emanating from the assembled representatives. They were acknowledging with gratitude that this was the man who had the original dream and who pursued it. Dunlea found Wilson's address quite inspirational, especially his interpretation of the twelve traditions, which were still being explored in Australia.

That the assembled members gave their founder a rousing standing ovation of several minutes didn't at all surprise the contingent from down-under. What did surprise them somewhat was seeing Bill come back to the dais to make an important announcement. In an atmosphere of silent expectancy, Wilson declared that the first country outside the United States to show an interest in their movement was none other than Australia. He lauded the Australian-American alliance during World War II. In that climate of friendship and mutual help, news of the AA Movement surfaced in Sydney.

Wilson cited Archie McKinnon, Dr Minogue and Dunlea as the founding fathers: "These wise and compassionate people saw its possibilities to alleviate and hopefully solve a problem they had been long concerned about." He then called on his good friend, Father Tom, to address the conference as its second keynote speaker. This, of course was a great honour and, as was not unusual on the big occasion, Dunlea came up to expectations.

Although his heart and joints had been giving rather ominous signals en route to Canada, the enthusiastic warm-hearted welcome set the adrenalin flowing and the magic working. The setting called for flamboyance and flourish and flowery language of which Dunlea was master. It also called for something else, something deeper and something that would touch people in their own inmost being. As Ken Scully noted above, the stream of love and all that is great and good flowed from his lips, infiltrating the minds and hearts of the assembly so that they hung on his every word. They loved, too, the anecdotes and experiences that he recounted with humour and panache and a humility particularly dear to the AA philosophy.

This was a momentous occasion among many such in Dunlea's life and, sadly, it was also the last such keynote address he was to give. He couldn't wait to brief his friends in Sydney: the Cardinal, Archbishop Freeman and Harry Kennedy the secretary. His short pithy notes are full of excitement at the honour shown Australia at this great international gathering.

He reported, too, that the clergy from different churches who attended found, in their brokenness, a new source of unity. The fact that they all had to face and deal with the same weakness gave them a sense of solidarity and brotherhood that made their theological differences, in a sense, irrelevant. He became convinced that ecumenism will grow and develop not from positions of strength, but only from the humble admission of weaknesses and a common dependence on a Higher Power. As Paul said, "My power is at its best in weakness ... it is when I am weak that I am strong" (2 Cor 12:9,10).

The glowing accounts of the convention were followed some weeks later by news of recurring health problems. The first, in September 1965, was from Limerick, reporting an ankle sprain sustained in a street-side accident. That was followed by a letter from a Dr McMahon, St Patrick's Place, Cork, indicating that Dunlea was suffering from osteo-arthritis of the right hip joint. The treatment by the Cork doctor and extensive physiotherapy with the Blue Nuns at St John's Hospital Limerick seem to have brought about a good recovery, sufficient for him to begin the trip back to Australia.

En route through London, he had evidently arranged an audience with none other than Her Majesty, the Queen, who would personally invest him as an Officer of the British Empire. Everything had been finalised, even the day and the hour when he would be welcomed with fitting pomp and ceremony at Buckingham Palace! He looked forward to it, feeling somehow that this would be a suitable and fitting denouement in his dramatic and eventful life.

However, it was not to be. Before he reached the Palace, he was stricken with "a sudden chill followed by a great depression, related apparently to my old heart condition". His letters to the Cardinal and Harry Kennedy were from his bed in the Catholic Nursing Institute in Waterloo SE.

He recovered quickly, however, and by mid-November 1965, he was on a plane to Paris, where he was met by his young friend, Tony Newman, who was the assistant priest at the Bois-Columbes parish in Paris. With Tony as interpreter, he entertained and delighted the parish staff with stories of his weird and wonderful experiences. Two fabulous days of sightseeing with Tony were brought to a fitting finale with a banquet in the revolving restaurant atop the Eiffel Tower.

Before he had left Australia, his friend Nicholas McNally, the Chaplain to Lewisham Hospital, had quipped that "Tom was off to Rome to give an audience to the Pope!". Not managing to audition the Holy Father, he was admiring the frescoes in the Sistine Chapel in Rome when he heard his name called, only to find his good friend Bishop Thomas Muldoon similarly engaged. Muldoon was in Rome for the last session of the Vatican Council. Like Dunlea, Muldoon had a deep resonant voice and was an entertaining speaker with a capacity for wit and embellishment. He was a fine theologian, had compiled his own theology textbook, and was making his mark in the pre-Vatican II seminary scene. Like some other clergy who had the gift of articulating the faith with clarity and panache, however, Muldoon didn't tune into the aggiornamento or factor it into his theology.

He didn't see any need to, nor did the Australian Bishops. Unlike what was happening in Europe, Catholic life was flourishing in Australia. What was needed was more of the same, not updating or opening up to the winds of change. The popular choice of Muldoon as auxiliary Bishop of Sydney could be taken as indication that updating was not a high priority for the Sydney Church.

Although considerably younger, the new bishop and the visiting priest were in many ways kindred spirits. They were both exuberant and somewhat ostentatious and rather fond of the limelight. Dunlea, however, as a supporter of Roger Pryke and Tony Newman, was enthusiastic about the changes already flowing through in the area of liturgy and freedom of conscience. The people he met in Paris and Rome were abuzz with excitement about the new Church emerging from the Council, but not so Sydney. Yet the push for change was strong among a small number of vocal lay people and some younger clergy. Groups of priests living together and working as a team was proposed, but didn't eventuate, except in Redfern, where Dunlea's friend, Ted Kennedy, was pastor.

In fact, there was more excitement about the discovery of minerals and oil than about anything else. Dunlea had visited the Pilbara region of Western Australia and seen the iron ore being mined, but it was only while he was away that the vastness of the mine field had been discovered. The Hamersley Ranges held the world's richest iron ore deposit. Arthur Maher filled him in on the oil beginning to flow from the Moonie field, west of Brisbane, and Bass Strait and Barrow Island in Western Australia. All this, being very good for the economy, would be a big feature in returning the Coalition to Government after the election in late 1966.

Dunlea was delighted to hear that the Labor Party had abandoned the White Australia policy and was against Australian involvement in the Vietnam War. Dunlea was all in favour of the massive protests about sending troops to Vietnam, but couldn't take to the streets himself because of his arthritic condition. The main election issue between the two parties was the sending of troops to Vietnam, and the victory of the Coalition meant that it would remain a bone of contention for some years to come.

A system of quasi-conscription was introduced, calling up selected twenty-year-olds, using a ballot involving their birthdays — maybe the most ironic birthday present the nation ever gave to young men. Several parishioners from St Michael's were among the names pulled out of the ballot box, and Dunlea made a point of keeping in touch with them. A letter to one of them, Philip Byrne, shows how tuned in to nature Dunlea was and how observant of female beauty:

> Philip, mother and I are having a Sunday morning cuppa — waited on by one of Aussie land's leading jockeys. The sun is shining, 11 am: birds singing, radio music, planes and birds above in an Austral blue sky. Mother looks as lovely as when she was a

teenager. Our Masses and Novena will remember as they have been dedicated to our people at Hurstville, at home or abroad. God love you, Phil — to bring you back to us. From your old family friend, Tom Dunlea. (Lea Scarlett p135).

When Tony Newman arrived back in Sydney after two exciting years working in Paris, he found that many of his contemporaries had left or were about to leave the ministry. Disillusioned with the pace of change and feeling that, without conciliar updating of doctrine and practice, the Church was becoming irrelevant to modern men and women, they opted for the lay state and, often, for the family lifestyle.

Tony Newman liked the French pastoral way of focusing on things spiritual, and especially spiritual direction, which had occupied much of his time in Paris. This way of priesting he found rewarding and fruitful, but it was not valued much in Sydney where practical matters like parish visitation, Housie-Housie, first Friday confessions and the like were regarded as all-important. Tony found the Sydney Church way more than he could cope with. He tried several parishes and, in desperation, asked the Cardinal to appoint him to St Michael's with Tom Dunlea. Dunlea invited him to participate in parish life and he did so, minimally, but he felt somehow it was no longer his scene. Although Dunlea probably didn't fully understand what Tony was on about, he was happy to have him and made sure his small room at the back of the presbytery was comfortable.

When his current curate, Paul Fitzgerald, was due to be promoted to administrator at the parish of St Martha's Strathfield, Dunlea asked the Cardinal for a very special favour, something he hadn't done before. It had to do with the replacement for Paul Fitzgerald. Up to then he had been happy to accept whoever was sent to him. But now his heart condition was reminding him of his fragility and gradually deteriorating grip on life. With Arthur Maher in residence and Tony Newman coming and going, he may have been afraid of missing out on a replacement, in view of the fact that so many young priests were leaving the ministry.

To succeed Fitzgerald he needed someone who knew St Michael's and understood Dunlea, and the one, par excellence, who filled those requirements was none other than Peter Morrissey. Peter had been in Hurstville for two years in the mid 1950s and he had kept in touch with Dunlea since then. Although Dunlea realised there was a long tradition against reappointing a man as curate in the same parish, he knew he was in the Cardinal's good books and he would understand that the request, in his case, was warranted.

An opportunity came at the Golden Jubilee of priesthood celebrations of a contemporary of Dunlea's: Monsignor Pat Crowley, who was for a few years the Vicar General of the Archdiocese. The Monsignor, in many ways, was quite dissimilar from Dunlea. He dressed impeccably and lived similarly. Although a County Cork man, his accent sounded somewhat uppercrust British. As Vicar General, instead of challenging the Archbishop and expressing the priests' point of view, he was said to acquiesce meekly in everything proposed. (True or otherwise, this was the perception.)

At the celebration meal after the Jubilee Mass, Dunlea was called on to propose the toast to the jubilarian. To the large gathering of clergy present, he related how in Ireland he had gone through a cemetery looking at the headstones and had come upon a priest's grave. It was somewhat overgrown and he had some difficulty making out the inscription. However, once he had pushed aside the long grass and weeds, the words stood out boldly. and they well repaid the effort entailed in exposing them. They were only four short words followed by an exclamation mark. He paused, a dramatic Dunlea pause, while he pursed his lips and with that half-serious Dunlea smile, gazed on the expectant faces awaiting his disclosure with bated breath. The words were: He loved his Bishop!

It brought the house down! A spontaneous burst of boisterous laughter and clapping erupted from the assembly. Every priest and bishop present knew those four words perfectly encapsulated a core characteristic of the jubilarian. They fitted like a glove. Although priests in general respect and obey their bishops, "loving him" is not normally part of the arrangement. In fact, if a priest is perceived as loving his bishop, he could be regarded as dangerous. He could be seen as eavesdropping and thus inhibiting the normal clergy pastime of complaining about and criticising the bishop — a practice found to be therapeutic and healthy, especially when there is a slight suspicion that it may be the clergy themselves who are falling behind and letting the side down.

"He loved his bishop" kept ripples of smiles and laughter on clergy faces for hours and even for years as the story, forever associated with the name Dunlea, circulated far and wide. When clergy are in a happy mood, they're far less likely to bring troublesome problems to the bishop, and so the cardinal, feeling indebted to Dunlea, was in no position to refuse his request for the curate of his choice.

26

Weakness accepted — power released

Writes Tony Newman:

> I had the great honour to live with Tom Dunlea during the last year and a half of his life. I count it one of the most enriching experiences of my life. His heart was reaching the end of its functional life and so his death was inevitable, but the powers of his spirit were reaching their highest development — as is the law of life. There is a balance between weakness accepted and power released.

When referring, in a sort of light-hearted way, to his own demise, Dunlea used the language of space travel, like being launched into the heavenly orbit. In July 1969 he watched Neil Armstrong walk on the moon. He was fascinated. He was so thankful that he had lived to see the day when that small step became a great leap for mankind. That very morning, Monday, the clergy day off, he had a surprise visit from Mary Rose of Boys Town days. She had visited him from time to time over the years, generally with one or more friends from Sutherland. This time she had her daughter, a fine-looking twenty-something, who was wearing a style of dress that had lately appeared in Australia, called the mini-skirt.

The model, Jean Shrimpton, had caused quite a sensation at the Rosehill races when she sported the brief skirt (c 12 cm above the knee), seen for the first time down-under. Many younger women followed suit, including some members of Paul Fitzgerald's Catholic Youth

Organisation (CYO), much to the disapproval of their parents and others. Mary Rose was hoping Dunlea would express his distaste to her daughter but, on the contrary, he complimented her on looking so attractive. Some of his assistant priests were offended by the mini-skirt and spoke out against it, but not Dunlea.

When asked to comment on it, he admitted honestly that in some perverse way he found it fetching and even alluring, but not threatening. His attitude, he felt, might have something to do with his age and poor health. He admitted that for young male members of the CYO, it could possibly be overly seductive and tempting, and for that reason, he didn't encourage it, but neither did he condemn it.

Even in his declining years, when moving about was quite painful for him, he was never short of one or two attractive young female shoulders to lean on. His laborious shuffling from place to place was thereby transformed into a rather pleasurable activity for Dunlea. On one occasion his curate thought he would be quite shocked when he showed him page three of the *Daily Mirror* where one of his glamorous helpers was featured modelling a two-piece swimsuit. Far from being offended, Dunlea reached for the phone to tell her how stunning she looked!

When clergy talk of this quaint Dunlea habit of linking with young females, they do so with a degree of merriment mixed with derision. This might indicate the presence of some frustration or even regret on missing out themselves on this rather exotic aspect of celibacy.

To Mary Rose's dismay, Dunlea seemed to give the nod of approval to her daughter, but that and other lesser matters disappeared into oblivion as the three of them sat in the presbytery lounge room gazing in sheer awe and wonder at the surface of the moon and human footsteps being etched into it. Deeply conscious that they were watching a momentous event, the most critical happening in his lifetime, one that would have decisive consequences for the human family, Dunlea drifted into silent prayer. After sharing a cuppa with his friends, he asked them to join him in the Rosary. As he said goodbye, he kissed both of them affectionately and observed that in the not-too-distant future he himself would be launched into orbit.

"I was often his driver," records Tony Newman, "taking him to AA meetings in the evenings. He considered that Sydney had the most beautiful nights of any city he had visited in the world. 'Whatever the weather during the day,' he used to say, 'after nightfall Sydney is mild and inviting'. So he would accept the invitation of the city he loved so much and go forth and find life."

Newman goes on to describe how he normally would sit at the back during the AA meetings, "often tense and anxious with my own struggle towards freedom". The rapt attention with which the members listened to Dunlea's rambling words puzzled Newman until he "understood that they were listening, not to his logic, but to his love, his peace, his confidence about death and his sureness of touch as a doctor of souls. There were many of us who fidgeted with impatience as we sat through his long sermons; but it was the little dark roots of human vanity that were rankled and caused us to suffer, rather than his longwindedness."

Joe O'Shea, a West Cork man, refers to a meeting they both attended in 1967. It was a gathering of an Irish Cultural group called The Ashling Society:

> The atmosphere of the room seemed to be electrified by his presence. His charisma was such that everyone seemed to be drawn to his every utterance. Indeed he was a man of great goodness but you didn't have to know his contributions to arrive at that conclusion. On meeting him you knew his powerful aura was structured from working for the underprivileged or some such activity. You knew, Joe goes on enthusiastically, that the welfare of people's lives was his driving concern. He was no back-room number-cruncher but a man who knew what coalface activity was all about. On meeting him you realised he was a

man of action who would leave no stone unturned in pursuit of a satisfactory outcome. I'm happy to say that, even now [2002] he remains one of my mentors when confronted with painful decisions.

There is no doubt but that the sufferings Dunlea had to face had a big impact on who he was and what he accomplished. Newman quotes a passage from Isaiah that is applied to Jesus, though it was written many centuries before Jesus was born. He feels that, *mutatis mutandis*, it can in some way be applied to Dunlea:

> The Lord has been pleased to crush him with suffering. If he offers his life in atonement. ... through him what the Lord wishes will be done. His soul's anguish over he shall see the light and be content. By his sufferings shall my servant justify many, taking their faults on himself, (Isaiah 53:10–11).

Newman often heard Dunlea tell his story openly at AA meetings. His melodramatic misdemeanours brought much laughter. But the members laughed with him, too:

> Our laughter contained a lot of relief and happiness that those days were over for him and for us too. But it was those years of suffering that had matured him, making him the giant among men that we felt him to be. His shoulders were broad from carrying his own cross, and he was able to take the weight of other people's burdens on his own back, and help them accept and so overcome their faults.

Newman goes on to indicate that Dunlea was not unaware of his limits. There were times when the state of his health or the perverse pestering of the supplicant or the importune timing led to a negative response. Newman remembers:

> One Sunday afternoon, as he sat in the dining room after lunch, one of the gentlemen of the road came to the front door of the presbytery. "Is Father Tom at home?" he queried. "Tell him it's so and so" he

> ordered me, mentioning a name that I had heard many times at inconvenient hours. I went inside and a look of mock theatrical despair marked the parish priest's face. He took out his wallet, gave me two dollars and told me to pass it on to the caller. "Tell him I'm indisposed," he said. "I haven't got the patience to face up to X again. I would not be able to stop myself giving him a hearty lecture on the evils of drink, and it would do him no good, while it would be disastrous for my heart condition. It's better that you deal with him — you are more understanding." I took the money and went back to the door, reflecting that I should have taken the note out of my own pocket — that was just how much more understanding I was.

Newman points out that condemning people was not the Dunlea way. He made his assessments of persons and situations, but did not sit in judgement. Jesus didn't presume to judge and condemn people, and neither should he. Encouragement, mercy and compassion shaped Dunlea's attitude and dealings, even though this seemed to be at variance with the accepted standards of behaviour in dealing with some types of people.

* * * * * * * *

Dunlea, Newman observed, wasn't averse to being alone:

> Father Tom loved his room and the chance it gave him to be by himself. He had a lot of interesting books, loaned or given to him by his friends. He enjoyed listening to the radio, which Roy Maurus had specially adapted for him, and the TV at the end of his bed kept him in touch with the events and faces of the world. His bedside telephone would ring and be engaged for long periods, as he sympathised with someone who needed encouragement.
>
> Mystic that he was, he certainly had not abandoned the world, but he had learned to live in it without desire, demand or need. Every day had

become full of magic for him, spent either by himself or in the midst of people. He always seemed happy to wait and see what life and the day would bring to him.

And many did come, all shapes and sizes, continues Newman: "I felt myself one of them, a seeker after his secret. What had he discovered in his great suffering, his descent in degradation? I felt all his visitors looked upon him as one who had gone close to God and could now tell them what he had seen. If they could not get close to God themselves, they could at least drink the wisdom of one who had and then perhaps they could see for themselves".

Veronica, his private secretary, picks up on the theme: "He gave himself continually," she writes. "He even gave his mind, his time and his personal possessions ... " Among those who came to him in need, Veronica specifies: "the boy, the old man, the derelict, the alcoholic, the cadger and the great". Father was a "pushover", she says, "for the sad story. Whether he knew he was being conned never mattered. He always gave — every man was Christ in disguise to him."

In a letter to Ray, an AA friend mentioned earlier, Dunlea touches an even deeper aspect of the mystery of Christ's identification with the poor:

> A Protestant lady, Lady Gregory, of my little home country who, as you know, was the founder of the old Abbey Theatre used to say "never deny the one because the other might be the Christ" and I have often thought that whenever I have had the opportunity to do what might be called a good deed, instead of my feeling chest proud, that I should have gone on my knees ... thanking God for allowing me a sinner not only the mercy but permitting me to dispense to Him mercy.

For Veronica, working with Father Tom Dunlea was, to say the least, the most wonderful experience a girl could have enjoyed.

Father Dunlea was indescribable. There were many characters in this wonderful man. He was first and foremost a priest. He never once dictated a letter wherein he failed to mention the name of God. Listening to him speak was like listening to a symphony. The Irish voice was soft and musical, genuine and sincere. His dictation was akin to an author about to embark upon a Nobel Prize.

Pat Kenna testifies likewise:

> Dunlea was never heard swearing or using uncouth language. This was not because he was genteel, pompous or holier-than-thou, but rather because he seemed to regard words with the same respect — indeed reverence — that he gave to every person or animal or place. Quite simply, language for him was sacred. He would roll around in his mouth a recently discovered expression or a new surname with all the glee of a young boy sucking a boiled lolly. Every word, you felt, was, as far as Dunlea was concerned, wondrous, delightful, memorable, to be savoured, respected.

Although obviously capable and competent with words herself, Veronica feels her utterances about this great man, whom she saw in tears over the plight of a young boy, are quite inadequate. "He was humble," she concludes, "dedicated to his fellow-man, brilliant without a trace of business sense, trusting all; he loved every creature."

That universal focus of his love is a theme that runs through most of the correspondence. Max Lambe does not seem to realise that he's exaggerating when he writes "... everyone knew him, he knew everyone. He touched everyone's life ... a man among men." Anne Cuddy, impressed with his personal charm, charisma and good humour, declares without qualification, "He loved everyone". Laura Lennox couldn't believe that one man could do "... so much for so many and loved what he was doing". As far as Mary Dolan (née Colbran) and her friends were concerned, Father Dunlea was a saint on earth ... "who loved and was loved by all".

This impression of his all-embracing love is a fairly consistent one in the minds of many people who knew him. Whether the reality corresponded with the impression or not, there must have been something very special in the way he lived and spoke and maybe looked at people; something that etched itself deeply in the minds and hearts of his friends.

Pat Kenna again:

> After a Cronin baptism in Gerringong, I was asked by one of the visiting party did I know Father Dunlea. She then proceeded to tell me that she had known him in Hurstville parish. Her husband, a sports journalist, had left her with several young children to rear single-handed. Whenever Tom would meet her in the street, he'd say, "Valerie, be brave". Of course, it was the way he would have mouthed those three words, looking at her with deep compassion, that had the effect of buoying her up, enabling her to keep going. A good example, I believe, of Tom's quasi-sacramental use of words. A rare gift.

27

Fifty golden years

Early in May 1970, Ron Rathbone, Mayor of Rockdale, received a phone call from his counterpart, Ed Curliss, Mayor of Hurstville, suggesting a meeting to discuss a matter of importance to both councils. Relieved that it had nothing to do with finance or roadworks or parklands common to both municipalities, but about honouring a resident, Rathbone readily agreed to meet and discuss. When the resident turned out to be Thomas Vincent Dunlea, Rathbone was surprised and pleased. When both mayors announced at their respective council meetings that in June Dunlea was celebrating his Golden Jubilee as a priest, they were delighted at the positive reaction of their members. One after another, the councillors, of differing political and religious loyalties, glowingly referred to Dunlea's outreach to the underprivileged, his confidence in the generosity of the Australian people and the blessing his open-ended, inclusive ministry had brought to so many citizens of both municipalities.

As a lasting memorial of his unsurpassing service to the community, they resolved to take the unprecedented step of having an illuminated address executed and presented to him under the Common Seal. The presentation was to take place on Sunday June 21, at the Illawarra Catholic Club, Hurstville.

It was the last function of what came to be known as Jubilee Week. People had been praying for months that the guest of honour would last the distance and, indeed, their prayers were answered. His heart was weaker and his joints more painful but, as Tony Newman pointed out, his spirit was keen and robust. He managed to be principal celebrant at two special Masses, one for the clergy on Wednesday June 17, and an open-air Mass for parishioners and friends on Saturday afternoon, June 20.

The homilist at the clergy Mass was his good friend and confessor, Dick Funcheon, parish priest of Sutherland. Like Dunlea himself, Funcheon had a way with words. They flowed out of him effortlessly. With precision and sincerity, mixed with not a little humour and charity, he etched in beautiful technicolour a picture of Dunlea that was factually based, even though a little embellished and enhanced as the occasion demanded. His words about Dunlea's almost childlike humility were certainly echoed by many others. His courage in the face of disappointments, setbacks and apparent failure was another key element in the life of the Jubilarian that was noted and seen to be inspirational.

The Cardinal and several bishops joined with one hundred and fifty priests, whose numbers had to be limited because of the limited capacity of the function centre, where lunch was served to all present. Peter Morrissey and Tony Newman and committee who organised the clergy function knew it was important for Dunlea to be accepted by his brother priests, who tend to resent a colleague who dares to be different, or whose name is frequently featured in the media. Although, in some ways, Dunlea was a challenge to them, he was also a source of comfort.

Priests are often dissatisfied with the way they deal with the down-and-outs who regularly come to the presbytery, looking for the fare to some distant location where they have urgent business. The priest sometimes contacts the members of the St Vincent de Paul Conference or, more often, gives them the money himself. As he watches them shuffle along the footpath towards the local, he feels a qualm of conscience that he has just taken the easy way out. Although he might regard Dunlea's ministry as somewhat extreme, he doesn't feel good about his own rather impersonal, uninvolving and indeed unChristlike efforts either. The fact that at least one colleague was taking the time and the trouble and making the effort to be Christlike in this regard was a source of consolation.

The Jubilee Mass for parishioners and others had to be celebrated in the open air because no church or hall could accommodate the people from all walks of life and of all ages, especially the young, who signified their intention to be there. The weather, always a hazard in mid-winter, turned out to be mild and dry. As Dunlea got up to express his thanks to various people, the clouds moved and the sun bathed them in brilliant light for some minutes. His brief hesitant words, showing signs of the emotion he was feeling, brought tears to many eyes. He managed to finish, however, with an amusing motion of his hand towards heaven, thanking God for the rays of sunshine he enjoyed for most of his life, rays reflected in the eyes and smiles and love of the good people with whom God had blessed him.

Arthur Maher, one of those allowed to pay a brief anecdotal tribute to Dunlea, told of an invitation to dinner he received when first a patient at St John of God Hospital Richmond. It came from a Sydney parish priest who called to drive Arthur and another priest the forty miles down to St Michael's Presbytery Hurstville. On the way back the driver, (the jubilarian) took Arthur to Reuben F Scarf's clothing store in Parramatta and had him fitted out in brand new suit, hat and overcoat. Dressed in full pontificals, as Arthur put it, he arrived back in Richmond and his recovery took a new leap forward from that day. People might think that dress, especially the sober black clerical dress of those days, might not mean much to a priest. The fact is, however, that like most other humans, especially women, comfortable, well-fitting, stylish clothing gives the clergyman, even an ailing clergyman, a feeling of confidence and self-worth that can lead to better mental health. Pat Kenna remembers Dunlea remarking: "If you dress people in second-hand clothing, they become second-hand people".

Dan Minogue, Member of Parliament and proprietor of the White Horse Inn, one of the two much-frequented Irish pubs in Surry Hills, brought felicitations from the Liberal Prime Minister John Gorton and the Labor Opposition, of which he was a member. With some humour and a strong County Clare accent, he recounted how the AA activities of the Jubilarian deprived him of some of his most lucrative customers in Surry Hills!

Dunlea's nephew, Gerard from Brisbane, told how his uncle had knocked on their door in Cronulla after midnight when Gerard was a little fellow. As Gerard's mother opened the door, the visitor simply said, "I'm hungry". Being caught up with other people's problems during the day, he had forgotten to have something to eat!

Years later, when the priest sometimes came to visit Gerard's home in Brisbane, Gerard had great difficulty in getting him to the return plane on time. He couldn't bear to leave until he had paid at least one visit to a stray dogs home. Gerard noted how his uncle left the canine company energised and happy, satisfied that man's best friend was well looked after! As Gerard was speaking, all eyes were on Dunlea's three-legged dog, Fred, languishing contentedly in the sanctuary at his master's feet.

They hadn't got round to changing the altar in St Michael's Church in accordance with the liturgy norms of Vatican II. For the outdoor Mass however, they had an altar table facing the people, together with an ambo and president's chair. While he found the new arrangements a bit disorientating in the beginning, Dunlea liked the idea of facing the people while celebrating Mass. He felt the eye contact made for a sense of solidarity and unity; an awareness that the people were taking the bread, blessing it, breaking it and consecrating it with him.

On the following afternoon, Sunday June 22, the gathering was at the Illawarra Catholic club. As Arthur Maher notes:

> People came in knots and groups of two or three to greet him. He wasn't too fast in receiving them and

not too slow. From 2.15 pm to 5.30 p.m. they filed before him, with the exception of time off for the Austrian Ladies song and the presentation of the illuminated address from the Rockdale and Hurstville municipalities. (Lea Scarlett p144)

Among Hurstville and Sutherland parishioners present at the weekend functions were many former Boys Town boys and helpers, AA members, Matthew Talbot Hostel clients, and a host of friends, many of whom were from other churches or had no church affiliation. Great spontaneous applause greeted a cable from the Reverend Neil MacLeod. He was travelling in Europe, in Dalmatia actually, at the time, but as Dorothy Coleman notes, "He did not forget an old colleague".

During the weeks after the jubilee celebrations, Dunlea still received people at the presbytery, but more frequently from the bunk rather than in the parlour. Pat Kenna refers to an outing during this time which he calls an unforgettable LAST SUPPER. It was a formal dinner in Dunlea's honour at the Brighton-le-Sands unit of Frank and Pat Newman (Tony's parents). With them was another couple, as well as their son Tony (in clericals for the last time, apparently):

> Dunlea looked magnificent in suit and cuff-links and hair swept back. His post-meal discourse was stream-of-consciousness stuff, in which he drew in each person around the table. Affirmations galore. It was prolonged and in technicolour. As Tony and I were driving away over Taren Point Bridge, Tony remarked: "Much of what he was saying was b---s---. But there were pieces of pure gold in there".

A happy but short-lived interlude, and Kenna's last contact with him. Back in the presbytery, Dunlea barely managed to hobble to the church each day, leaning on shoulders, mostly female and young. When he ascended the altar steps to celebrate Mass, Bill Tearle's head, or that of other tall altar servers, provided the necessary fulcrum.

As well as the arthritic pain in his right hip, sometimes very intense, his heart was deteriorating so rapidly that he had to be admitted to hospital once more.

Frances Massey LCM was on hand:

> After many trips to Lewisham Hospital, this was the last one. I recorded his ECG — he was gravely ill, but spoke to me by my first name and wanted to speak. One morning he had felt so ill that he knew that would be his last Mass. In spite of this he dressed and vested and began mass (Latin rite). After the prayers at the foot of the altar, he attempted the step, put his foot on it, but collapsed. His mind was very clear, but that Mass was continued on his bed — his one desire to be united with Jesus on the Cross. That prayer gives a clue to Father's joy and peace: "I will go to the altar of God — the God who gives joy to my youth". That was it! Father Dunlea had the heart of a true child of God — nothing could shake it — that childlike trust with his heavenly Father.

His heart was so weak that his doctor told him he had to rest it by not speaking. So instead he began to write. One of his first epistles was to the Star of the Sea School Hurstville to say how dear the Sisters, staff and children were to him and how he would like them to have a free day for the occasion of his jubilee. It was a short message as he wasn't up to penning a long communique, so he asked Arthur to send it as a telegram. As Arthur was busy during the day and didn't get round to sending the telegram, he delivered the handwritten copy to the Sisters personally that evening. "When I saw Father the next day (the Tuesday before his death), he scolded me for not having sent his telegram," says Arthur, explaining how Dunlea remained lucid in his mind right to the end. That same Tuesday a telegram from staff and pupils of St Marys made up for Arthur's *faux pas*:

> MANY THANKS FOR HOLIDAY GET WELL SOON WE MISS YOU.

A second chance was given to the errant messenger, this time with a rather longer telegram to Father Jim McLaren of Concord whose mother was buried that morning. Father Maher obeyed and the message was despatched from Sydney at 10.32 a.m. Received at Concord at 11.13 a.m., it is now treasured by the McLaren family. It reads:

> "Dear Jim, your sorrow has big share in my sad heart as I sorrow for one who did so much to help Boys Town when friends were few. To your sister my sympathy. To Dad and Mum my head is bowed in prayer and respect.
>
> Tom Dunlea."

Although the precarious condition of his heart left him in no doubt but that the Angel of Death was very close, his concerns were not focused on his own imminent demise, but on those whom he loved most, namely, children — the children at Hurstville and the children at Boys Town whom he was able to provide for through many generous helpers. Mrs McLaren personified all those wonderful men and women who had believed in him, and who slogged and strained and struggled to bring to reality his dream for homeless boys. That dream which took shape as a town run by boys in Engadine defined his life to such an extent that, in the minds of those who knew him, the name Dunlea and Australia's first Boys Town are forever inextricably linked.

Perhaps his very last letter was a whimsical note to his friend in Nowra, John Purcell, arriving the day following Dunlea's death. Pat Kenna writes: "Did John hold on to this 'treasure'? Not a bit of it! (But he could quote it verbatim)".

The last entry in his notebook, which he penned on the very eve of his death, when he saw the heavenly armies gathered to transport him into the great unknown, reads:

> The procession is forming for the trek eternal
> Yes, close ranks — make room;
> The invisible line, you can't see them,

But they are coming
All on the move.

Peter Morrissey gave him the Viaticum, the special Eucharistic food for the trek eternal, his last Holy Communion. As a final prayer, Peter quoted lines from Cardinal Newman which Dunlea himself loved to use as a blessing on appropriate occasions:

May God support you all the day long
Until the shadows lengthen and the evening comes
And the busy world is hushed and the fever of life is
  over ...
And God in his mercy grant you safe lodging — a
  Holy Rest,
And peace at last.

28

His final gift

At 6 a.m. on Saturday morning, St Michael's telephone rang. It was August 22, 1970. A call was indeed expected, even awaited and feared. Peter Morrissey hesitated for some moments, afraid to pick it up. Tony Newman and Arthur Maher heard it, but both refrained from taking it, although in normal circumstances, they would have. The one who did answer it was the housekeeper. She took the message and went to look for Peter and Tony who had dressed and moved into the common room. As soon as they saw her face, they knew. Between sobs she was able to whisper, "Father died at 5.50 this morning". Peter had a later Mass so he had time to go straight away to the hospital to say the Prayers of the Dead with the sisters, including Frances Massey, who were still in Father's room when Peter arrived.

"The death of Tom Dunlea", writes Tony Newman, was a mysterious affair: full of mystery and significance.

> I can remember many details, but I shall recount only two. Firstly, I remember the feeling of pointlessness that came over me when I entered his room in the presbytery after his death. Life and effort and purpose seemed inventions of man, and death seemed to mock them all as it scattered a man's bones amongst his unfinished plans. It was an empty feeling as I looked down at his empty bed. But it was succeeded in the days that followed by a much deeper and stronger conviction, which was symbolised by the most striking impression I have ever had of Father Tom. Peter Morrissey had told me

that the plans were to lift the lid off the coffin as the body lay in St Michael's Church. I circled the church several times on various diversionary messages, but eventually I got up my courage and walked past the open casket, letting my fearful eye fall on his face. The eyes were not quite closed and light was glinting on them — indeed they seemed to be sparkling underneath the lids.

The expression on his face was his accustomed half-serious smile. Then I knew that all those little pieces of Tom Dunlea's life were part of a jigsaw and that they had been put together and completed at last. The picture was designed and drawn by two artists who had finally met. (Coleman p35)

The poet, Wendell Berry, writes, "I almost understand, I almost recognise as a friend the great impertinence of beauty that comes even to the dying, even to the fallen, without reason sweetening the air".

Death can bring sadness and a deep sense of loss. Notwithstanding, it can sometimes sweeten the air, as the poet says and produce an impertinence of beauty, or on the other hand it can sometimes make the air sour and stale. The death of one person can be like a threatening sky brightened by the colours of a rainbow, the death of another can be unrelieved darkness.

It is said that one dies as one lives. If one lives with resentment, cynicism and meanness of spirit, that's what people will experience at one's obsequies. That's the tone or the feeling that will colour the sky. If one lives graciously, as Dunlea did, with a positive optimistic outlook, one's death brings light and freedom, enabling people to get on with their lives with less fear and less guilt. If one encourages people, especially the young, as Dunlea did, admiring their energy, their beauty and their achievements, without a trace of envy or bitterness, one's death becomes a source of hope, bringing new courage and liberation to others.

Henry Nouwen, one of Dunlea's favourite spiritual authors, writes:

> We ourselves are responsible for the way we die. We have to choose between clinging to life in such a way that death becomes nothing but a failure or letting go of life in freedom so that we can be given to others as a source of hope. This is a critical choice and we have to work on that choice every day of our lives. Death does not have to be our final failure, our final defeat in the struggle of life, our unavoidable fate. If our deepest human desire is, indeed, to give ourselves to others, then we can make our death our final gift.

Dunlea's giving to others continued right up to the day he died, when death became his final gift: the brilliant picture designed and drawn, as Tony Newman observed, by God and himself, was in his death releasing light and colour into the air and into the lives of those around him.

News of his death reached the media and was soon a talking-point in many parts of Sydney. People were surprised and shocked, especially those who weren't aware of his medical prognosis. They couldn't believe it, explains Bruce Aley, because "he seemed so indestructible".

The good-will messages (the surviving ones) sent to the hospital were very optimistic, with the emphasis on getng well. For Gladys his recovery was very important: "Remember, there are so many who rely on seeing you or speaking with you". Nancy who looks forward to seeing him on her next visit to Sydney, signs off with "must away dear heart" and addresses her "get well soon" message to my dear Thomasheen.

Marge quotes from a poem on friendship by Kahil Gibran which finishes with:

> ... and in the sweetness of friendship
> Let there be laughter and sharing of pleasures
> For in the dew of little things
> The heart finds its morning and is refreshed.

Marge and Bunny from Mareeba in Queensland sent a telegram that would have cheered him greatly: "Looking forward to seeing you soon have nominated you for open buck-jump Nareeba rodeo". The Gray family featured a likeness of Smokey their Scotch Terrier which would have amused him. Audrey from Al-anon assured him that she prayed for him thro-out (sic) the night. Ted M from AA's Central Office had a personal message: "Father Tom, I just wanted to say personally how much I enjoyed the special meeting at Recovery House and wish that your talk had been taped". The greetings from Frata House was signed by the fifteen members present. The Seven Hills AA invited him to their 11th anniversary meeting on September 14, 1970.

The wake took place at Hurstville, St Michael's Church and presbytery. All day Monday, August 24, people, many of them young, including a large contingent of former Boys Town boys, filed past the open coffin — to look, to pray, to touch, and even to kiss his forehead or hands. They too, like Tony Newman, noticed the half-serious smile and the glint in the eyes, and they thanked God that some of his light and freedom had been passed on to them. The three-legged dog, Fred, occupying the space under the coffin, resisted all attempts to oust him, even during the Vigil Mass celebrated on the Monday evening. Pat Kenna and some friends who travelled from Wollongong could only get as far as the door because of the crowd.

After Mass there were some very moving scenes as people said goodbye. Seeing his face for the last time was a touching and heart-rending experience for people who loved him so much. To provide an opportunity to comfort one another, Peter Morrissey invited them to the hall for supper, while the undertakers put the lid on the coffin and started on the journey to Sydney.

As St Michael's Hurstville was much too small for the Funeral Mass, the quest for a bigger church had been going on for some days. Eric Drew and some others suggested the newly completed church of Our Lady of Fatima in the next-door parish of Kingsgrove. Monsignor Cronin of Kingsgrove, however, didn't think Kingsgrove was a good choice, as the new church hadn't been officially opened and blessed and the grounds were still in a mess. The Cardinal's private secretary, Eamon Barrett, settled the matter when he rang to say the Cardinal felt the appropriate place was St Mary's Cathedral, the mother church of Australia and the largest in Sydney.

The Cardinal himself had a word with Peter Morrissey. He spoke with feeling and emotion about Dunlea and how much he would miss him. He didn't think, however, that he was the appropriate one to give the homily. Although it was his normal practice to preach at priest's funerals on the theology of death and resurrection and the necessity to prepare for one's demise, he didn't believe in saying anything very much about the deceased priest. Dunlea's Requiem demanded something different, something more personal and, rather than establishing a precedent himself, he would prefer Peter to do the honours.

Having served two terms with him, Morrissey knew him well and, like Dunlea, had a compassionate heart and the luminous vision of a mystic. He was the right choice for the challenging task. With a rich vibrant voice and a fine choice of words that would have delighted Dunlea, he painted a picture of the deceased that had the packed Cathedral (over three thousand, Dorothy Coleman claims) glued to their seats and nodding in approval. Some of his pearls of wisdom are quoted in different parts of this work.

Cardinal Gilroy presided at the Mass on Tuesday August 25 at 11.00 a.m. In the sanctuary with him, Peter Morrissey was joined by Arthur Maher, Michael Kennedy, who worked with Dunlea in AA, Con Keogh, who founded GROW, Bishop Tom Muldoon, John McRae, who worked with him in Boys Town, and one of the largest collection of priests ever seen at a Requiem in St Mary's. Also present was Reverend Neil MacLeod, who had returned from Europe to be there, and other St George and Sutherland Shire ministers, some of whom had also attended the Vigil at St Michael's. The chief mourners were his older brother, John Dunlea from Melbourne, now a widower and aged 83 years, and various nephews and nieces. As Dorothy Coleman remarks: "It must have been a sad but proud day for them".

The one person present who surprised and delighted everyone was Dorothy Day, editor of New York-based the *Catholic Worker*. Her being there was so appropriate and much appreciated, because her spirit was in many ways, akin to Dunlea's. Even back as far as the 1930s in her work for the very poor, she was a sort of role model for him. She too set up centres for the homeless and the hungry, people who were, for whatever reason, "beaten by life", as she said. She believed:

> Every parish should have its Works of Mercy Centre, where the poor are fed daily, without question, in the name of Jesus Christ, who himself was hungry and homeless at times on this earth.
>
> Proceeding with faith and with simplicity, we will be able to continue, if we recognise that it is Christ in us who is doing the work.

Then she goes on in Dunlea fashion:

> Of course we do not know where the money is coming from or who will support it. Let Divine Providence take care of that. (*Catholic Worker* 3/38)

The presence of Dorothy Day (who died in 1980) and her travelling companion, Eileen Egan (died 1999), was due to Roger Pryke, the Catholic Chaplain to the University of Sydney. Pryke sponsored her visit as part of a programme to inspire and motivate university students who, concerned about academic success, often overlook the homeless and hungry in their midst.

* * * * * * * *

"All traffic lights were extinguished en route from St Mary's Cathedral in Sydney to the Woronora Cemetery in Sutherland," writes Arthur Maher. A police escort on motor bikes led the cortege through the 25 km trip south by Botany Bay to the Princes Highway and Tom Ugly's Bridge. Many people from the Sutherland Shire who could not get to the Cathedral, joined the cortege south of Tom Ugly's; others went straight to the cemetery, where they waited. This led to quite a traffic jam when the cortege arrived.

Although lots of people are normally present in the church for a priest's Requiem Mass, the number continuing to the cemetery is generally small. With Dunlea the number present at the cemetery was quite massive. The Boys Town boys were to form a guard of honour from the cemetery gate to the office, but the traffic chaos made that too dangerous. Among the multitude present, Dorothy Coleman noticed Eric, the first Boys Town boy, as well as Irish Kevin and his pretty wife Roslyn who had travelled from Canberra. Some people from Sutherland and Engadine, going to the wrong part of the Woronora cemetery, arrived at the graveside as the service was being conducted, thus adding to the huge crowd already assembled there.

Peter Morrissey intoned the final invocation:

> May the angels lead you into paradise
> May the martyrs come to welcome you
> And take you to the holy city
> The new and eternal Jerusalem.

Dick Funcheon, the local parish priest, made apologies for various Dunlea admirers who, because of severe illness, were unable to attend, including "Percy, who had suffered so many anxieties and frustrations in the early years as secretary to the Boys Town Committee". He then concluded, as people were pouring a little earth on the lowered coffin:

> May choirs of angels welcome you
> And lead you to the bosom of Abraham;
> Where Lazarus is poor no longer
> May you have eternal rest.

It was so fitting that the name Lazarus, the man who languished in dire poverty outside the rich man's door in the Gospel story of Dives and Lazarus (Luke 16:19), should be mentioned at the grave of one who ministered with such love and patience to every Lazarus who came to his door. As the final Ave was said, Irish Jim from Forty Acres days, unwrapped his piano-accordion and filled the air and the hearts of those present with the haunting lilting melody of *Danny Boy*. In the deep silence that followed, many tears watered the brown earth of Woronora.

Dorothy Coleman called to mind the words of Cardinal Gilroy at the end of Dunlea's Jubilee Mass for priests: "No priest has done more than Father Dunlea to make the Church loved".

Tony Newman felt Kahlil Gibran's reflection on giving could form a suitable epitaph:

> Then said a rich man,
> Speak to us of Giving.
> And he answered:
> You give little when you give of your possessions.
> It is when you give of yourself that you truly give.
> There are those who give little of the much which they have —
> And they give it for recognition and their hidden desire makes their gifts unwholesome.
> And there are those who have little and give it all.
> These are the believers in life and the bounty of life,
> And their coffer is never empty.
> There are those who give with joy, and that joy is their reward.
> And there are those who give with pain, and that pain is their baptism.
> And there are those who give and know not pain in giving,
> Nor do they seek joy, nor give with mindfulness of virtue;
> They give as in yonder valley the myrtle breathes its fragrance into space.
> Through the hands of such as these God speaks,
> And from behind their eyes He smiles upon the earth.
>
> *The Prophet.*

I passed my brother and cousin:
They read in their books of prayer;
I read in my book of songs
I bought at the Sligo fair.

When we come at the end of time
To Peter, sitting in state,
He will smile on the three old spirits,
But call me first through the gate;

For the good are always the merry,
Save by an evil chance,
And the merry love the fiddle,
And the merry love to dance.
The Fiddler of Donny, W B Yeats

29

He returns to Boys Town

It was only weeks since the golden jubilee celebrations, when so many letters and telegrams of congratulations had arrived at St Michael's. Now they began to arrive again, this time in sorrow and deep gratitude for a helping hand, a smile of recognition, a word of encouragement, a loving presence. Many correspondents, including Mary Rose and others from Sutherland, referred to his being there for them; even though they might not have contacted him that often, the fact of knowing that he was there when they needed him was the source of much comfort and strength.

Most messages came to St Michael's Hurstville, with a few also going to Cardinal Gilroy. Typical of the latter was a short communique from Mr Morrison, State Member for St George, and an avowed secular humanist: "We all regret the loss of Father Dunlea, who learned his humanity by being human and who passed his own wealth of compassion on to young and old alike". To which the Cardinal duly replied: "Very few learnt the art of giving without counting the cost as he did, there were no bounds to his charity". Terence Jennings SDB, Provincial of the Salesians, recorded the condolences of his congregation: "I do know the esteem in which he was held by the late Father Ciantar. I assure Your Eminence, he will be remembered by us among our own dear dead".

As Terence Jennings was writing his letter of sympathy, he had a phone call from Engadine to inform him that there was a move afoot to have Dunlea's body removed from Woronora and reinterred at Boys Town.

"Always the subject of controversy in life," notes Dorothy Coleman (p38), "in death it remained the same and Father Tom's body was not to rest long in Woronora Cemetery".

Flora Wickham, a Hurstville parishioner, attests that before the funeral, a group approached the Cardinal to indicate that Boys Town would be the appropriate place to bury Dunlea. Although he could see why that was so, Gilroy had a thing about the cult of personality, that is, a priest (or bishop, for that matter) being so acclaimed that he might end up as a sort of cult figure. If Dunlea's body were treated differently from that of other priests, Gilroy felt, his grave might become a sort of shrine or a place of pilgrimage. And so the priests' section of Woronora was deemed the most suitable resting-place, until, that is, Roy Maurus got a brainwave.

Maurus, a Hurstville parishioner and good friend of Dunlea, had all the skills of a handyman and used them generously around St Michael's. He followed the funeral procession to Woronora and was one of the last to leave the graveside. Although he hadn't even heard about the group who had approached the Cardinal regarding Dunlea's burial place, he had a gut feeling that something was amiss. He couldn't put his finger on it, but it continued to haunt him throughout the night after the funeral. He twisted and turned until just before daybreak, on Wednesday, August 26. Then it suddenly dawned on him. He turned to his half-asleep, half-awake wife and exclaimed: "Father is buried in the wrong place. He doesn't belong in Woronora, he belongs in Boys Town. It is there he would want to be buried".

That very day Roy went to see his friend, Mick Croote of the Hurstville Council, about the possibility of exhuming and re-interring the body. Mick explained the formidable negotiations that would have to be entered into, the various authorities that would have to be consulted and the mountain of red tape that would have to be dealt with — procedures that would have frightened off anyone less passionate than Roy Maurus. For days and weeks he hung in there, till the authority to exhume the body was signed and sealed. With similar reluctance, Cardinal Gilroy gave his permission on condition that the re-interring was done privately, without fuss and publicity. The Salesians were very happy with the proposal and suggested the beautiful garden in front of the chapel as the most appropriate burial place.

The re-interment ceremony took place within a month of the original burial. A few priests officiated, with Peter Morrissey and Dick Funcheon conducting the ceremony in the presence of the boys and staff, some old parishioners, Roy Maurus and Dunlea's old and faithful friend, Eric Drew. As the Rosary was being led by the Town Mayor, a dog followed by a pet sheep ambled towards the grave "and rested peacefully on the fresh brown earth, a symbol" — Dorothy Coleman believes — "of the abandoned ones Father Dunlea had in mind when founding Boys Town". Or maybe it was a silent tribute to a shepherd who went after the sheep that was lost and on finding it, placed it on his shoulders and brought it back to the fold, and called his friends and neighbours to celebrate with him. (Luke 15:4–7)

> When the almond tree blooms,
>   and the locusts grow sluggish
>   and the caper tree is without effect,
> Because man goes to his lasting home,
>   and the mourners go about the streets;
> Before the silver cord is snapped
>   and the golden bowl is broken,
> and the pitcher is shattered at the spring,
>   and the broken pulley falls into the well,
> and the dust returns to the earth as it once was,
>   and the life breath returns to the God who gave it.
>   Ecclesiastes 12: 5–7

*On the day when
the weight deadens
on your shoulders
and you stumble,
may the clay dance
to balance you.
And when your eyes
freeze behind
the grey window
and the ghost of loss
gets in to you,
may a flock of colours,
indigo, red, green
and azure blue
come to awaken in you
a meadow of delight.
When the canvas frays
in the currach of thought
and a stain of ocean
blackens beneath you
may there come across the waters
a path of yellow moonlight
to bring you safely home.
May the nourishment of God's earth be yours,
may the clarity of Christ's light be yours,
may the fluency of the clean spring water of the Holy
Spirit be yours,
may the protection of the ancestors be yours
and so may a slow
wind work these words
of love around you
an invisible cloak
to mind your life.*

Anam Cara John O'Donohue

Epilogue

For one week in early December 1945, the year World War II ended, I was the bell ringer at St Patrick's College Manly, the former Sydney seminary situated on the North Head of Sydney Harbour. Being the junior of about one hundred and fifty clergy who were on retreat that week, my task was to call the clergy to their different exercises by several pulls on the thick rope that connected with the bell on the high tower.

Unfortunately, my watch wasn't very reliable. I had purchased it earlier that year for fifteen shillings in South Africa's Cape Town, the only stop on our wartime eight-week voyage from Liverpool England to Sydney Australia. My timing on bell duty was often awry, sounding the bell either too late or too early and, on the Wednesday morning, I slept in and failed to sound the first call of the day at 6.30 a.m.

As a result, my standing among the clergy and Archbishop Gilroy was rather low. In this strictly silent retreat, they would have had a distracting thought: if he's incapable of doing a simple task like ringing the bell on time, what good is he going to be in a parish?

After the retreat concluded on Friday, when some other young clergy and myself were travelling on the ferry from Manly to Circular Quay, an older priest joined us. His eyes and smile were welcoming and fraternal and full of good-natured concern for our welfare. He called me by my first name and as I introduced my companions, he reminded me that his name was Tom Dunlea.

He had spoken to me once during the retreat. It was on the morning I failed to ring the bell. He had whispered that it was the Lord himself who had kept me from ringing the bell because of his love for the older clergy who don't sleep too well in those strange narrow beds and who badly needed a sleep-in!

Even then his friendliness and kindly attitude impressed me and removed completely any misgivings about my bad bell-ringing record.

The next significant meeting with him was in March 1947. I was having an after-golf drink at St Michael's course, Little Bay, in eastern Sydney. Of the seven young clergy sitting at the table, six had volunteered to go to Japan for five years as missionaries. It was a scheme devised by Archbishop Gilroy to keep afloat the almost priestless post-war Japanese Church, until such time as the foreign missionary orders regrouped after the war and were in a position to send out full-time trained missionaries. Volunteering more or less because my best priest-friends had done so, I wasn't at all sure that I'd be able to cope with the rigours of war-torn Japan. At the time, I was quite happy to call Australia home, but now I was leaving behind so much about Australia that appealed to me and venturing into the threatening unknown.

Although not a golfer himself, Dunlea sat with us, and we felt quite at home with him, an older and rather famous priest. His cheerful presence gave us a lift, a buzz, you could say. Speaking in glowing terms about the exciting venture we were about to embark on, he assured us we had made the right decision. In fact, he felt we were fortunate that the call to do something beautiful for God (as he put it) came in our time. If it had come in his time, he wouldn't have missed it for quids.

This was just what I, and I think the others, needed to hear. This man, I felt, was God-sent to encourage and enthuse us.

Being out of the country for over six years, I had no further contact with Tom Dunlea until Peter Farrelly, my classmate and former neighbour in Japan, became his curate in Hurstville in the early 1960s.

In the mid-1970s, when I became parish priest of Kingsgrove, next door to Hurstville, I was quite surprised at the number of older parishioners who, six years after his death, spoke about Dunlea. As they did so, their eyes sparkled and a glimmer of a smile lit up their faces. Thinking of him obviously evoked happy memories. These they readily shared with me and, although I have forgotten most of them, some are included in this book.

Maurice, a member of the Kingsgrove St Vincent de Paul Conference who helped at the Matt Talbot Hostel went to Hurstville for years to a group called "The Dunleana Society". The group met regularly, under the tutelage of Father Maher, to perpetuate the memory and work of Father Tom, to imitate his way and to support his motto: Every Australian a saint. Their stated ambition was: "the people will have canonised Father Dunlea; we hope for the Church's pronouncement yet...".

There's a saying in Church circles that "there's no-one more dead than a dead priest". In other words, a priest is quickly forgotten, not having a family of his own to remember him. The Dunleana people were going to great pains to make sure this didn't happen to their late beloved parish priest.

It never occurred to me to attend the meeting, but the fact that it was happening aroused my curiosity at the time, especially when they told me how much they enjoyed it and how the volume of remembered stories never seemed to dry up. I tried to suss out some of these stories for this book but, amazingly, there doesn't seem to be any written material in circulation.

In his June 1988 letter to the clergy, Cardinal Clancy intimated that the Salesians were hoping to compile some material on Father Dunlea on the occasion of the golden jubilee of Boys Town, occurring the following year. The Cardinal believed there was much oral and documented material on Dunlea that needed to be collected before his contemporaries died.

In the same month, June 1988, an article appeared in the *St George and Sutherland Shire Leader*, headed "Shire priest, a legend today". It announced that Father Dunlea research was being undertaken on behalf of Boys Town by Anne Bezzina, a social worker at the Town from 1981 to 1986. Father Frank Bertagnolli, then Director of Boys Town, appealed to anyone who had any personal recollections of Father Dunlea or knew people who had some association with him to contact Anne Bezzina or himself.

Some of the clergy who responded were friends of mine, and their reminiscing and re-telling of the stories made very entertaining conversation. The dark picture of one or two who couldn't remember anything good about Dunlea was negated by the multi-coloured exciting image emerging from the others. All this renewed my own interest. I am grateful to Robert Bossini SDB, the present Superior of the Salesians in Engadine, for giving me access to Anne Bezzina's handwritten synopsis of replies from various respondents.

Two years later, in 1990, a similar appeal was made by Pat Kenna, the parish priest of Kiama in the South Coast. As a young priest Pat was a personal friend and admirer of Dunlea. Having found that the name still rang bells for people in many South Coast parishes even twenty years after his death, Pat decided to collect material with a view to writing an article or even a book. He never did get round to putting the resultant material together, but the fact that he had it in mind and that the Dunlea memory continued to be alive and healthy, while that of others, prelates of even greater and more prestigious stature, was fading into oblivion, impressed me greatly.

As had the Salesians, Pat Kenna generously allowed me access to his material. Pat, like Dunlea himself, is mystically inclined, has a way with words and is an excellent raconteur. Had he proceeded to write, he would have done Dunlea proud — as indeed would have his good friend in Sydney, Peter Morrissey, from whom I received the Kenna material.

When my other book, *A Meddling Priest* (a life of Father Therry, Australia's first chaplain), was published two years ago, I was surprised and delighted at the number of ordinary non-academic people like myself who enjoyed it. Many of them would never have tackled a more scholarly, annotated, historical work. They were attracted to it because they perceived it as, what they called, "an easy read". They became its best promoters. They even went to the trouble of writing or ringing to thank me for enticing them to dip their toes into early colonial history. The fact that *A Meddling Priest* was their only door into John Joseph Therry's life and times was an incentive to me to try again. Although I knew that Dunlea was a book waiting to be written, I hesitated, because there were others, as I indicated above, who were more in tune with the Dunlea personality and lifestyle.

However, when it became apparent that no-one else was putting pen to paper, I asked Shirley, my honorary private secretary, to seek information and stories as Anne Bezzina and Pat Kenna had previously done. The *Catholic Weekly*, the *Irish Echo* and the *St George and Sutherland Shire Leader* were contacted, as were some Irish radio programmes. The response was spontaneous and enthusiastic. Dunlea was still remembered with affection and even with a modicum of mirth.

Among the correspondents a proportion had responded to all three appeals. Most responded in their own handwriting on pages running from to one to a half-dozen. Some sent photographs, cuttings and copies of the *Voice of Boys Town*, with Flora Wickham sending the very first issue. Ron Harden, Dunlea's successor as pastor of Hurstville, lent me "Father Dunlea's approach to dealing with young people in difficulties". From Hurstville also I received a copy of the *Faith of the Forest* by Errol Lea Scarlett, a history of St Michael's parish published in 1990. Brian Lucas, the Archdiocesan Chancellor, allowed me access to the Dunlea files in the Cathedral Archives. Ted Cooper's book, *Grateful Heirs*, on the history of the Australian Salesians, was very helpful, as were Chris

Riley's notes on the care and rehabilitation of youngsters, with special reference to the Dunlea method. Archie McKinnon's book, *Castle of Shadows*, detailed the beginnings of Alcoholics Anonymous in Australia, and Con Keogh's *Grow Comes of Age* was a mine of information about the beginnings of that wonderful self-help programme.

The most useful of all, however, was *The Priest of the Highway*, penned by Dorothy Coleman shortly after Dunlea died. This small pamphlet is lyrical and poetic, as befits Dunlea, and has happily recorded what significant people thought of Dunlea over thirty years ago — people like Peter Morrissey, John McRae, Tony Newman, Eric Drew and others.

As I was arranging the pieces of the jigsaw, gleaned from the above sources, I found that even though these pieces fitted together, they didn't quite complete the picture. Here and there pieces were missing, pieces that time and distance had hidden. The only way I could find them was to go back in time, walk a few kilometres in Dunlea's shoes and even be Dunlea for a while. That was very difficult and not too successful, because I've come from a different mould.

Dunlea was inimitable; there was only one Dunlea. Having produced Dunlea, that unique mould wasn't used again. Even though a few may say "Thank God" to that, countless others would say, with Cardinal Gilroy, "What a pity! More than ever, we need priests with Christmas hearts who, like Dunlea, have the gift of making the Church loved!".

Bibliography

- Coleman, Dorothy 1973. *Priest of the Highway*. Devonshire Press.
- Cooper, Ted SDB 1999. *Grateful Heirs*. Baugham Press Sydney.
- Cuddy, Anne 2003. *Fr Thomas Vincent Dunlea*. Annals Australasia Sydney.
- Keogh, Con 1982. *GROW Comes of Age*.
- Lea Scarlett, Errol 1985. *The Faith of the Forrest*. St Michaels Hurstville.
- McKinnon, A.V. (Archie). *Castle of Shadows*. Devonshire Press Sydney.
- Petrus Magazine 1962. *Memories of the Australian Mission*. St Peters College Wexford.

Selected References

Alban, Brother — FSC director	85
Alcoholic Foundation	100
Alcoholics Anonymous Convention	220
Aley, Bruce — driver	58
Allen, Steve — Boys Town	21
Anderson, Alf	68
Araluen Valley	175
Archbold, Pat — priest	179
Ballina County, Tipperary	9
Bezzina, Anne	260
Boyle's cottage — Sutherland	41
Boys Town, Nebraska	39
Caldwell MHR, Arthur	112, 144
Chifley, Ben — Prime Minister of Australia 1945–1949	112
Cistercians	13
Clune CP, Francis	147
Clune, Edward (Ned) — parish priest	33
Cooper, Walter	43
Cuddy, Anne (nee Macinante)	58
Curlewis, H R — Judge	85
Curtin, John — Prime Minister of Australia 1941–1945	112
Daily Telegraph — newspaper	51

SELECTED REFERENCES

Day, Dorothy — New York	249
Depression, The Great	32
Drew, Eric	262
Dublin Lad — racehorse	54
Eucharistic Congress, Dublin	34, 132
Farrelly, Peter — priest	258
Fedrigotti SDB, Father B M	118
Forest, Fred	66
Forty Acres	110
Funcheon, Dick — priest	237
Game, Sir Philip	24
Giles, Joe — priest	155
Gilmore, Dame Mary	55
Ginger Meggs, cartoon	26
Green, Eric — first boy	63
Hayden, Tommy — priest	73
Jewish Cross	219
Kendall, Henry	175
Kenna, Pat — priest	260
Kennedy, Ted — priest	175
Keogh, Con — priest	183, 262
Kingsgrove-Bexley North, Parish of	33
Kinnane, Alice	36
Lawson, Henry	175
Mair, Alex — Premier of New South Wales	61
Marien, Brian — journalist	47
Massey LCM, Frances	211
McCosker, Frank — priest	74
McGovern, Joe — priest	76
McKell, William — Premier of New South Wales 1941–1947	51
McKinnon MBE, A V (Archie)	93, 262

McLeod, Reverend Neil 165
McRae, John — priest 57, 110
Merritt, Joseph 66
Merton Street, Sutherland 36
Michell, Mary 128
Miles, Dr Eric 19
Minogue MHR, Dan 51, 112
Minogue, Dr S J 91
Mirror — newspaper 51
Mount Melleray 13
Murphy SJ, Richard 94
Newman, Tony 155
O'Regan, Dick — priest 17
Papal Cross 219
Paterson, Banjo 117, 174
Phar Lap — racehorse 25
Rooney, Mickey — actor 39
Rose Bay, Parish of 17
Russell, June — hairdresser 54
Scarf, Reuben F 97
Scully, Ken — journalist 20
Sisters of Charity 152
Society of St Vincent de Paul 3
St Patrick's College, Manly 70
St Peter's Wexford, Seminary 13
Sturge Harty, Frank — radio presenter 94
Sunday Sun — newspaper 26
Sydney Harbour Bridge 24
Sydney Morning Herald — newspaper 119
Talbot, Matt — Dublin 141
Tearle, Bill 193

Tearle, Sheila	121
Tent Village, Loftus	53
Tracy, Spencer — actor	39
Truman, Harry S — President of the United States of America 1945–1953	106
Tuomey, Dr Pat	24, 28, 156
Vianney House	102
Walsh, Jim — Hurstville	39
Wells System	158
White FSC, Benignus	82
Woronora Cemetery	51